XBETHL00491556

The Washington Journey

GIBBS SMITH EDUCATION
TO ENRICH AND INSPIRE HUMANKIND

First Edition
© 2010 Gibbs Smith Education
All rights reserved.

No part of this book may be reproduced
by any means whatsoever,
either mechanical or electronic,
without permission from the publisher.

23 22 21 20 19 18 17 16 15   10 11 12 13 14

Published by
Gibbs Smith Education
PO Box 667
Layton, UT 84041
801-544-9800
www.gibbssmitheducation.com

Project Editor: Charlene S. Kerwin
Editorial Assistants: Hollie Keith, Courtney Thomas
Cover and Book Design: Michelle Pierce
Photo Editor: Wendy Knight
Maps and Graphs: Michelle Pierce

Front Cover Photos: On the trail to Paradise Valley, courtesy of the
Library of Congress Prints and Photographs Division.
Back Cover Photos: Cascade Mountains, Stephen Strathdee/Shutterstock.
Inset Photo Summit of Pinnacle Peak, courtesy of the
Library of Congress Prints and Photographs Division.

Gibbs Smith books are printed on either recycled, 100% post-consumer waste,
FSC-certified papers, or on paper produced from a 100% certified
sustainable forest/controlled wood source.

Printed and bound in the USA.
ISBN-13: 978-1-4236-0622-2
ISBN-10: 1-4236-0622-1

Contributing Authors:

Laurie Winn Carlson, PhD, has an MEd from Arizona State University, an MA in history from Eastern Washington University, and a PhD from Washington State University. She has taught students at all grade levels and published 14 nonfiction books, for which she has received many national awards.

Michael K. Green, PhD, was born in Spokane and has spent the past 34 years teaching the history of the Pacific Northwest. As professor of history at Eastern Washington University, he helped prepare college students to teach in the public schools. Dr. Green earned his PhD at the University of Idaho.

Charlene S. Kerwin has an MA in history from the University of Delaware and a BA in journalism from Northeastern University. She has taught history and economics courses for more than 10 years at high schools in Delaware and Pennsylvania.

Reviewers:

Tina Kuckkahn-Miller has served as the founding director of the Longhouse Education and Cultural Center at The Evergreen State College since 1996. Affiliated with both Lac du Flambeau Band of Lake Superior Chippewa (enrolled) and the Lac Courte Oreilles Band of Lake Superior Chippewa tribes, Tina works with a multitude of Northwest Tribes in her roles at Evergreen. She holds a Juris Doctorate from the University of Wisconsin Law School.

Gwen Perkins is the Education Specialist at the Washington State Historical Society. She is responsible for coordinating the History Museum's school program. In that role, she writes the museum's online curriculum materials, which includes gathering primary sources and other documents for use by students and teachers. She also serves as assistant editor for COLUMBIA Kids, an online magazine that explores the history of the Pacific Northwest.

Contents

Washington PORTRAIT

Maps and Charts

Go to the Source

WASHINGTON SOCIAL STUDIES SKILLS

Setting the Stage

"To see the earth as it truly is, small and blue and beautiful in that eternal silence where it floats, is to see ourselves as riders on the earth together, brothers on that bright loveliness in the eternal cold."

—Archibald MacLeish, American poet

One of Washington's most famous photographers, Edward Curtis, took this photo of an Indian fishing camp more than 100 years ago. The house is made of tule. Tule is a plant that grows in Washington. **How do you think the boat was made?**

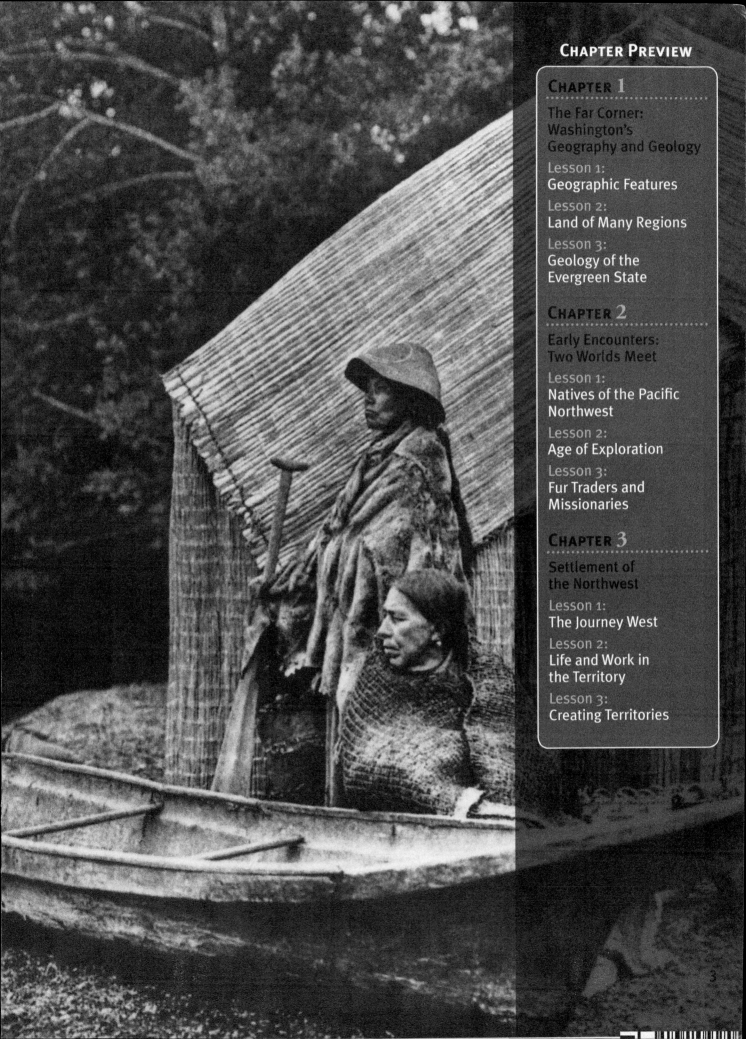

Essential **Question** ?

How does Washington's geography and geology affect the way we live?

The Far Corner:
Washington's Geography and Geology

Chapter 1

Washington is a mix of unique geographic and geologic features. Our state shares common features with other states in the Pacific Northwest. Trade connects us to other countries around the Pacific Rim.

The state's mountain ranges, valleys, plateaus, rivers, and coastline were shaped millions of years ago.

These unique features played a role in the settlement patterns and activities of the people of Washington past and present.

Palouse Falls is pictured here at Sunset. **What are the features of the land around the falls?**

KEY IDEAS

- Natural and political boundaries separate Washington from its neighbors.

- Geography influences where people live and what they do.

- Over time, people have changed the land and resources of Washington.

KEY TERMS

cultural characteristic
headwaters
hydroelectric
physical characteristic
spatial pattern
temperate
tributary

The Northwest Corner

The location of a place is like an address. Washington is located in the northwest corner of the United States. It is between the 46th and 49th parallels north latitude. It is between 117 degrees and 125 degrees west longitude.

Washington covers 68,139 square miles, including some of the most diverse geographic regions in the country.

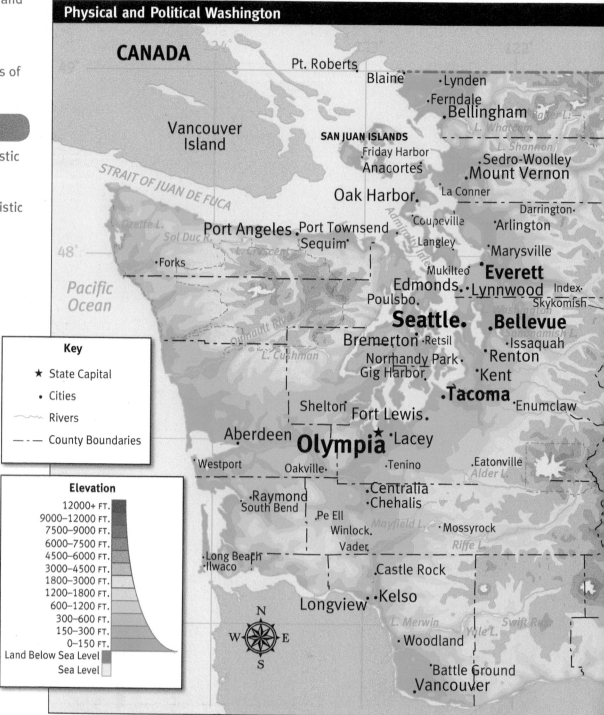

Physical and Political Washington

Key
- ★ State Capital
- • Cities
- Rivers
- –·– County Boundaries

Elevation
- 12000+ FT.
- 9000–12000 FT.
- 7500–9000 FT.
- 6000–7500 FT.
- 4500–6000 FT.
- 3000–4500 FT.
- 1800–3000 FT.
- 1200–1800 FT.
- 600–1200 FT.
- 300–600 FT.
- 150–300 FT.
- 0–150 FT.
- Land Below Sea Level
- Sea Level

Boundaries

Some of Washington's boundaries are natural features of the land. Others are political boundaries, which means they were decided by people.

- British Columbia, a Canadian province, is north of Washington. The line separating the United States from Canada is a political boundary.

- The Pacific Ocean and the Strait of Juan de Fuca are natural boundaries.

- The Columbia River forms most of our southern boundary and separates us from Oregon.

- Idaho is on the eastern side of our state. Is the border between Washington and Idaho a natural or a political boundary line?

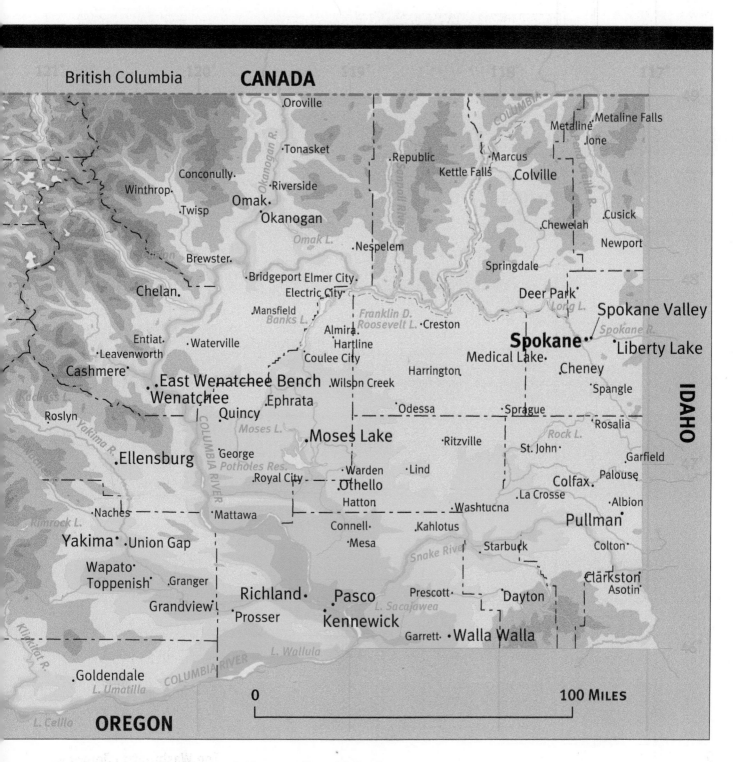

The Far Corner: Washington's Geography and Geology

This is a view of downtown Bellevue from Lake Washington. **What geographic features made this a good place for people to settle?**

Mt. Rainier is seen in the background behind this barn outside of Seattle. **Why might this be a good place for a farm?**

Spatial Patterns

Geography is all about spatial patterns. *Spatial patterns* are the location and arrangement of natural and human features of the land. All locations have *physical characteristics* that make them different from other places on Earth. Physical characteristics are natural to the environment. Washington has a striking diversity of physical characteristics. There are rocky beaches, islands, miles of forests, mountains, volcanoes, deep river gorges, deserts, and rich farmland.

The location of the land's physical features has a lot to do with where people live and work. Large cities, small towns, farms, orchards, highways, dams, and bridges have not always been here. When people moved to Washington from other places, they brought their languages and ways of living with them. These human features of the land are part of its *cultural characteristics*.

Where Do People Settle?

Washington's coastline, rivers, deserts, and mountains have always influenced where people live and what they do for a living. Our land also influences the kinds of recreational activities people seek.

Consider how challenging nature's obstacles were for the people who traveled by boat, foot, and wagon. It must have been terrifying to cross wide, fast rivers, never knowing if you would be swept downstream in a moment. It must have been discouraging to try to clear a path through steep mountain passes with rocky cliffs falling hundreds of feet below. It was common for settlers to view the environment as an obstacle that needed to be subdued.

This is Diablo Dam on the Skagit River. **How does this dam change the river and the land around it?**

Factories make the things we all want. **How are the factories pictured here affecting the environment?**

What Do You Think ?

Only in the late 20th century did most Americans come to recognize that our environment is more delicate than we had realized. How can we protect the environment, but still continue to build and grow?

Washington's coastline and rivers make fishing a big industry. **How does this image support concerns about overfishing?**

The Columbia River

One of our state's most famous physical characteristics is the Columbia River. Indian tribes and early fur trappers relied on the river for transportation in their large canoes and as a source of food. The river became the source of a thriving salmon industry. Railroads followed its route through the Cascades, while steamboats braved its wild waters. Explorers Lewis and Clark bravely rode down parts of the wild river to the Pacific Ocean in the early 1800s.

The Columbia River flows to the Pacific Ocean, forming the border between Washington and Oregon.

The River's Route

The source, or *headwaters*, of the river is at Columbia Lake, high in British Columbia, Canada. The river enters Washington flowing south and then sweeps around the "Big Bend" where it meets with the Snake River. Carrying the water of both rivers, the Columbia turns west. Cutting through the Cascades in the Columbia Gorge, the river flows to the sea.

Tributaries

When summer arrives and mountain snow melts, what happens to all the water? Much of it flows in thousands of tiny streams into larger streams, then into rivers. These *tributaries* eventually become part of the mighty Columbia River, and the water then flows into the Pacific Ocean. In this way, the Columbia River drains water from the mountains like the drain in a sink.

Dams Produce Electricity

The river's huge volume of water, together with its very steep fall in elevation, makes it the most powerful river in North America in terms of hydroelectric energy. *Hydroelectric* refers to electricity that is produced by waterpower. Major dams on the river

produce more electricity than any other state. By the late 1900s, the Columbia had been so altered by dams it was called an "engineered" river.

Roosevelt Reservoir, behind Grand Coulee Dam, and Banks Lake, behind Dry Falls Dam, are man-made lakes that bring water to dry regions, but also provide recreation.

The Grand Coulee Dam was built on the Columbia River to help irrigate farmland and provide hydroelectric power to the region.

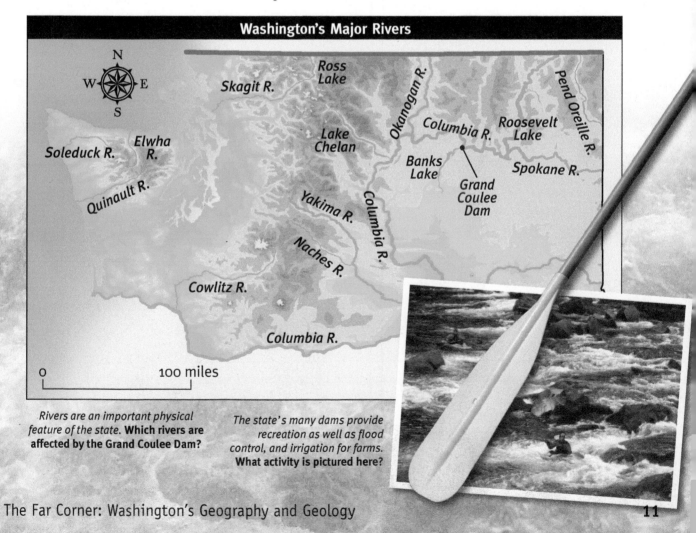

Washington's Major Rivers

Ross Lake
Skagit R.
Okanogan R.
Pend Oreille R.
Columbia R.
Roosevelt Lake
Soleduck R.
Elwha R.
Lake Chelan
Banks Lake
Spokane R.
Quinault R.
Grand Coulee Dam
Yakima R.
Columbia R.
Naches R.
Cowlitz R.
Columbia R.

0   100 miles

*Rivers are an important physical feature of the state. **Which rivers are affected by the Grand Coulee Dam?***

*The state's many dams provide recreation as well as flood control, and irrigation for farms. **What activity is pictured here?***

The Pacific Coast

The coastline is one of our state's important physical features. Washington has only 157 miles of ocean coastline, but there are over 3,000 miles of coastline along the Strait of Juan de Fuca, the numerous bays and inlets of Puget Sound, and around the islands.

Washington has more deep-water harbors than either California or Oregon. Shipping goods in and out of our harbors links Washington to the rest of the world.

The Pacific Ocean and Puget Sound are the sources of the state's fishing industry. Salmon accounts for about one-third of the fishing income, followed by oysters, crabs, and shrimp. Other fish caught in ocean waters are halibut, flounder, tuna, and cod.

The Ocean Affects Our Climate

More important than the beautiful scenery it provides, the ocean has an important influence on our land and climate. Winds from the ocean give Washington a *temperate,* or mild, climate. This is because the temperature of large bodies of water does not change as quickly as the temperature of the air. The warmer water of the ocean warms up the air next to it. Winds pick up the warmer air and carry it across the land. Away from the ocean, in eastern Washington, the climate is more dry. Eastern Washington tends to have colder winters and hotter summers than western Washington, and it has much less rain.

There are lots of different kinds of seafood to buy at Pike Place Market in Seattle. **What kinds of seafood do you see?**

Salmon are caught in large numbers by Washington fishermen.

Washington has a rugged and rocky coastline along the Pacific Ocean.

Compare the wet rainforest along the coast to the dryness of the land east of the mountains. **How does the ocean affect the climate?**

What Did You Learn? ①

1. What boundaries separate Washington from its neighbors?
2. How does geography influence spatial patterns?
3. What changes have people made to the land and resources of Washington?

KEY IDEAS

- Washington is part of the Pacific Northwest and the Pacific Rim.
- Washington has five land regions, all with very different features.
- Most of Washington's population lives in the Puget Sound Lowlands.

KEY TERMS

commerce
lowlands
metropolitan
Pacific Rim
plateau
prominent
region

What Region Is Washington Part of?

Washington is part of several regions. *Regions* are places that share common features. There are political regions, economic regions, and land regions. People who live in a particular political region have similar governments. Being part of an economic region is to be connected by trade activity. Land regions share common physical features.

The Pacific Northwest

The Pacific Northwest is a region of states that share common physical, political, and economic features. Washington, Oregon, and Idaho have tall snowy mountains, rushing rivers, evergreen forests, dry grasslands, and farming valleys. The region is divided from the rest of the United States by the Rocky Mountains.

The Pacific Rim

The *Pacific Rim* is an economic region. All the countries of the Pacific Rim border the Pacific Ocean. This makes trade between Pacific Rim countries easy. Each country around the rim makes and sells products that other countries want to buy.

For example, the people of the United States buy clothing made in China and the Philippines. We buy cars, televisions, and electronic equipment made in Japan. Washington ships aircraft, machinery, lumber, wheat, fruit, and computer software to China, Japan, Korea, and many other countries on the Pacific Rim.

Seattle has one of the busiest ports in the country.

The Pacific Rim

ASIA

NORTH AMERICA

SOUTH AMERICA

AUSTRALIA

The Pacific Northwest

WASHINGTON

OREGON

IDAHO

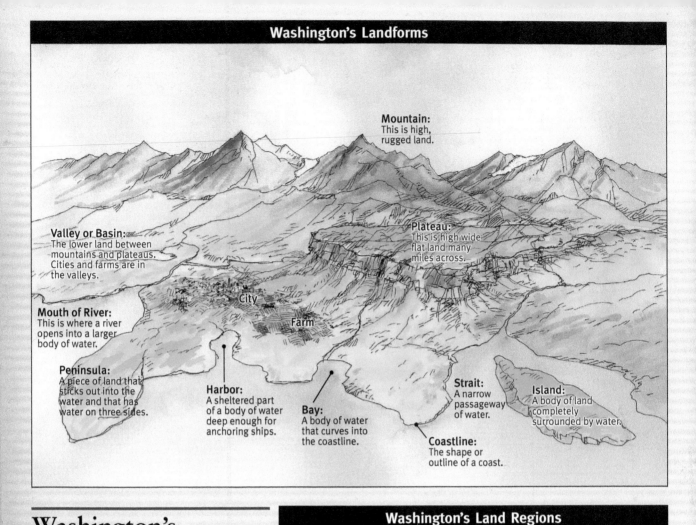

Mountain: This is high, rugged land.

Plateau: This is high wide flat land many miles across.

Valley or Basin: The lower land between mountains and plateaus. Cities and farms are in the valleys.

City

Farm

Mouth of River: This is where a river opens into a larger body of water.

Peninsula: A piece of land that sticks out into the water and that has water on three sides.

Harbor: A sheltered part of a body of water deep enough for anchoring ships.

Bay: A body of water that curves into the coastline.

Strait: A narrow passageway of water.

Island: A body of land completely surrounded by water.

Coastline: The shape or outline of a coast.

Washington's Five Regions

Washington can be divided into five land regions. Each region has at least one main physical feature but may contain more. These features, also called landforms, include valleys, mountains, and *plateaus* (high, wide, flat areas hundreds of miles across). As strange as it may seem, the rivers, oceans, and lakes are also called landforms because they are natural features of the Earth.

Starting at the western coast and moving east across the state, the land regions are:

Washington's Land Regions

Coastal Range

Puget Sound Lowlands

Cascade Range

Rocky Mountain

Columbia Plateau

The Coastal Range

Puget Sound Lowlands

Cascade Range

Columbia Plateau

Rocky Mountains

The Coastal Range is home to rainforests. **How can you tell this is a rainforest?**

The Coastal Range

This narrow region along the Pacific Coast includes several landforms, including a rainforest, the snow-capped Olympic Mountains, and other forests. Olympic National Park is part of the region, and the region itself is part of the Olympic Peninsula.

The rainforest in this region has so many different types of plants that one naturalist said it was "the greatest weight of living matter, per acre, in the world."

There is little industry in the region since most lumber mills have closed and commercial fishing is in decline. The small towns rely on tourism.

Coastal Range

The sun sets on Shi Shi Beach on the Pacific Coast of Olympic National Park.

North Head Lighthouse was built to help ships see the entrance to the Columbia River.

16

Puget Sound Lowlands

The Puget Sound Lowlands

The *lowlands* make up the plains and valleys of the Puget Sound region. The land here is fertile and there is access to rivers and deepwater seaports.

As a result, cities such as Seattle, Tacoma, Bellevue, Bremerton, Bellingham, Everett, and Olympia, the state capital, make this region the population center of the state. Seattle is the heart of the region. The region boasts one of the highest per capita income levels in the country. Microsoft, the world's largest corporation, has its headquarters in this region. This is a bustling, crowded, exciting, and prosperous region.

Deepwater seaports on Puget Sound and other ports on the Columbia River are important for the shipping industry. The bays, harbors, and San Juan Islands are popular recreation and vacation places.

Of course, not everyone in this region lives in cities. One of the state's richest farming areas is the Skagit River Valley. Tulips and daffodils are the most famous crop. Peas, carrots, cauliflower, broccoli, and other crops are grown for their seeds or are canned or frozen. The Cowlitz and Chehalis River Valleys are also farming regions. Dairy cattle and chickens are raised for profit.

Seattle is in the heart of the Puget Sound Lowlands. **What famous landmark is pictured here?**

A Seattle ferry arrives at Friday Harbor in the San Juan Islands. The ferries carry cars and people between the mainland and the islands.

The Cascade Range

The Cascade Mountain range, with its high volcanic peaks and many glaciers, is considered Washington's most *prominent*, or well known, geographic feature. These rugged mountains divide the land sharply. They are a barrier to *commerce*, which means trade, and travel.

The mountains are sometimes called the "Cascade Curtain." This term recognizes the very different interests of the large seaport and manufacturing cities in the West and the less-populated farming regions in the East.

The mountains also contribute to the startling differences in climate and rainfall between the eastern and western sections of the state. The land to the west of the mountains is rainy. Hemlocks, firs, and cedar forests grow in the damp climate. The forests of the western slopes are thick with mosses, ferns, and bushes growing beneath the trees. The eastern mountain slopes get

Cascade Range

much less rain, so the forests there have fewer trees than the western sections.

Five famous mountains are part of this region—Mt. St. Helens, Mt. Rainier, Mt. Adams, Mt. Baker, and Glacier Peak. Lake Chelan is also part of the region.

Two national parks, the North Cascades and Mt. Rainier, bring thousands of visitors to view the breathtaking beauty of the mountains. You will read more about Mt. St. Helens in the next lesson.

The Cascade Mountains have many physical features. **Describe the features you see here.**

Mountain Travel

The Cascades are not the great obstacle to travel they were in past years, though two of the five mountain passes are closed in the winter. Early wagon roads across the mountains were a dangerous adventure. Railroads carried people over the mountain passes in the 1800s.

Now the four-lane Interstate 90 goes over the mountains and through Snoqualmie Pass. When winter snows pile up and the threat of avalanches is great, however, Snoqualmie Pass can be closed for days at a time. Travelers just have to wait.

Travel over Snoqualmie Pass was quite different in 1919 than in 2009. The trip from Seattle to Spokane took three days in 1919. It takes four or five hours today.

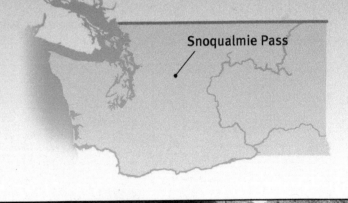

Snoqualmie Pass

The Palouse Falls are one of the key features of the Columbia Plateau. **How have the falls changed the land here?**

Washington's vineyards produce many variety of wine. **What is grown in the vineyard pictured here?**

The Palouse Hills provide some of the most fertile land in the state.

The Columbia Plateau

On the east side of the Cascades is the large Columbia Plateau region. The high, flat plateau covers most of eastern Washington and parts of Oregon and Idaho. It includes some of the driest land in the Pacific Northwest. Natural vegetation ranges from grassland to desert sagebrush.

The region includes the wheat-growing area of the Palouse. These irrigated lands grow a large variety of crops, including apples, cherries, grapes, corn, and alfalfa.

Spokane is the *metropolitan*, or city, center of the Columbia Plateau. Spokane is the commercial, financial, and medical center of a large region covering parts of surrounding states and southern British Columbia. Other cities on the plateau are Yakima, Moses Lake, Walla Walla, Pullman, and the Tri-Cities (Richland, Pasco, and Kennewick).

What Do You Think ❓

Why do you think the cities on the Puget Sound Lowlands attract more people than the Palouse farmland on the Columbia Plateau? What factors of geography affect where people start cities, where industry thrives, and where farming is successful?

Columbia Plateau

The Rocky Mountain Region

This region in the northern corner of the state is sometimes called the Okanogan Highlands. The steep hills are foothills of the great Rocky Mountains.

People in this region rely on farming, mining lead and zinc, ranching, and lumbering to make a living. There are a few small towns that depend on tourism.

Peopling the Land

As you read, the landforms of Washington's five regions have a lot to do with the spatial patterns of the state. People tend to live in the regions with natural features that enable them to provide for themselves and make a living. As a result, you find that Washington's greatest population is in the Puget Sound region, where fertile land like that of the Skagit Valley makes farming profitable.

In those regions where the natural environment is not as friendly, such as in the Palouse of the Columbia Plateau region, people make changes and adapt the land to meet their needs.

The sun sets on a farm in Addy in the Colville River Valley of the Rocky Mountain region.

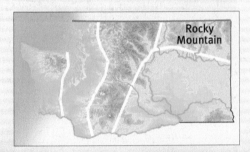

Rocky Mountain

What Did You Learn? 2

1. What common features and activities make Washington part of both the Pacific Northwest and the Pacific Rim?

2. Compare and contrast two of Washington's five land regions.

3. Why does most of Washington's population live in the Puget Sound Lowlands?

A view of the Rocky Mountains from Addy-Gifford Road in Stevens County.

KEY IDEAS

- Most of Washington was under water at one time.
- Earthquakes, volcanoes, and floods shaped the mountains, valleys, and plateaus of our state.
- Fossils provide clues about the animals and plants that once lived in Washington.

KEY TERMS

aquifer
coulee
dormant
fault
fissure
fossil fuel
lahar
loess
molten
subterranean
tectonic

A Jigsaw Puzzle

Eastern Washington used to be part of the coast of the North American continent millions of years ago. Spokane would have been on that seashore long ago.

All of the land to the south and west of the North American Continent shown on the map was under water at one time. Land was exposed as a result of collisions between the continent and the floor of the Pacific Ocean. These collisions caused the old coastal plain to be crushed into a long belt of folded rock. This created the Kootenay Arc. The Okanogan and North Cascade micro-continents (very small continents) were formed next.

Scientists believe that the North Cascade Micro-Continent broke away from Asia. Many of the fossil remains found there are similar to remains found in Asia. Also, the rock in the North Cascades is different from the rock of the rest of the Cascade Range.

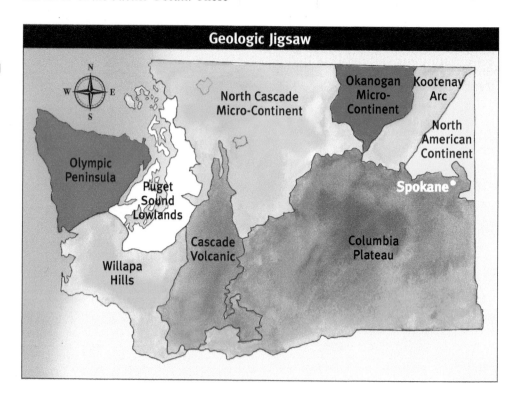

Geologic Jigsaw

A Timeline of Washington's Geologic History
*MYA means millions of years ago

500 mya	500 mya	400 mya	300 mya

Precambrian Era (85% of the earth's time period)

Paleozoic Era (570–240) MYA
- The Pangaea supercontinent divides.
- Shallow seas cover most of North America.
- Trilobites, amphibians, and reptiles live in the seas.
- Coal is formed.

Mountain Formations

Mountain ranges were uplifted, tilted, and folded in various ways. You can see the folded and tilted layers of rock as you explore mountain canyons. The uplifting is partly the result of the tectonic forces. *Tectonic* refers to the forces within the earth that cause movements of its crust. These forces pushed huge ridges of land against each other. Where the two landmasses met, land ridges were forced upward.

After the mountains were formed, erosion by moving wind, water, and ice started immediately. That is why older mountains are more rounded, and younger mountains are more jagged.

The Rocky Mountains are the oldest mountains in the West. Both the Cascades and the Olympic Mountains are much younger. The Olympic Mountains at one time were islands peeking out of the ocean.

Mountain Chains of the Pacific Northwest

Olympic Mts.

Cascade Mountains

Rocky Mountains

N W E S

Earthquakes!

Tectonic forces left *fault* lines—fractures in the earth's crust—in the Puget Sound region and off the Pacific Coast. A shift in one of the landmasses causes earthquakes every few years.

About a thousand years ago, there was a major earthquake where Seattle is now. More recent large shakes occurred in 1949, 1965, and 2001. The potential for a "big one" is always there.

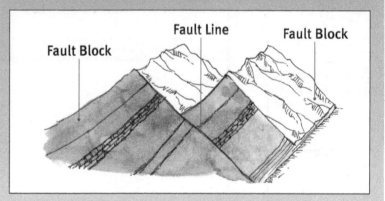

Fault Block   Fault Line   Fault Block

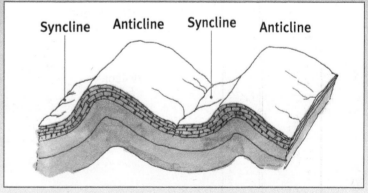

Syncline   Anticline   Syncline   Anticline

A syncline is formed when rock layers come together at their lowest point and push upward. Synclines can be as small as the side of a cliff or as large as an entire valley. An anticline is formed when rock layers push downward from a common crest. Anticlines can be as small as a hill or as large as a mountain range.

---

200 mya   100 mya   Present

Mesozoic Era (240–65) MYA
• Sedimentary rock is formed.
• The Rocky Mountains begin to take shape.
• The Okanogan Micro-Continent joins North America.

Cenozoic Era (65 MYA to present)
• The North Cascades Micro-Continent docks against the mainland.
• Volcanic activity forms the Cascade Range.
• Lava flow forms the Columbian Plateau.
• Ice Age glaciers blanket northern Washington.
• Glaciers carve valleys. Melting ice forms lakes.
• The Pacific Coast changes as ice melts.
• Grand Coulee and Dry Falls were eroded by floods.
• Olympic Mountains are formed.
• Humans hunt mammoths in the Pacific Northwest.

EUROPE

ASIA

NORTH
AMERICA

ATLANTIC
OCEAN

AFRICA

PACIFIC
OCEAN

INDIAN
OCEAN

SOUTH
AMERICA

ATLANTIC
OCEAN

AUSTRALIA

Pacific Ring of Fire

ANTARCTICA

Mt. Baker has one of the highest peaks in the Cascade range. Its elevation is 10,750 feet.

Mountains of Fire

Mountains were also formed by volcanic action. After the uplifting, folding, and faulting, volcanic activity occurred in both the Cascade and Olympic mountains. They are part of a great Ring of Fire that includes volcanoes in Indonesia, the Philippines, Japan, Alaska, and the west coast of North and South America.

How were these tall mountains formed? Steam and gases expanded inside the earth until the pressure was too great. **Molten** (liquid) rock called lava rose to the surface of the earth in a violent explosion. The lava flowed down the mountainside, building it higher and higher.

The Cascades include Washington's five "sleeping giants." Mt. Baker, Glacier Peak, Mt. Rainier, Mt. Adams, and Mt. St. Helens are **dormant**, or inactive, volcanoes now. No one knows when they will "wake up" and again cover the land around them with lava, mud, and ash.

> "Volcanoes are one way the earth gives birth to itself."
>
> —Robert Gross

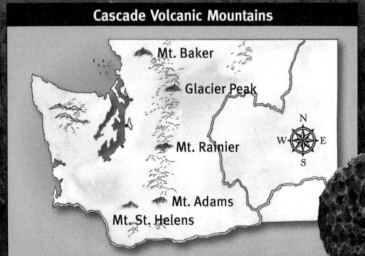

Cascade Volcanic Mountains

Mt. Baker

Glacier Peak

N
W • E
S

Mt. Rainier

Mt. Adams

Mt. St. Helens

Volcanic rocks have a bubbled texture like this.

The Washington Journey

Volcanoes Shaped Columbia Plateau

Volcanic activity formed more than mountains. Lava also helped change the relatively flat Columbia Plateau. It is one of the largest and most spectacular volcanic regions in the world.

Repeated eruptions from long *fissures*, or cracks in the Earth's crust, covered the plateau with lava that spread out more than 100 miles.

Rich Soil of the Palouse

After the lava flows ended, another feature changed the landscape. Rich soil was formed by deposits of glacial loess. *Loess* is a mixture of fine volcanic ash and dust carried by wind. Soil up to 150 feet deep gradually covered large regions of rock. Today, this is the Palouse wheat-growing region in eastern Washington.

Palouse Hills

Columbia Plateau

Basalt

Basalt is igneous rock, formed of hardened lava. Overlapping basalt layers of the plateau are more than 4,000 feet deep, leaving geologists to wonder what might be buried beneath them.

Basalt takes many forms when it cools. **How would you describe the form of these rocks?**

Volcanic lava helped to create the rich soil of the Palouse. **What is the main crop of this region?**

THE LESSON OF MT. ST. HELENS

It was May 18, 1980. Mt. St. Helens awoke with an eruption equal to 21,000 atomic bombs like the ones dropped on Japan at the end of World War II. This mountain was the youngest of the Cascade volcanoes and had been fairly active over the past 300 years. It was so active, in fact, that Indians had been afraid of the mountain and so stayed away.

No lava flowed from the mountain during the eruption.

A few months before the eruption there were tremors deep in the mountain. This signaled that an eruption was likely. By early May, a large bulge began to form on the side of the mountain. A week later, a large patch of the mountain turned into a churning brown liquid mass and began to slide downward. Then came an enormous explosion and a chain reaction of devastating events.

The collapsing mountain filled the north fork of the Toutle River with debris 600 feet deep. *Lahars*, or huge mud flows containing boulders and uprooted trees, filled the river. The load was carried down to the Columbia River, where the mud clogged up the river. Ships could not travel on the Columbia as a result.

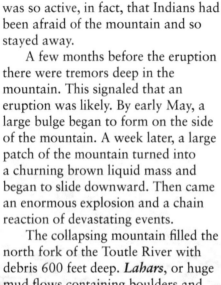

The damage from the eruption was caused by gas, ash, and flowing mud.

A towering cloud of ash and gas from the erupting volcano rose 12 miles into the air. Winds carried the ash and gas across the continent. Ash choked automobile air filters, causing vehicles to stall. In Spokane, 200 miles to the east, visibility was reduced to 10 feet and the airport was forced to close.

In the immediate blast area, ice and snow were melted quickly. Tens of thousands of stately Douglas firs six feet in diameter and 200 feet tall were laid flat over an area of 250 square miles. The earth beneath them was blown away to bedrock. All the wild land animals, fish, and birds were killed.

Deadly Consequences

Fifty-seven people lost their lives in the eruption. Probably the first to die was David Johnston, a geologist who was observing the mountain from a distance of six miles. Johnston had greatly underestimated the wide range and force of the eruption. He had time for one brief radio message. "Vancouver, Vancouver, this is it!" were his last words. His jeep, trailer, and his body were never found.

Mt. St. Helens loomed tall before the eruption.

Why did people risk their lives by staying so close to the mountain? The story of 84-year-old Harry R. Truman provides one explanation. Truman had operated a resort on Spirit Lake since 1926. When he was urged to leave, Truman stubbornly refused. He had a lot of money invested in his lodge. He had 16 cats that depended on him. This was his home, filled with memories of his wife who had died. As he put it, "If the mountain did do something, I'd rather go right here with it." Truman was buried under several hundred feet of volcanic debris.

The Mountain Today

Nature destroys, but it also heals. Plants and animals are slowly reclaiming the scarred landscape, and the mountain has become a place to study volcanoes, earthquakes, and changes to the environment.

Visitors to the three Mt. St. Helens visitor centers typically ask two questions. The first: "Will the mountain explode again?" The answer is: "Yes." The second: "When?" The answer is: "We do not know."

In geologic time, the eruption was an ordinary event, typical of the forces that have always shaped our physical environment. It serves as a powerful reminder that geologic forces continue to work.

The top of Mt. St. Helens was blown away, leaving only a huge crater. Spirit Lake is now filled with debris.

Hot gases reaching about 660º Fahrenheit shot out of the volcano along with pulverized pieces of mountain. The debris traveled at speeds up to 300 mph.

The valleys below Mt. Shuksan were carved by glaciers. **What features of the valley are shown here?**

A mile is 5,280 feet. Glaciers were over a mile thick in some places.

Olympia

Lake Missoula

Lake Lewis

Lake Condon

Columbia Gorge

Lake Allison

Pacific Ocean

Approximate southern extent of continuous ice sheet

Ice Age Washington

A long time after the major lava flows ceased, the air got much colder. Snow fell much of the year. Snow and ice accumulated, and the polar ice cap moved southward. The continental ice sheet moved into what is now Canada and the northern areas of what is now the United States. The cooling and warming happened over and over again. We call the last glacial period the Ice Age. It happened about one million to 10,000 years ago.

The moving glaciers shaped the Puget Sound Lowlands, filling in some areas of the landscape and carving out others. The ice sheet was 5,000 feet thick over the place where the city of Bellingham is today. It was 4,000 feet thick over the place where Seattle is today, and 1,800 feet over the Tacoma region. The Ice Age glaciers ended south of present-day Olympia.

The Great Floods

Glacial action also produced great floods. The ice sheet blocked the Clark Fork River near the Idaho-Montana border, forming an ice dam half a mile high. The water backed up and formed a prehistoric lake. Lake Missoula was larger than any lake in the western United States today. It was about half as large as Lake Michigan.

When the rising water from glacial melt became deep enough, the force of the water tore over and through the ice dam, unleashing an immense flood. Ice, dirt, rocks, and water rushed out at speeds of up to 50 miles per hour.

The movement of the glacier created a new dam and formed a new lake that produced another flood. Every 50 years or so for 2,000 years the process was repeated. As a result, the site of today's city of Spokane was repeatedly covered by water more than 500 feet deep. Today, Spokane draws its water from a huge *aquifer* created by the great floods. An aquifer is a deep layer of rock that holds water.

Millions of years ago, the falls were the largest in the world. Tons of water spilled over the basalt cliffs.
Why is this area called Dry Falls?

Grand Coulee

Large sections of eastern Washington were sculpted by ice and floodwater. The ice plugged the Columbia River, causing the water to overflow the riverbanks. Water flowed across the Columbia Plateau and wore down the rock of the Grand Coulee. A *coulee* is a dry streambed.

Today, the Grand Coulee is one of the state's most spectacular geologic features. It is between one and six miles wide and 50 miles long. Halfway down the channel is Dry Falls, site of the largest prehistoric waterfall the world has ever known. During Ice Age melting, water spread out more than three miles, thundering over the 400-foot-high falls.

Geologists now think that during the huge floods the cliffs of Dry Falls were actually submerged for a time. As the glaciers melted and the ice dams broke up, the waters retreated, leaving the coulee region high and dry. This process was repeated many times.

Fossils Are Clues to the Past

Fossils tell us what kinds of animals and plants once lived in a region. Sometimes thousands of shells are found in layers of rock. Sometimes entire skeletons of ancient animals are uncovered.

Shells and bones from ancient sea life tell us that oceans once covered our land. Fossils of ferns and other plants in central Washington indicate that a large tropical rainforest once flourished there.

Washington PORTRAIT

J. Harlen Bretz
(1882–1981)

The story of the great floods is a geological detective story. America's leading geologists could not agree that the floods existed.

There was one geologist, however, who spent most of his life trying to convince others that the floods had actually happened. From the early 1920s through the 1960s, J. Harlen Bretz argued the case of the Spokane Flood. His peers laughed at his ideas, but he stuck with them. How else could the immense water-scoured coulees, the enormous gravel bars topped with giant ripple marks, and the huge, dry waterfalls be explained?

Slowly, the Bretz theory came to be accepted. By then, Bretz was nearly 90 years old. Today, geologists call the great floods the Bretz Floods.

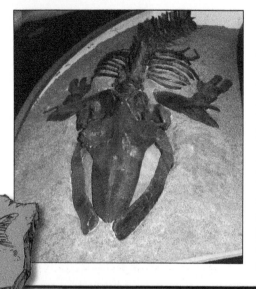

The bones of the oldest-known fossil of a toothless whale were discovered in a quarry on the Olympic Peninsula in 1993. The bones are on display at the Burke Museum.

Fossil Fuels

Coal was formed by the combination of prehistoric plants, heat, and pressure over millions of years. In the wet climate of prehistoric times, ferns and other plants lived and died. In time, rock and earth covered the plants. Later, when mountains were thrust upward, the rock sometimes contained layers of coal. Other deposits stayed under the ground. Such *subterranean* deposits of coal and other fossils that can be burned are considered *fossil fuels*. Today, there are fairly large coal deposits in King, Kittitas, and Lewis counties.

Fossil Fuels and Global Warming

Carbon dioxide is one of the greenhouse gases that is produced when fossil fuels are burned. For example, our cars emit carbon dioxide into the atmosphere as a result of the burning of gasoline, which contains petroleum (another fossil fuel). Environmentalists warn that greenhouse gases produced by the burning of fossil fuels are a significant contributing factor to global warming.

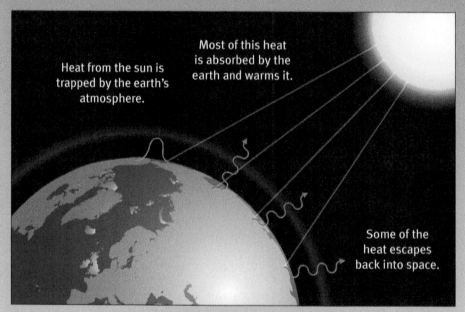

Heat from the sun is trapped by the earth's atmosphere.

Most of this heat is absorbed by the earth and warms it.

Some of the heat escapes back into space.

Greenhouse gases, like carbon dioxide, trap heat from the sun. The planet gets warmer when the amount of carbon dioxide in the atmosphere increases.

What Did You Learn? ③

1. Where was the coast of Washington millions of years ago?
2. Identify the main forces that shaped the landscape of our state.
3. What have geologists learned about Washington from fossils?

Go to the Source

Where Do People Live?

Why do people choose to live in certain places? What geographic, cultural, or economic features draw people to an area? Often, areas with a large population tend to share common features as do areas with small populations. Examine the map and see what conclusions you can make about Washington's population.

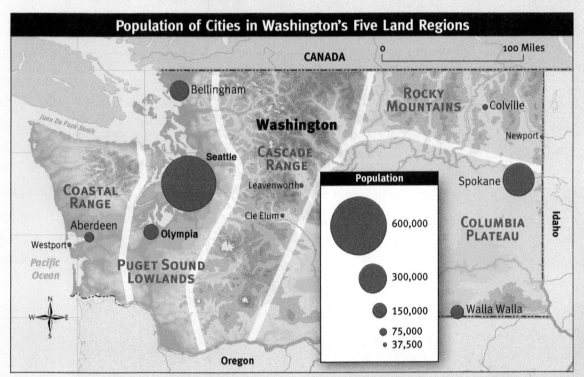

Population of Cities in Washington's Five Land Regions

Observe ----- Evaluate ----- Conclude

Observe	Evaluate	Conclude
• How is the map organized? • Identify three cities with the greatest population. • Identify three cities with the smallest population.	• What do cities with a large population have in common? • What do cities with a small population have in common?	• What conclusions can you draw about spatial (settlement) patterns in Washington?

Using Maps as a Resource

Maps are an essential tool of geography. Maps have many purposes. Road maps help us know where we are and get to where we want to go. But maps can do more than that. Maps are like pictures . . . they say a lot with few words. Maps can help us see the Earth's spatial patterns. They can give us information on physical features, climate, natural resources, economic activity, political boundaries, and topographic features that help us distinguish steep terrain from flat land.

Although maps may show different kinds of information, they typically share some common features:

- A title that indicates what kind of information the map will show.
- A compass rose, which helps determine the orientation of a map by showing North, South, East, and West.
- A scale of miles to estimate distances.
- A legend or key with symbols to help identify cities, rivers, forests, regions, major religions, main ethnic groups, and other things.

Some maps also include a grid showing lines of latitude and longitude. The intersection of those lines helps determine the absolute location of a place. For example, the absolute location of Seattle is 48°N latitude and 122°W longitude.

Your Turn

Two examples of maps are shown here.

1. What title would you give to each map?

2. What do the keys show for each map?

3. Write a brief paragraph describing three significant pieces of information you learned from each map.

4. Flip through the pages of *The Washington Journey* and find at least three examples of maps. Be sure they represent different types of maps. Compare your list with a partner. What did you find? Which maps did you find most informative? What observations can you make about your state based on the maps you found?

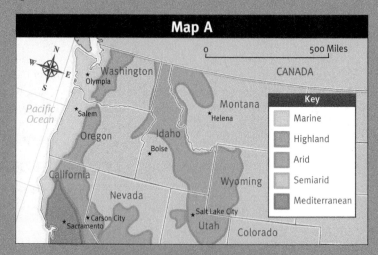

Chapter Review Questions

1. What are the three most common types of landforms in Washington?
2. Identify at least three important ways the Pacific Ocean affects the people and economy of Washington.
3. How has Washington's environment been affected by human activity?
4. List Washington's five land regions.
5. Describe three ways the eruption of Mt. St. Helens changed the land.
6. How did lava flows help form the Columbia Plateau?
7. Why have the Palouse Hills become the state's wheat-growing region?
8. How do fossil fuels contribute to global warming?

Becoming a Better Reader

Previewing a Textbook

One of the most important reading strategies is hardly reading at all! It's called previewing. Previewing a textbook helps you prepare to read. Preparing to read helps you better understand what you read. When previewing a textbook, it is good to browse the table of contents. Also, look at the essential questions in each chapter as well as chapter introductions. After previewing this book, write a paragraph about what you might learn by reading *The Washington Journey*.

A journey of a thousand miles, must begin with a single step. —Lao Tzu, Chinese Philosopher

You Are the Geographer

Calculating Distance

Examine the map of Washington on pages 6 and 7. Use the scale of miles to calculate approximate distances. Compare your answers with a partner.

1. What is the distance between the coast of Washington and the border of Idaho?
2. What is the distance from Washington's border with Canada to its border with Oregon?
3. How far apart is Seattle from Spokane?
4. How far apart is Seattle from Olympia?
5. How wide is the Strait of San Juan de Fuca?

Essential
Question **?**

What brought explorers
and settlers to the Pacific
Northwest and how did
their arrival affect native
cultures?

Early Encounters:
Two Worlds Meet

Timeline of Events

1776
Captain Cook sails to
the Pacific Northwest.

| 2000 B.C. | 1592 | 1776 |

◄— 4,500–2,000 B.C. —
Coastal and Plateau
Cultures emerge.

1592
Juan de Fuca claims to
have sailed the coast of
the Pacific Northwest.

Chapter 2

Long before white settlers came to live in the Pacific Northwest, there were many Indian tribes living along the Pacific Coast and inland river systems. Theirs was a world of fishing, hunting, gathering, and trading.

By the late 1700s, these native groups would meet outsiders from Europe and America. The encounter changed their lives forever.

*Prehistoric drawings in the rocks were made by the coastal Makah tribe who lived on the Olympic Peninsula. These drawings can be seen at Cape Alava in Olympic National Park. **What images did the Makah draw?***

1792
Robert Gray explores the Columbia River.

1803
The United States buys the Louisiana Purchase.

1811
The Pacific Fur Company builds Fort Astoria.

1831
Four Indian men travel to St. Louis to request Christian missionaries.

1838
The first Catholic mission is started in Oregon Country.

1800

1820

1840

1804
Lewis and Clark explore the Louisiana Purchase.

1812
The War of 1812 is fought between Great Britain and the United States.

1824
The Hudson's Bay Company builds Fort Vancouver.

1834
The first Protestant mission is started in Oregon Country.

1836
Marcus and Narcissa Whitman start a mission.

1780s–1840s
The fur trade

KEY IDEAS

- The Coastal Indians developed a unique and rich culture along the rivers and coastline of the Northwest.
- The land and climate of the Columbian Plateau shaped the lives of the Plateau Indians.
- Indian groups interacted through trade and sometimes war.

KEY TERMS

camas
longhouse
migration
potlatch
spoils
tule
weir

Native Americans

When European explorers first came to the Pacific Northwest, there were many groups of native peoples living all over the land. The native lifestyles were alike in many ways but different in other ways. Some spoke related languages, and some spoke entirely different languages.

Groups were divided by geographic landforms such as mountains and large rivers. The climate varied greatly. These natural features greatly affected native culture.

The Coastal People

During the 2,000 years before contact with white explorers, natives of the Northwest Coast—an area extending from California to Alaska—created a unique and rich culture. The Pacific Ocean provided for a marine economy. The ocean was full of fish, shellfish, and sea mammals. Its moist air assured an abundance of plant life, including the giant red cedar—a source of shelter, clothing, and transportation. The mild marine climate made life easier than life in other places. Large semi-permanent villages were found at the mouths of every river.

Most of all, the ocean's resources gave the Coastal tribes the extraordinary gift of leisure time in the winter months. The winter months could be spent on recreation and on artistic projects. Winter was also the time for elaborate ceremonies, a basic feature of coastal social life.

Salish

The largest group of Indians on the coast was the Salish-speaking people. The mild climate and plentiful food from the sea made life easy. The coastal Salish thrived living next to the ocean. They occupied all of Puget Sound and most of western Washington.

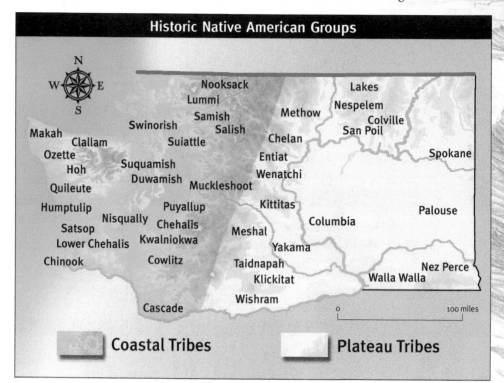

Historic Native American Groups

Nooksack
Lummi
Samish
Swinorish
Salish
Suiattle
Makah
Clallam
Ozette
Hoh
Suquamish
Duwamish
Muckleshoot
Quileute
Humptulip
Puyallup
Nisqually
Chehalis
Satsop
Lower Chehalis
Kwalniokwa
Chinook
Cowlitz
Cascade

Lakes
Nespelem
Methow
Colville
San Poil
Chelan
Entiat
Wenatchi
Kittitas
Columbia
Meshal
Yakama
Taidnapah
Klickitat
Wishram
Spokane
Palouse
Nez Perce
Walla Walla

0   100 miles

Coastal Tribes   Plateau Tribes

Chinook

Along the Columbia River lived various groups of the Chinook. They spoke Penutian, an ancient language.

The Chinooks were the great middlemen in a vast network of Indian trade. They traded slaves from California to Vancouver Island for canoes and prized dentalium shells. The shells were long and narrow and were strung on long rope necklaces that were worn by both men and women. They were used in trade as we use money.

To make trade and communication with other groups easier, the Chinook developed a language known as "Chinook Jargon." This was a spoken language understood by dozens of tribes over a vast stretch of western North America. You will read in chapter 4 how Chinook Jargon was the language used in treaties between Indian tribes and the U.S. government in the 1850s.

Chinook Jargon

How did sailors and coastal Indians talk when neither knew the other's language? The problem was complicated by the many different languages the Indian tribes spoke and the variety of countries the traders came from. American Indians who spoke different languages were already speaking a trade language when white trappers and settlers came. Called Chinook Jargon, the language had about 500 words.

Here are a few words from Chinook Jargon:

Chinook Jargon	English
Boston	American
cultus	worthless
muckamuck	food; eating
skookum	strong
tillicum	man
tyee	chief
gleece	grease
pire	fire
gleece-pire	candle
mahkook	trade
chuck	water
tenus	small
hyas	big

Access to the Pacific Ocean and rivers made life easy for the Coastal people. **What animal does the boat seem to represent?**

Early Encounters: Two Worlds Meet

37

A Chinook longhouse was home to several related families. A hole in the center of the roof let out smoke from the cooking fire. The people made cattail and cedar mats that formed movable interior walls. **What other features of the longhouse do you notice?**

Makah

On the very tip of the Olympic Peninsula lived the Makah. They were a division of the Nootka, a tribe that occupied much of the west coast of Vancouver Island.

The Makah, Nootka, and a few neighboring tribes were the only Coastal peoples to pursue gray whales. The largest of all sea mammals, gray whales regularly migrated along the coast. *Migration* is the seasonal movement of a group of animals from one place to another. They hunted the whales in large cedar canoes so well built and decorated that they became prized trade items. Ceremonial rituals were held to prepare for the hunt.

Homes of Cedar

The Coastal Indians used wood as their basic building material. Red cedar was the most important wood. Red cedar was easily split into wide,

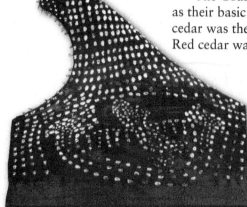

The Makah created a lot of ceremonial art, including this whale saddle. The decorations and carvings on the saddle were believed to be spiritual.

straight planks for building houses and ceremonial lodges.

Longhouses, or long dwellings where many people lived, were built by overlapping cedar planks. Planks or cedar shavings covered the dirt floors. Several related families lived together in one longhouse that faced the sea.

Family, Wealth, and Slaves

The basic social unit was the extended family. Wealth was important to social ranking. A wealthy family might own more canoes, tools, weapons, and animal skins. Wealthy people also had slaves. Group leaders were nearly always wealthy. As a person got more possessions, he moved up in social status.

No single person ruled the group. Councils met and made decisions together. There were chiefs, nobles, commoners, and slaves in the communities.

Slaves were usually women and children who were stolen from other groups. Slaves lived in the house with the rest of the family and did the hardest work. Sometimes they were sold to other groups.

The Plateau People

Large groups of native people lived east of the Cascade Mountains. The land and climate of the plateau shaped the lives of the people who lived there just as the marine environment influenced the lives of the Coastal Indians. The plateau's hot, dry summers and cold, snowy winters meant that the people moved, or migrated, with the seasons and changed clothing and shelters.

The plateau's most prominent natural feature, the Columbia River system, was a major transportation route and was also the Indians' most important source of food.

The Plateau people often moved around in search of food.
What time of year does it appear to be?
How are the natives preparing for what is to come?

Two Language Groups

Plateau tribes were divided into two main language groups. The Salish-speaking tribes of the northern plateau included the Spokane, Kalispel, Coeur d'Alene, Colville, Okanagon, Columbia, and Wenatchee. Most of the tribes of the southern plateau spoke a different language. These groups included the Nez Perce, Yakama, Palouse, Klickitat, Kittitas, Umatilla, and Wanapum.

Coastal Indians lived in the same place all year, but the Plateau Indians moved around. They lived in winter villages for years but often spent months at a time on long food-gathering trips. At these times, they lived in tepees that could be taken apart and moved to a new place.

A painting of Palouse Falls that the artist titled Falls of the Paloos River.
Who is pictured on a cliff overlooking the falls?

Pit Houses

At times, the Plateau people built more permanent dwellings called pit houses. This type of house was widely used until the early 1800s.

The house was built partially in the ground and partially above ground. The walls were made of tall poles covered with thinner poles or, in other places or later years, with woven grass mats. The builders placed a large notched log down through a hole in the top of the house to be used as a ladder.

The person who wanted to build the house asked all his neighbors to help. Twenty or more came, so that the building was sometimes completed in a single day.

Tule Houses

After the early 1800s, tule houses replaced pit houses. *Tule* is a grasslike plant that grows in swampy areas. Tall bunches of tule were cut, dried, and laid flat side by side. The ends were tied to form mats. Tule mats were laced to a log framework and overlapped to provide protection from wind and rain.

Gender Roles and Equality

Women gathered roots and berries, dried meat and fish, prepared animal skins, made the family's clothing, and cared for young children. Men fished and hunted, made tools and weapons, built the houses, and, if necessary, went to war.

While men and women had defined roles, there was a great deal of equality between them. The woman was always free to reject a marriage proposal. And, in some groups, the women could propose marriage.

Within the family, women had greater authority than men. For example, food was the wife's property. Even if he had provided it, the husband needed permission to take even a small piece of dried meat.

The interior of a pit house. **What are the main features of the home? How might this home provide good protection during bad weather?**

The Potlatch

Nothing showed the wealth of Coastal people more than the potlatch. A *potlatch* was a huge celebration hosted by a family for a special event. There were marriage, birth, and death potlatches. A large feast for the entire village and the presenting of gifts were basic features. The people of the highest social status received the most expensive gifts first. Those of the lowest social status got smaller gifts.

Linking the Past to the Present

In what ways do people today use wealth as a way of measuring a person's worth? Do we look down on the poor? Do poor people get the same respect and opportunities as people with more money?

Coastal and Plateau Indians meet for intertribal trading. **What items are they trading?**

Unlike the Meadow Death Camas, the Common Camas shown here is edible.

Trade Connections

Trade took place at the intertribal fishing sites at Kettle Falls and Celilo Falls, as well as at major camas-gathering fields. *Camas* is an edible, flowering plant. Goods were exchanged as ritual gifts, bartered for other goods, and won or lost through gambling. Gambling was so widespread that some scholars believe it was the primary method of trade.

Coastal tribes carried on extensive trading activities, none more so than the Chinook. Up the Columbia River at The Dalles, there was a thriving exchange between the Chinook and the various Plateau tribes. It was almost like a giant flea market. The Dalles became one of the most important inter-cultural trading sites in all of North America.

The lives of both the Coastal and Plateau Indians were enriched by trade. But there was a downside to the exchange. As Indian trading networks expanded, they became routes for deadly germs.

The salmon were speared, caught in nets or weirs, or scooped up in large baskets beneath waterfalls. *Weirs* were fences put across streams to stop fish from getting away.

Kettle Falls•

Celilo Falls

The Dalles

The fishing was excellent near waterfalls on the Columbia and other rivers. **What methods are these Indians using to catch fish?**

Spanish Bring Horses to North America

Horses were brought to Mexico by Spanish explorers. By 1700, horses had been traded to the Shoshoni in Idaho. The Cayuse people brought the horse to the Columbia Plateau. By 1750, most Plateau tribes had at least a few horses.

The Nez Perce and Cayuse, whose territory contained extensive grazing lands, had large herds. *Cayuse* became a term generally used for the tough, wiry ponies of the region. Coastal Indians had little use for the horse. However, there were some horses around Puget Sound.

Horses changed Indian life in many ways. Food gathering became more efficient. On horseback, it was possible to travel greater distances to hunt, and it was easier to bring back food to winter camps. Many tribes traveled to the Great Plains to hunt buffalo. An 1824 hunt consisted of more than 800 Indians with 1,800 horses. Dried buffalo meat and buffalo robes became important trade items.

The Last of the Buffalo *was painted by German painter Albert Bierstadt.*

Artist David Govedare's sculpture, Grandfather Cuts Loose the Ponies *includes 15 life-sized steel ponies overlooking the Columbia River in Vantage. The sculpture can be seen by travellers on I-90.*

An Indian Legend

Southern Columbia Basin tribes tell a colorful legend that explains how they got horses. Like all oral Indian history, this legend was passed down from generation to generation by what the people called "Grandfather Tales."

Speelyi, the Coyote Spirit who created the Indian world, decided one day that his people in this part of the country had walked long enough.

Summoning one of his favorite shamans to a cave, he gave the medicine man a basketful of ponies and told him to turn them loose as a gift to his people. The shaman tipped the basket on a high bluff, where they spread to all the inland tribes as Speelyi's special gift.

While the benefits of the horse were many, there was also a downside. Greed for horses greatly increased the scale of violence. Horses became *spoils*, or rewards, of war. Stealing horses became an important test of bravery. The Shoshoni began regular raids for horses and slaves. The Oregon Klamath people became fierce slave and horse raiders. "We found that we could make money by war," as one warrior put it, noting that "we rather got to like it anyhow."

What Did You Learn? ①

1. What enabled the Coastal people to develop their culture?
2. Why did the Plateau people move with the seasons?
3. In what ways did the native peoples interact?
4. How did horses affect the lives of Indians?

European Explorers

The first Europeans to come in contact with the natives of the Northwest were explorers. They were in search of a shortcut between Europe and Asia. Discovery of the *Northwest Passage* would make it much easier for European traders to reach the markets of China and India.

Instead of traveling east over land from Europe to Asia, merchants and government leaders spent money trying to find a shorter and faster water route. In fact, Christopher Columbus was looking for a new water route to Asia when he accidentally "discovered" North America. Columbus and his crew sailed west from Europe. They didn't realize there was another continent between Europe and Asia.

Once North America was discovered, explorers from several countries kept searching for the *elusive* (hard to find) Northwest Passage. Many explorers spent years trying to discover it, often with disastrous and tragic consequences.

Although the passage was finally discovered, it took sailors through the icy waters of the Arctic Circle and not through the rivers of the Pacific Northwest. Traversing the passage today requires navigating thousands of icebergs—a dangerous, costly, and time-consuming trip.

Juan de Fuca

The Spanish may have been the first to sail ships along the Pacific Coast. Juan de Fuca claimed that Spain had hired him to be the captain of a ship to explore the Pacific Coast. He described a narrow water passage, or *strait*, along the coast. He told of a *pillar*, or a natural structure of rocks, that stood at the entrance to the passage.

Whether or not Juan de Fuca actually found the strait, mapmakers in Europe added his name to their maps, creating the Strait of Juan de Fuca—at least on paper.

KEY IDEAS

- Spanish and English sailors were the first to explore the Northwest coast.
- An American explorer named the Columbia River and claimed the land around it.
- Lewis and Clark helped map the terrain of the Northwest.

KEY TERMS

elusive
extensive
lucrative
Northwest Passage
pillar
strait
terrain

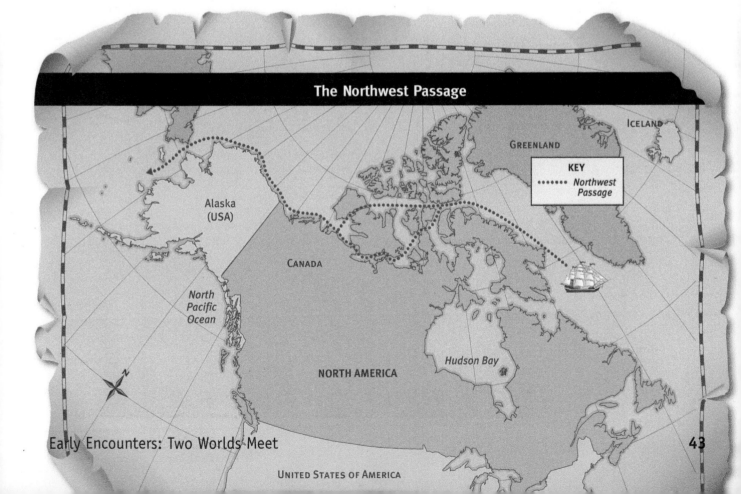

The Northwest Passage

ICELAND

GREENLAND

KEY
...... Northwest Passage

Alaska (USA)

CANADA

North Pacific Ocean

Hudson Bay

NORTH AMERICA

UNITED STATES OF AMERICA

James Cook was a famous British sea captain who twice sailed around the world.

Captain Cook

In 1776, the same year American colonists were fighting the Revolutionary War along the East Coast, a British sea captain, James Cook, left the coast to sail around the tip of South America.

He was already a famous explorer who had been around the world twice, in both directions. Cook had even discovered a group of islands in the Pacific that he named the Sandwich Islands. (They were later renamed the Hawaiian Islands.)

Sailing to what is now called Vancouver Island, Cook discovered that the Spanish were already there, trading with the Indians.

Captain Cook was looking for the Northwest Passage. Whoever discovered it for Britain was to receive a cash prize equal to nearly a million dollars today.

Feeling the trip had been a failure, the crew traded trinkets for some sea otter furs. The furs made warm bedding and clothing for sailing in such a cold climate. The ships returned to the Sandwich Islands, where Cook was killed in a fight with natives.

After Cook's death, his crews left the islands and headed to China, where they were delighted to learn that the Chinese paid very high prices for the sea otter pelts from the Pacific Northwest.

While Cook's men did not find the Northwest Passage, the word about the *lucrative*, or profitable, fur trade was out. More people were soon on the way.

Gray Discovers Columbia River

Robert Gray, who had heard about the huge profits to be made by trading furs in China, sailed out of Boston with a load of trade goods bound for the Pacific Coast. It was his second voyage to the Pacific Northwest.

After a long trip around the tip of South America and up the coast, Gray and his men discovered what seemed to

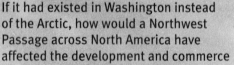

American explorer Robert Gray

Robert Gray's ship, the Columbia Redivia, *as it approaches the mouth of the Columbia River.* **How do you know this ship is American?**

What Do You Think?

If it had existed in Washington instead of the Arctic, how would a Northwest Passage across North America have affected the development and commerce of our state and our country?

be a river, but the water was so rough the ships could not sail into it. They sailed on to a wide inlet "which had the very good appearance of a harbor."

A few days later, the crew again tried to sail into the Columbia River. Sandbars filled the passageway between the sea and the river. Gray waited until the ocean tides were high, then carefully guided a small boat, and then his ship, over the foamy white waves. This time he made it, named the river, and claimed all of the land on both sides of the river for the United States.

The crew spent nine days on the river, trading with the Chinook Indians for furs. Realizing that the Indians captured the valuable sea otters in the ocean and not on the river, the group did no further exploring of the great Columbia.

British Sailor Names Vancouver Island

In that same year, a British sailor, George Vancouver, also sailed up the coast, passing the mouth of the Columbia River. Later, hearing of Gray's entrance into the Columbia, Vancouver returned and sent a small ship to cross the dangerous sandbar

Pirates!

Pirates sailed the Pacific Northwest Coast, too. Between 1575 and 1742, there were at least 25 different pirate ships preying upon ships along the West Coast of North America. Pirates came from England, Holland, and France. They were looking for Spanish ships to plunder, meaning to rob. Spanish ships on their way back to New Spain were filled with expensive goods from China and the East Indies.

and explore farther up the river. "I never felt more alarmed and frightened in my life," wrote one of the sailors. Vancouver spent the summer exploring and mapping the Puget Sound region.

Vancouver claimed all the land on both sides of the river for Great Britain and named Vancouver Island for himself. Among Vancouver's friends were men with last names of Baker, Rainier, Whidbey, and Puget. Do you recognize these names?

Washington Place Names

One advantage to being an explorer is getting to name places for yourself and your friends. Many of the early Spanish names have survived. Are you familiar with these Spanish names?

San Juan Islands—named for Saint John the Baptist

Guemes Island—named for the viceroy of Mexico

Rosario Strait—named for Our Lady of the Rosary

Port Angeles—named for Our Lady of the Angels

Cape Alava—named after the governor of Acapulco

George Vancouver spent a summer exploring and mapping the Puget Sound region.

Lewis and Clark

In 1803, France sold the Louisiana Purchase to the United States. It was an immense piece of new territory that needed to be explored and mapped. President Thomas Jefferson sent explorers to see if river travel all the way to the Pacific Ocean was possible and to learn about the *terrain* (land), plants, animals, and native people.

Jefferson chose his secretary, Captain Meriwether Lewis, to lead the expedition. Lewis, age 29, was a quiet man and a lover of nature. He chose an old friend from his army days, Lieutenant William Clark, as a partner. Clark, an outgoing redhead, was eager to take part in the adventure.

The rest of the party consisted of 28 "good hunters, stout, healthy, unmarried men . . . capable of bearing bodily fatigue." York, Clark's black slave, was part of the group as well.

The men traveled north from St. Louis and spent their first winter in the Dakotas—land of the Mandan Indians. There they met a 16-year-old Indian woman named Sacajawea and her French-Canadian husband. They joined the expedition as guides and interpreters. (Years before in what is now Idaho, Sacajawea had been stolen from her people by another tribe.) Sacajawea carried her baby son, Pomp, on her back the entire trip.

The group traveled by boat on the Missouri River and then trekked across the Rockies of northern Idaho. There Sacajawea met her long-lost brother, who had become a chief. His horses helped the group across the mountains.

Indians give Lewis and Clark the gift of a white horse.
Do Lewis and Clark have anything to offer in return?

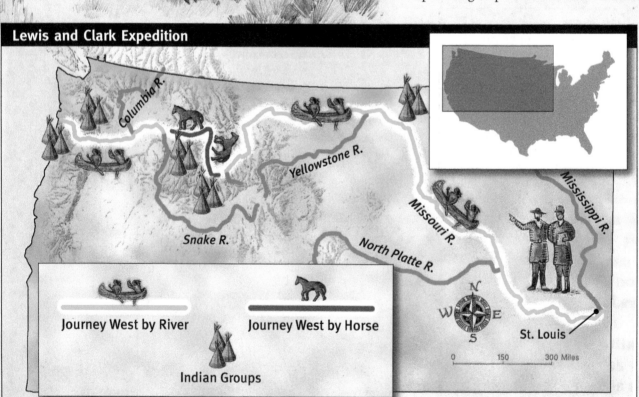

Lewis and Clark Expedition

Columbia R.

Yellowstone R.

Snake R.

Missouri R.

North Platte R.

Mississippi R.

St. Louis

Journey West by River

Journey West by Horse

Indian Groups

0   150   300 Miles

Clark's Diary

November 6, 1805

A . . . rainy morning. The Indians of the two lodges we passed today came in their canoes. . . . I purchased two beaver skins for which I gave five small fish hooks. . . . Dried out our bedding and killed the fleas which collected in our blankets.

November 7, 1805

A cloudy, foggy morning. Great joy in camp. We are in view of the ocean, this great Pacific Ocean which we have been so anxious to see.

Lewis and Clark on the Lower Columbia was painted in 1905. The dress of the Indians and the decorations on the boat are not quite right for the time period and location. **Why do you think the artist painted the scene this way? What other observations can you make about this painting?**

Worn out but still hopeful, the group came to the winter camp of the Nez Perce Indians along the Clearwater River. The Nez Perce gave Lewis advice about the best route to the Pacific and provided vital food and assistance with building boats. The explorers then made their way to the rough Columbia River and continued to the ocean.

It was November 1805 when the explorers finally reached their goal—the blue waters of the Pacific. It had taken more than a year and a half to get there. The group hoped to meet a ship to take them back to the East but none appeared. The entire party, including York and Sacajawea, voted to build a small shelter, called it Fort Clatsop, and waited for spring.

The Journey Home

The next spring the group began the long trip home. Along the way, they drew maps, collected plants, and made notes about the native people. They even sent a live prairie dog and dinosaur bones back to President Jefferson.

When the explorers finally arrived in St. Louis over two years after they had started, local people were astonished. Many thought the explorers had died. However, it was not until their *extensive* (lengthy) journals were published—many years after their deaths—that Lewis, Clark, and Sacajawea became heroes.

Lewis and Clark first saw the ocean from Washington, then the group voted to cross the Columbia River into Oregon, where the weather was milder to wait for spring.

What Did You Learn? ②

1. Why were explorers looking for a Northwest Passage?
2. How did Gray's discovery of the Columbia River impact the United States?
3. List three accomplishments of Lewis and Clark's travels.

Early Encounters: Two Worlds Meet

KEY IDEAS

- Fur trading was the chief economic activity along the Pacific Coast in the early 1800s.

- Missionaries had limited success in converting Indians to Christianity.

- Diseases brought by missionaries and others took a toll on the Indian population.

KEY TERMS

barter
Continental Divide
epidemic
extinction
immunity
intrusion
predominant
subsidiary

American Fur Traders

Fur trading was the *predominant*, or main, economic activity of Americans, British, and French who established trading posts along the Pacific coast and the Columbia and Willamette rivers in the early 1800s.

The first American trading post was established by the Pacific Fur Company. The company was a subsidiary of the American Fur Company founded by John Jacob Astor of New York. A *subsidiary* is a company that is owned by another bigger company. Astor wanted to expand his company to the Pacific Northwest so he hired Captain Jonathan Thorn, a strict military man, to sail from New York to open a trading post on the Pacific Coast.

After the long trip around South America and up the coast, Thorn's ship sailed through a storm to the mouth of the wild Columbia River. Instead of waiting for better weather, Thorn ordered five men to get into a small boat and find a safe passage into the river. The boat flipped over in the white foam, and the men drowned. Three other men and a second boat were also lost in the raging waters.

The main group finally made it through and landed the ship. Thorn left some men there to build Fort Astoria, named for John Jacob Astor. They built the fort on a hill with a magnificent view of the river below.

Impatient to begin trading with the Indians for furs, Thorn took the rest of the crew and sailed on to Nootka to trade. Later in the summer, word came back that Thorn had made some local Indians so angry that they killed him and all of his men.

Fur traders were among the first to settle in Oregon Country. **How can you tell this man is a fur trader?**

Americans and British Shared Oregon Country

When the United States and the British fought each other in the War of 1812, the Astorians were forced to sell their fort to the British. At the end of the war, Great Britain and the United States signed a treaty that gave both countries ownership of Oregon Country. The land stretched from the Rocky Mountains to the Pacific Ocean.

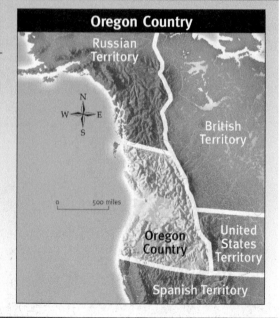

Oregon Country

Russian Territory

British Territory

Oregon Country

United States Territory

Spanish Territory

N W E S

0   500 miles

British Fur Traders

The Hudson's Bay Company, or HBC, controlled the fur trade in Canada and in the Oregon Country. An excellent trapper, medical doctor, and ambitious leader, Dr. John McLoughlin traveled by canoe and horseback across Canada for four months. He built a new fort near the mouth of the Willamette River and called it Fort Vancouver.

Fort Vancouver grew to contain small houses for fur trappers and their Indian wives, storehouses for furs, trade goods, and workshops for blacksmiths, carpenters, and other craftsmen. There was a sawmill to provide lumber and a gristmill to grind grain.

Outside the fort there were extensive orchards, farmlands, a dairy, and herds of cattle. Ships brought the latest news and supplies.

The people at Fort Vancouver came from many places. There were local Chinook Indians as well as Delaware and Iroquois Indian fur trappers who came from the East. Also, there were French Canadians, Hawaiian laborers, Indian women who had married HBC workers, and Scottish traders.

Many of the Hudson's Bay Company fur traders were from Scotland. A tall, red-haired Scottish Highlander in plaid kilts played bagpipes for the local Indians. It awed the Indians, who had never heard anything like it.

Fort Vancouver was located near the mouth of the Willamette River. It was used as a trading post by the Hudson's Bay Company. **How would you describe the activity at the fort in this image?**

Washington PORTRAIT

Ranald MacDonald
(1824–1894)

Ranald MacDonald's father was a Scottish trader with the Hudson's Bay Company, and his mother was the daughter of a powerful Chinook chief. He grew up at Fort Vancouver, where he met three Japanese fishermen. He heard about the exotic land of Japan and decided to go there someday, but at that time, Japan would not allow foreigners to enter the country.

Eventually, Ranald got a job on an American whaling ship. On the coast of Japan, he went ashore in a small boat. He had an English dictionary, a history book, and a world map that he thought would reassure the Japanese that he meant no harm.

Local villagers quickly discovered him and put him in jail. He was treated well, however, and spent his time teaching Japanese youths to speak English.

A year later Ranald was sent back to the United States, where he discovered his Chinook relatives had died from diseases.

49

A fur trapper makes his way through the snow. **How prepared is he for the winter weather?**

Fur was a popular fashion used in making top hats and coats.

What Do You Think ?

From what you have read about the fur trade, what do you think were some positive and negative effects on the development of our state? On the native people? On the animals? In the lives of the explorers and trappers?

Sea Otters

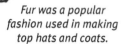

Between 1750 and 1790, thousands of sea otters were killed for their furs. Almost all of the otters were taken by explorers and trappers at sea before beaver trapping really got underway.

Why was there such a demand for the fur? Much of the fur was taken by ship to China, where it was traded for silk, spices, and tea. The Chinese used the soft, warm furs for coats and blankets during the bitter cold winters.

The sea otter fur trade stopped when there were no longer enough otters alive to make the sea voyage worthwhile.

Popularity of Fur

The main business of the forts was trading for furs. Company trappers traveled out along the many streams to kill animals and take their fur. Indians also brought furs to the fort and traded them for glass beads, muskets, and metal objects such as knives and cooking pots.

From Fort Vancouver, British traders **bartered** (traded) for furs from French and Indian trappers up and down the Columbia River. The fur in demand was the beaver pelt. Pelts were stretched, dried, and shipped to London, where the long, soft fur was made into felt. The felt was then made into hats. Top hats were a very popular style for men in Europe and the United States until fashion replaced them with silk hats.

End of an Era

The fur era was over by the late 1840s. The animals had been trapped almost to extinction. **Extinction** is the total loss of an animal or plant.

Pioneers were beginning to move into Oregon Country. They used the trading posts, trails, and information they got from traders. Soon, more people would come to the Pacific Northwest.

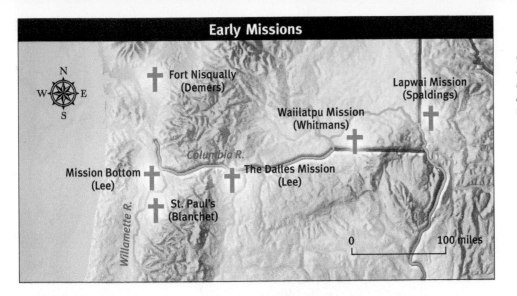

Early Missions

Fort Nisqually (Demers)

Lapwai Mission (Spaldings)

Waiilatpu Mission (Whitmans)

Columbia R.

Mission Bottom (Lee)

The Dalles Mission (Lee)

St. Paul's (Blanchet)

Willamette R.

0   100 miles

Both Catholics and Protestants opened missions in Oregon Country. **Along what rivers did the missionaries settle?**

Christian Missionaries

In the early 1800s, people in New England were excited about religion. The church was the center of village life, and crowds of enthusiastic worshippers attended prayer meetings and revivals. Preachers shouted out sermons, and congregations enthusiastically sang religious songs. Many people, especially women, supported a worldwide missionary effort. Missionaries and teachers were sent to Africa, China, and the American West. They tried to teach the people how to read the Bible and dress, speak, and live like Christian Americans.

A Request for Christianity

In 1831, four Indian men went to St. Louis to visit William Clark, who, along with Lewis, had visited them during the famous exploration trip. The Indian men asked Clark to send someone to teach the Christian religion to their people. They thought Christianity would help them understand the white people's ways and their powerful God. A religious newspaper printed the story.

Methodist Missionaries

Jason Lee and his nephew, Daniel Lee, both Methodist ministers from the East, were the first to answer the request of the Nez Perce. Instead of staying with the Nez Perce, the Lees decided to settle in the Willamette Valley. The Lees converted few Indians. The Indian people there did not take to the white people's religion or lifestyle, and their children did not like the strict rules of the mission school.

Jason Lee went back east and later returned with 50 more settlers. They opened new missions and started settlements. Lee was active in creating a new government for the settlements, and he educated the children in his mission schools. Accused of neglecting his commitment to the Indians, Lee was later recalled by the mission board, and his mission was closed.

"Hear! Hear! Who will respond to the call from beyond the Rocky Mountains? . . . Let two [suitable] men, [without] families, . . . live with them [and] teach Christ to them . . ."

—written in the journal of the Methodist Missionary Society

The St. Paul Indian Mission was built in 1859 near Kettle Falls. Missionaries there worked with Colville Indians. **How can you tell that this image is from the late 1800s?**

A missionary addresses a group of Indians. **Who else besides Indians is pictured in the group?**

Whidbey Island Mission

At the invitation of Chief Tslalakum, Father Francis Blanchet visited Whidbey Island. Father Blanchet was impressed by the crowd of Indians who attended his church services and sang hymns in Chinook Jargon.

Following services the next Sunday, there was a feast of salmon and venison. A peace pipe was passed around among various chiefs who had previously been at war. After the meal, a group of Indians dragged a huge cross—24 feet long—and planted it in the ground. The cross remained there until the 1900s, when a settler used it to make a fence.

Whidbey Island Mission

Catholic Missionaries

Some members of the Hudson's Bay Company were Catholic and wanted priests. Father Francis Blanchet answered the call. He spent most of his time with the French Canadian Catholics and not with Indians. Later, a Jesuit priest, Peter John de Smet, and other priests came and worked with the Coeur d'Alenes and Flatheads. Many of the Coeur d'Alenes were baptized Catholic, mixing in their own religious customs with that of their new religion.

What Do You Think

Do you think people should try to change the lifestyle and cultural practices of other people? Why might Christian missionaries have thought it was okay to convert natives to Christianity? How might their ideas and actions cause conflict?

Presbyterian Missionaries

Narcissa Prentiss was a kindergarten teacher in rural New York State who dreamed of being a Presbyterian missionary. A minister put her in touch with Marcus Whitman, a young doctor who was planning a mission in the West. Only married people were sent to missions, so the two agreed to marry. They set out to build a mission in the Rocky Mountains. They were joined by Reverend Henry Spalding and his wife, Eliza, who were also on their way to an Indian mission.

The two couples traveled to Oregon Country in 1836 with a party of fur traders. They were the first group to travel by wagon over the Oregon Trail. Eliza and Narcissa, traveling on horseback, were the first white women to cross the Continental Divide. The *Continental Divide* is located in the Rocky Mountains and divides water flowing west toward the Pacific Ocean from water flowing east toward the Atlantic Ocean.

After almost seven months of travel, the group finally arrived at Fort Vancouver. Dr. McLoughlin sold them supplies and advised them about where to locate a mission. The Spaldings went to live with the Nez Perce Indians along the Clearwater River. The Whitmans built a mission among the Cayuse Indians on the Walla Walla River.

Two years later, other missionary couples built a mission among the Spokane Indians in eastern Washington.

Missionaries built log houses and schoolrooms and taught the Indian men and women how to raise animals, grow and harvest crops, grind wheat to make flour, and weave wool into cloth. Missionaries translated the Bible into the Indian languages so they could teach the Indians to read.

Although some natives welcomed the missionaries and embraced Christianity, many resented the intrusion. An *intrusion* is a disturbance or interruption.

Missionaries translated the Bible into the Indian languages so they could teach the Indians to read.

Marcus Whitman

Narcissa Prentiss Whitman

Whitman College and Whitman County are named after the Whitmans.

This painting of the Whitman Mission was painted in 1865. **Describe some of the activities taking place.**

Early Encounters: Two Worlds Meet

Seven Alone

The Sager family's seven children were orphaned when their parents died while traveling west on the Oregon Trail from Missouri in the 1840s. One was only an infant. Another child was on crutches, having broken her leg when she was run over by a wagon.

Members of the wagon train cared for the children for the rest of the journey. Like most other pioneers, the group stayed for a while at the Whitman mission. The Whitmans, whose own daughter had drowned, adopted all of the children.

The Sagers later experienced the tragic murder of the Whitmans. Two of the Sager boys were killed during the assault. Years later, the Sager girls wrote about their experiences in their new land. A movie called *Seven Alone* was made about them.

Catherine Sager Pringle, Elizabeth Sager Helm, and Matilda Sager Delaney photographed in 1897 at the 50th anniversary commemoration of the Whitman Massacre. The doll on the right belonged to one of the sisters as a child.

Disease and Death

Something terrible and unexpected happened to the Indian people, especially children. The white explorers, fur trappers, missionaries, and early pioneers brought diseases such as smallpox, measles, cholera, influenza (flu), and malaria. Entire Indian villages along the coast were wiped away by sickness.

In 1847, nearly 5,000 pioneers passed through the Whitman's mission. The last wagon train of the season brought many sick travelers infected with measles. At the Whitman mission, both children and adults got sick, and several died.

At the same time, there was a measles *epidemic*, meaning a rapidly spreading disease, among the Indians. The Cayuse Indians near the Whitman mission had no *immunity*, or resistance, to the disease. When they came down with measles, over half the tribe died. It was horrible and frightening for everyone. Dr. Whitman, with his simple medicines, could do nothing to save the people he had tried so hard to help. Some Cayuse, in fact, accused Dr. Whitman of starting the disease and trying to kill the Indians.

The angry Cayuse attacked the Americans, killing Marcus and Narcissa Whitman and 11 others. They took 47 women and children hostage. After bargaining with the Hudson's Bay Company officials, the angry Indian men ransomed the prisoners for blankets, shirts, tobacco, and muskets.

The "Whitman Massacre" caused American settlers in Oregon to demand protection from the U.S. Army. The first war between Indians and whites erupted across the region. The Cayuse War lasted for two years. You will read more about this and other Indian wars in chapter 4.

What Did You Learn? ③

1. What two companies built forts for the fur trade in Oregon Country?
2. Which mission seemed to have the most success at converting Indians?
3. What impact did contact with whites have on Indian communities?

Go to the Source

The Whitman Massacre

Below is an excerpt from a letter written by Eliza Spalding Warren. In it she describes the 1847 Whitman Massacre. She was 10 years old when she witnessed the killings. She was one of 47 hostages held by the Cayuse after the killings. The image of the massacre was created by an unknown artist. Historians have criticized the illustration as inaccurate. Compare the image to the letter and answer the questions below.

. . . Dr. was sitting in the sitting room talking with Mrs. W. how gloomy things were, & things he had heard which were causing much anxiety, when there was some Indians came & sayed they wished medicine. He stepped into the kitchen where they were and were talking to them about their sickness & so on, when one of the Indians steped behind the Dr. and struck him on the head with a tomahock. That seemed to be the signal for the slaughter. One of the Sager boys was in the room with the Dr., he was struck down and his throat cut. Some men that were butchering a beef were shot and cut down. The miller at the mill was shot; a tailor working in his room was shot in his bowels and died that night. . . . Mrs. Whitman steped [sic] to the door window and was shot in the breast by a half breed that had stoped at the Dr. with the intention of staying all winter there.

Observe ------ Evaluate ------- Conclude

- What words and phrases from the letter are the most descriptive and emotional?

- Compare the image to the letter. What are the similarities? What are the differences?

- Why do you think the two accounts of the Whitman Massacre differ?

- Which account of the Whitman massacre seems more believable to you? Why?

- What can you conclude about how each account would affect the attitude of white settlers towards Indians?

Using a Timeline

You probably noticed the timeline at the beginning of the chapter. Timelines are helpful tools for learning history. They help us see the chronology of events. Chronology is the order in which things happened. But a timeline is more than a series of dates. Timelines can also help us see relationships between one or more events. A series of similar events on a timeline give evidence of a trend, such as a timeline of inventions. Some events on a timeline are related by cause and effect. Take a look at a timeline of events leading up to the American Revolution, for instance.

Timelines can be arranged in a number of different ways. Often timelines are organized thematically, meaning they show the progression of a particular topic, a person's life, a significant event, or an entire era.

Units of Measurement

Timelines are divided into equal parts, or units of measurement. Each part could stand for an hour, a day, a month, a year, a decade, or even a century. The unit of measure used depends on what the timeline is trying to show. For example, a timeline on the Age of Exploration might cover a whole century, but divide the century into 5- or 10-year increments.

Reading a Timeline

Using the timeline on pages 34 and 35, answer the following questions:

- How many different centuries does the timeline include?
- Why are there breaks (⌇) in the timeline?
- What trends or changes over time do you see?
- Select two events from the timeline and explain what they do and do not have in common.
- Which events caused the other events to occur?
- What entry shows a trend over an extended period of time?
- Are there any events that you think should not be included on the timeline? Why or why not?
- What conclusions can you make about the time period covered by the timeline?
- What title would you give to the timeline?

Your Turn

Create a timeline for a person, event, or trend that you read about in the chapter. Gather information from your textbook as well as an encyclopedia or other reliable source. Think about what you want your timeline to show. Consider the relationships of the entries on your timeline. How many years will your timeline cover? How will you show those units of measurement? Be sure to make them equal. You may even want to include pictures on your timeline.

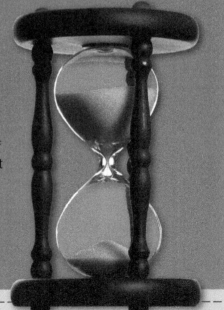

Chapter Review Questions

1. How did living near the Pacific Ocean influence the lifestyle of the Coastal Indians?
2. Why were the Plateau Indians more likely than the Coastal Indians to move around?
3. What was unique about the treatment of women in the Plateau tribes?
4. Create a chart identifying the explorers who first ventured into the Pacific Northwest. Be sure that your chart includes the country each explorer resprsented and what they accomplished.
5. Who asked Lewis and Clark to explore the Louisiana Purchase? Who was the Indian girl who helped guide Lewis and Clark?
6. Identify two factors that ended the fur trade.
7. Compare and contrast the successes and failures of the missionaries who tried to convert the Indians in Oregon Country.
8. How did disease affect Native American Indians?

Becoming a Better Reader

Set a Purpose for Reading

Good readers always set a purpose for reading. Part of setting a purpose for reading is thinking about what you already know about a subject. The next chapter is about the first settlers into the Oregon and Washington territories. Create a KWL chart to show what you know and what you want to learn about these early territory days. At the end of chapter 3, you will complete your chart by writing what you learned.

You Are the Geographer

On the Trail of Lewis and Clark

Using the map of the Lewis and Clark expedition on page 46 to answer the following questions.

1. Trace the route of the explorers from their start in St. Louis. What rivers did they follow?
2. Why do you suppose they traveled more by water than by land?
3. What were the biggest physical obstacles they faced in their journey?
4. Calculate the distance they traveled from their start in St. Louis to the Pacific Ocean.

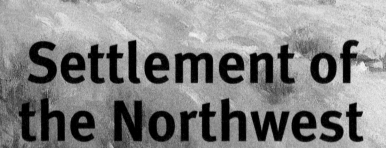

Essential
Question ?

Why did people move to the Northwest and what was life like for the early pioneers who settled there?

Settlement of the Northwest

Timeline of Events

1840

1842
Elijah White and 100 people travel the Oregon Trail.

1844
The George Washington Bush family moves to Oregon Country.

1846–1848
Mexican War

1848
• Oregon Territory is created.
• The California Gold Rush begins.

1850

1850
The Donation Land Act gives single white men 320 acres of free land and married couples 640 acres.

Young, adventurous men and their families from many places came to the Pacific Northwest along the Oregon Trail in the early 1800s. They came to start new lives as farmers, ranchers, merchants, miners, fishermen, and lumberjacks.

By the 1850s, settlers in Washington asked to have a new territory created. Their wish was granted and Washington Territory became a reality.

Pioneers traveled along the Oregon Trail on their trip to the Pacific Northwest. **What are the difficulties faced by these pioneers?**

1853
- Washington Territory is created.
- Isaac Stevens is appointed territorial governor of Washington and superintendent of Indian affairs.

1860
Abraham Lincoln is elected president.

1861–1865
The Civil War is fought between the United States and the Confederate States of America.

1860

1859
The Pig War between American and British settlers erupts in San Juan.

1862
The Homestead Act gives settlers 160 acres of land for $200.

1890

KEY IDEAS

- Thousands of pioneers traveled along the Oregon Trail to settle in the Pacific Northwest.

- Cheap land, business opportunities, and adventure were among the reasons pioneers moved west.

- The first wave of settlement was on farms and then small towns and cities began to grow.

KEY TERMS

diversity
homesteader
latitude
longitude
prime meridian
sow

Wagon Trains Head West

After the explorers, traders, trappers, and missionaries came to the Pacific Northwest, pioneer families in wagon trains walked to the rich new land. The first pioneers settled near Fort Vancouver or Oregon City, but later groups spread out over the fertile land.

Traveling across the flat plains was relatively easy. The main problems were crossing the wide rivers and dealing with the weather on the six-month journey. It was often hot and dusty or wet and muddy.

Crossing the high Rocky Mountains was difficult, however. Weary families who did not make it through before the snows fell had to wait until spring. Finding passage through steep mountain ranges was not easy. A government explorer found South Pass in Wyoming in 1832, and two men made it through the Blue Mountains of Oregon in 1840.

This opened up the way for more pioneers to follow.

The Oregon Trail

Elijah White, a former missionary to Oregon, brought a group of 100 settlers from Independence, Missouri, to Oregon's Willamette Valley in 1842. Their route became known as the Oregon Trail. For the next 35 years, the trail was used by more than 300,000 men, women, and children.

What Do You Think

How would a trip to a new place change a person's life? What changes would a person have to make to move to a place that was wild and unsettled?

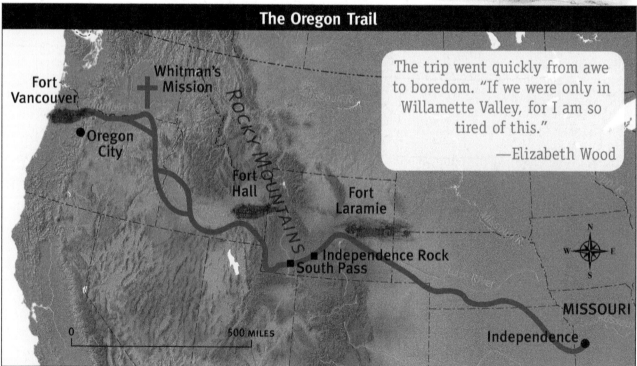

The Oregon Trail

Fort Vancouver
Whitman's Mission
Oregon City
ROCKY MOUNTAINS
Fort Hall
Fort Laramie
Independence Rock
South Pass
MISSOURI
Independence

The trip went quickly from awe to boredom. "If we were only in Willamette Valley, for I am so tired of this."

—Elizabeth Wood

0   500 MILES

Follow the trail from Independence, Missouri, to Oregon. **What rivers did the trail follow? What landforms did pioneers encounter? At what forts could they stop to rest and get supplies?**

Pioneers used oxen to pull their wagons along the Oregon Trail. **What other animals do they have with them?**

Father de Smet, a Catholic missionary, wrote that the trail was "as smooth as a barn floor swept by the winds, and not a blade of grass can shoot up on it on account of the continual passing."

Why Did People Go West?

- There was a chance to see new country and to be part of an adventure.
- Good farmland was available for a low cost.
- Merchants, doctors, and lawyers came to start businesses.
- Many people wanted to escape the problems of slavery.
- People wanted to live in a mild, healthful climate.

Many young people went west because their families did. Eugenia Zieber learned that she would be going on the Oregon Trail when she was a 16-year-old student at a school for young ladies in Pennsylvania. A letter came from her father just two days before Christmas, telling her about the plan. He wanted to move the family to a healthier climate.

Lucia Loraine Williams wrote in her 1851 diary:

*Some . . . were going for wealth and honors. Others, who had suffered from ill health for years, and to whom life had become a burden, expected to regain health . . . [Some people] wanted more action, more **diversity** (variety), more thrilling experiences with man and beast.*

Animals of Choice

Oxen were the best choice for pulling wagons. They ate prairie grass, could pull heavy loads, and were not as likely as horses were to be stolen by Indians. Those who could afford to took an extra team in case anything happened to the animals on the trip.

Cows were taken along to provide milk. One traveler wrote: "The milk can stood nearby and always yielded up its lump of butter at night, churned by the movement of the wagon from the surplus morning's milk."

Families took horses for riding and exploring in the area around their new home. Chickens, goats, and dogs also walked the thousands of miles to Oregon.

End of the Trail

As settlers arrived in Oregon Country, they settled south of the Columbia River. The British Hudson's Bay Company wanted to keep Americans out of the area north of the river. They hoped that the region would one day be under British rule. As a result, when settlers asked for guidance, company officials told them to settle south of the Columbia River.

At first, most people settled where Hudson's Bay Company officials suggested. Soon, however, settlers wanted the excellent harbors of Puget Sound for American ships. Some people settled around Puget Sound and in the Cowlitz River Valley. Places such as Tumwater, Tacoma, Olympia, Centralia, Alki Point (Seattle), and Port Townsend were founded.

"Sometimes the dust is so great that the drivers cannot see their teams at all though the sun is shining brightly."

—Elizabeth Wood

Washington PORTRAIT

Bush Prairie

The town of Bush Prairie was named after George Washington Bush.

George Washington Bush
(c. 1790–1863)

George Washington Bush was a war veteran and successful cattleman in Missouri. Then Missouri passed a law making it illegal for free blacks to live there. Afraid his property would be taken because he was black, Bush sold his home and business and outfitted six large wagons full of supplies.

George, his wife, Isabelle (a white woman who had been a nurse), and their sons left for Oregon Country. One of the Bush children later remembered his father hiding $2,000 in silver underneath the floorboards of a wagon. The money made the trip safely.

A few other families joined the Bush family, and the group joined a wagon train. When the Bushes arrived in the Willamette Valley, they discovered they could not stay. A law had been passed that said no blacks could live in Oregon, slave or free.

So the Bush party headed north of the Columbia River. They figured there would be few Americans there to challenge them. They were right. Bush and about 30 others spent another month walking beside their wagons to their new home.

The little group built log homes, plowed the ground, *sowed* (planted) seeds, and farmed. Nisqually Indians taught the new settlers to gather oysters, dig clams, and fish for trout and salmon. The farms prospered, but within a few years, the Bush family once again faced the loss of their land.

A law said that only white Americans and mixed-blood Indians could own land. New settlers wanted the Bush farm because it was so valuable. Fifty-three neighbors signed a petition asking that Bush be allowed to keep his 640 acres of land. Congress responded, giving Bush legal right to his original homestead.

A few years later, the Bush farm was one of the most productive in the area. George Washington Bush was always interested in improving his farm and spent his last years studying new techniques. Bush's son was elected to the state legislature in 1889.

George Washington Bush brought his family and neighbors to settle in the West. **What does Bush appear to be crossing with his family?**

"He provided the settlers with food for their first winter and with seed for the first sowing. If they had no money, he still supplied them with what they needed."

—Bush's neighbor

Settlement Patterns

The early years of territorial settlement were years of establishing boundaries. After American and British boundaries were established, and Washington Territory was separated from Oregon Territory, cities had to be laid out, homesteads marked, and maps drawn. How was this done?

In order to plot and map the land holdings for legal title, the land was surveyed, then marked on a grid pattern. That pattern was based on latitude and longitude. *Latitude* is the measurement of distances north and south of the equator while *longitude* is the measurement of distances east and west of the prime meridian. The *prime meridian* is a longitudinal reference line that runs through Greenwich, England. Once the grid was made, it was divided into townships and sections.

- A township was six square miles in each direction.
- A township was divided into 36 sections.
- Each section was numbered and measured one square mile, which included 640 acres. This was the amount of land given to married couples in the Donation Land Act.
- One section of each township was to be set aside for a school.
- Sections were subdivided into quarter sections of 160 acres each, which was the amount of land promised to settlers in the Homestead Act.

Settlers who got land because of the Homestead Act or other land grant program were called *homesteaders*. A homesteader checked with the land office in the nearest town and located on a map a quarter section he wanted to claim. After going out to see the land, he marked the corners. Corners could be marked by driving posts in the ground, or by marking a witness tree. A witness tree was the nearest tree to a corner. A homesteader sliced away a piece of bark and carved the township and section number with a knife.

After marking the land, the homesteader went back to register the claim at the land office. In order to make his claim official, he also had to advertise it in a newspaper so anyone else claiming that land could challenge him. During the homestead era, newspapers were published throughout the West because land claim advertisements were a source of profit for the newspapers.

6-mile-square township

6	5	4	3	2	1
7	8	9	10	11	12
18	17	16	15	14	13
19	20	21	22	23	24
30	29	28	27	26	25
31	32	33	34	35	36

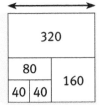

1-square-mile section

320
80
40 40
160

Life on a homestead could be difficult, but pioneers recall happy times as well. **Describe the work being done by this family.**

Towns and Cities

Seattle got its name from the leader of the Duwamish. His name was Sealth, pronounced like Seattle.

After the first burst of settlement on farmland, people began to locate in towns where they could sell goods or profit from offering services. They settled where shipping and transportation were available. In the mid-1800s, that meant along waterways. There were few roads—no good ones—and shipping by water was the easiest way to transport wheat, vegetables, animal hides, and even timber. Merchants also settled in towns that they thought would grow. More people meant more customers.

Cities competed with each other to be the largest. They wanted to be the seat of government and the place where successful businesses would open. Larger cities meant modern conveniences and a better supply of store-bought goods.

Walla Walla, a wheat-farming community, became a supply point for mining camps when gold was discovered in Idaho. It became the largest settlement in Washington Territory.

Olympia started out being called Smithfield. Mike Simmons, a friend of George Washington Bush, owned one of the two stores in town. Views of the stunning Olympic Mountains, however, soon led to the name of Olympia. Two years later and 26 miles away, the town of Tacoma was settled. Tacoma sounds like the Indian name for Mount Rainier.

Seattle grew as a shipping port for lumber. Dr. David Maynard was one of the first residents. He had visited Mike Simmons in Olympia and learned of the need for logs in San Francisco, California. After a trip there to investigate shipping logs to California, he returned with a ship full of goods and opened a store next to Simmons. He cut prices, too. Simmons' friends told Dr. Maynard that he should open a store somewhere else, and suggested a place at the mouth of a river several miles north. Dr. Maynard moved, and is credited with co-founding the city of Seattle.

Growth of Cities

Several things contributed to the growth of cities around Puget Sound and in eastern Washington:

Natural Resources	Human Elements
• Natural harbors	• Population growth
• Rivers	• Buildings
• Trees	• Roads
• Fish	• Railroads
• Farmland	• Ships
• Proximity to gold and coal mines	• Advertisements
• Mild climate	

What Did You Learn? ①

1. How was the trip west along the Oregon Trail both easy and difficult?
2. Why did so many people want to move west?
3. Who was George Washington Bush?
4. What was the process for claiming a piece of land?

An illustration of the Seattle waterfront in the 19th century. **What are the signs of an increasing population and industry?**

Hardships and Happiness

Surviving on a pioneer homestead was difficult. Chas Ross, a young man in Pierce County, described life on the homestead:

Pioneering here meant clearing land, hunting, fishing, and driving and feeding cattle. In this little home our family spent the most strenuous winter of our existence. That was the terrible winter of 1861–62. That winter opened with the freezing over of the Columbia River, which cut us off from the outside world. Then on top of this the snow began to fall and fell to the depth of four feet, then it would settle and freeze. For fear we would run out of matches, we kept the fire burning all night.

Life could be difficult as a homesteader. Everyone pitched in to help. **What does this image tell you about life for pioneer women?**

Disease

Many people came west for the clean air, clean water, and mild climate they thought would give them good health. In the mid-1800s, doctors did not know that germs caused disease. Most people thought sickness was caused by bad odors such as the smell from sewage or rotting garbage.

Eva Brown, a girl in Waterville, said, "To be sick was unfortunate for the patient. There was no doctor. The neighbors did what they could and the patient either got well or died."

Food

One boy on Whidbey Island remembered:

As late as 1866 pork—fresh, salted, or smoked—was about the only meat other than venison that was obtainable, except that occasionally a farmer would kill a beef and share the meat with his neighbors, who later would return an equal quantity of beef after butchering their cattle. Flour, for years, was almost unobtainable.

KEY IDEAS

- Although disease, bad weather, and poor crops could make like difficult, pioneers recall happy times.
- The mining, lumber, fishing, and whaling industries provided settlers with a way to make a living.
- Wheat and apples became important crops for farmers in Washington.

KEY TERMS

advocate
baleen
cannery
erosion
insatiable
livelihood
proximity

Fun and Games

Clara Gray was a teenager in Spokane in 1879. She told about getting ready for a neighborhood dance:

When I started to dress for the dance I found that the dress I wanted to wear was frozen fast to the side of the house, and it took me quite a while to thaw it loose with a hot iron. I had hung my spare clothing on nails against the rough boards. Two fiddlers played at the dance, and a collection was taken up to get money to build a schoolhouse.

"Horseback riding in the summer and skiing in the winter were the standby sports. I made my skis from barrel staves. I got about all over the country on them," one pioneer remembered.

Erskine Wood wrote about a game he played with the Indian youths. They used little whips to spin three or four egg-shaped stones. "They would start the rocks spinning on the ice with their hands and then whip them like everything and they would spin as good as a top."

Newsboys announced important headlines and sold newspapers.

Newspapers

The first newspaper in Washington was the *Columbian*, first published in 1852 in Olympia. Because the territory was so spread out, many people did not get a chance to read it regularly. "President Lincoln was assassinated a year before I heard of it," said Barney Owsley, a freight packer.

Mail Service

There was no mail delivery in rural areas until the 20th century. Mail might come and might not," one pioneer remembered.

Getting mail to the East meant sending it on the Columbia River by steamboat to Wallula. From there a pony express rider picked it up and raced overland on the Mullan Road to Montana. In Montana, the letter was put on a steamboat headed down the Missouri River to St. Louis. The mail then went eastward by boat, stagecoach, or railroad. Sometimes letters were sent aboard ships that had to round the tip of South America before reaching the East Coast. Letters could take a year to reach their destination.

Linking the Past to the Present

Compare the games you play today with those of pioneer times. How have activities changed?

Mail from the Pacific Northwest could take up to a year to reach someone in the East. **Why do you think mail delivery took so long?**

POST OFFICE

Earning a Living

When settlers first came to the Northwest, fur trading was the predominant economic activity. But as you read in a previous chapter, the fur trade came to an end by the 1840s due not only to changing fashion, but also to the near extinction of fur-bearing animals. Without the fur trade, what could settlers do to earn a living?

Abundant natural resources were key to the growth of industry and agriculture in Washington. As a result, the lumber, fishing, and whaling industries provided a *livelihood* (a way to make a living) for many. Additionally, in years with good weather, farming also provided a good income.

Coal Mining

Coal was discovered in the Puget Sound Lowlands and the Cascade Mountains. Coal was burned to heat homes and to provide the power that ran machines in factories. Some of the early miners were Chinese. Others came from England and Wales. The first large group of African Americans in Washington came to dig coal. Even children were hired to sort the pieces of coal.

Discovery of high-quality coal in 1886 in Kittitas County led to the rapid development of the Roslyn coal field. Two towns, Roslyn and Cle Elum, sprang up overnight. Coal mining was important well into the 1900s.

Gold and Silver Mining

Washington and Oregon never developed significant gold- or silver-mining districts. However, three Washington cities—Walla Walla, Spokane, and Seattle—were greatly affected by mining rushes in other places. Merchants grew rich by supplying food, tents, tools, and clothing to miners on their way to the gold fields of Canada, Alaska, and Idaho.

Some ordinary people struck it rich in the mines and returned to Washington to spend their money. For example, May Arkwright Hutton and her husband, Al, put their savings of a few hundred dollars into a mine in Idaho. To their surprise, their Hercules Mine became one of the richest strikes in Silver Valley, and the Huttons became overnight millionaires. Mrs. Hutton also became a very outspoken *advocate*, or supporter, of women's rights.

Trees, Trees, Trees

There were so many trees in Washington when the early settlers came that they thought they would never run out. Therefore, they did not replant trees. They were not concerned about how much wood they wasted.

One man wrote:

We cut down good, solid Douglas Fir, White Fir, Hemlock, and even Tamarack, lopped the limbs and burned it, leaving barren areas that today have grown up to brush. I'm ashamed of the wasted wood fiber . . . the loss of soil through erosion, the loss of trees that result in higher temperatures that melt snow swiftly and produce greater floods.

All those trees helped fuel a very profitable lumber industry, especially along the waterways where waterpower could run the gigantic saws needed to cut the huge logs into smaller pieces. The *proximity*, or closeness, to water also aided in the transport of logs to customers throughout the Northwest. As a result, Washington was the nation's leading lumber state by 1905.

Seattle had grown up as a sawmill town around Henry Yesler's steam-powered sawmill. Soon larger mills were built throughout the Puget Sound region. Tall timber next to deep water meant that trees could be cut, milled (sawed into boards), and easily exported by ship.

In California, the demand for lumber seemed insatiable. To be *insatiable* is to never be satisfied. Huge log rafts were towed to San Diego, where the lumber was processed. Timber companies were helped by the Northern Pacific Railroad. Huge tracts of timberland, first given to the railroads by the federal government, were sold at bargain prices to timber companies.

Timber companies found a wealth of trees in the Pacific Northwest. **What was the effect of tree harvesting on the land?**

Timber companies also benefited from the passage of the federal Timber and Stone Act, which they abused. Timber companies found out-of-work sailors and hobos and paid them to file homestead claims on forest lands. Then the sailors and hobos gave the land to the timber companies for $50. In some cases, the price was as low as a large glass of beer. One timber company acquired more than 100,000 acres with this scheme.

Down south, in San Francisco, the gold rush of 1848 gave a huge boost to the timber industry. Logs were needed to build docks, buildings, and sidewalks. The huge forests of the Pacific Northwest were cut down near waterways, the logs floated downstream, and then bundled together and towed by ship to San Francisco.

San Francisco had the misfortune of burning down in six major fires between 1849 and 1851. Each rebuilding effort meant greater demand for northern lumber. This meant more mill workers were needed in Puget Sound. More people moving to the area meant increased sales of local farmers' milk, vegetables, and hay. Coal and oysters both found ready markets in San Francisco.

Once the tree was down, it had to be cut into smaller sections. What dangers do you think these men faced?

Logs were shipped to places like San Francisco, where the lumber was needed to build docks, sidewalks, and buildings.

Linking the Past to the Present

One of the most successful sawmills in Washington was Puget Mill Company's Port Gamble facility. With its new steam sawmill, it could cut timber much faster. Men boiled water in huge boilers. The boilers gave off steam that pressed against moving parts of engines that moved the saws. Port Gamble was Washington's oldest continuously operating sawmill in the United States until it closed in 1995. Nearly 200 workers lost their jobs. The mill's equipment and two tugboats were put up for auction. Today, the community is designated as a Rural Historic Town and is a popular tourist destination.

One Fish, Two Fish

The great Pacific Ocean was the natural home to fish that could be harvested by American Indians and settlers. Fish were sold to local people and dried and shipped to other cities.

The fishing industry changed quickly when Robert Hume built a plant that used cans and high heat to preserve fish. Salmon was canned in over 30 **canneries** that sold salmon to faraway places in South America, Great Britain, Australia, and China.

C. O. Rhodes was a teen when he went salmon fishing with his uncle on the North Palix River in the 1880s.

In those days there would be tens of thousands of these fish in shallow streams. . . . Not being content to stand on the bank, I crawled out on an old slippery log that projected out into the creek some ten feet, right among the fish. I picked out a good big one and did I hook him! He landed me right off that log among all those fish. *The water was only about two feet deep, and there were fish over me, under me, and on all sides of me, and as fast as I'd gain a footing, down I'd go again with fish splashing salmon eggs in my ears, eyes, and mouth.*

Today, Washington residents are working hard to bring back wild fish runs that have become smaller from overfishing.

As the fishing industry grew, salmon became a popular symbol of the Pacific Northwest region. The fish had been the basic food source for most of the region's Indian tribes. Then fish became not only a food source but also a way to make money. Fresh, canned, and dried fish were sold to other states and countries. Most of the fishermen were Scandinavians and Finns.

Like the lumber industry, fishing was a victim of careless disregard for a natural resource. The huge salmon runs on the Columbia River were already in decline by 1900, long before the dams were built. Overfishing was the major reason. Also, water pollution and destruction of fish-breeding grounds by mining and logging companies contributed to the decrease in fish.

Fishing became one of the state's biggest industries in the 1800s. **What concerns about the industry does this image illustrate?**

Fishermen relax inside the mouth of a recent catch. **What were some of the uses for whale?**

The Whaling Industry

Indians who lived on the northern coast of Washington had a long tradition based on whaling. An early settler, Jim Hunter, wrote about the Makah people at Neah Bay who were whaling when whites arrived.

The killing of a whale meant a great celebration in the village at Neah Bay. The capture of these immense animals was attended with great danger, and only the Indians skilled in casting the harpoon or in rowing the large canoes were permitted to engage in the hunt. One of the most successful hunters was "Lighthouse Jim," who at the end of his life had established the reputation of having killed 59 whales.

During the early 1800s, American whaling ships set sail from New England ports. During peak years, 700 whale ships embarked on a voyage that averaged four years. Ships sailed from New England around the tip of South America and up the Pacific to hunt whales off the coast of Washington State and Alaska.

Whale oil was the most valuable product. It was used for home lighting and was very expensive. A ship full of barrels of whale oil brought $100,000.

Baleen was another valuable whale product. Baleen whales didn't have teeth. They had baleen instead, which strained a whale's food. *Baleen*, which is a flexible whalebone, was used for carriage springs, corset stays, fishing rods, hoops for skirts, ribs for umbrellas, and horse whips.

So many whales were killed that it became hard to find enough to hunt. Then, in 1859, petroleum oil was discovered in Pennsylvania. It could be made into kerosene for home lighting. Whaling was no longer a large industry.

Whalers traveled from New England to the shores of the Pacific Northwest in search of the giant mammals. **What dangers did these whalers face?**

Settlement of the Northwest

Our state is known for its delicious apples.

Growth of Agriculture

From its earliest beginnings in the Walla Walla Valley, wheat farming spread rapidly across the Palouse region of eastern Washington in the late 1800s. Soon wheat made up 45 percent of the value of all Washington crops. Whitman County, in the heart of the Palouse, was the wealthiest county per person in the United States. Later, a series of rainy years encouraged farmers to raise wheat in the drier Big Bend region.

Farmers put wheat in sacks and hauled it in wagons to landings on the Snake and Columbia rivers. Then steamboats took the wheat to Portland. Later, wheat was shipped by rail to the ports of Tacoma and Seattle.

A family of farmers is harvesting its wheat crop.
Why do they need so many horses?

Most wheat farms were small by today's standards, averaging 160–320 acres. There were dozens of small farm towns, most of which have disappeared.

Apples

Washington apples had become an important crop by 1900. Irrigation projects made it possible to run successful orchards in the Yakima, Wenatchee, and Okanogan valleys. Washington fruit growers planted over one million trees in one year. The transcontinental railroad and the development of refrigerated cars in 1902 made it possible to ship fruit to eastern markets before it spoiled. By 1917, Washington led the nation in apple production.

Ranching and Dairying

After farmers started growing wheat on the Palouse Hills, cattlemen could no longer graze their cows on the grass there. In other places, new settlers filed land claims along the rivers and streams and then fenced their land so cattle could not get to the water. Cattlemen retreated to the drier uplands and the foothills of the Cascades.

Harsh winters thinned the herds in the 1880s. The winter of 1889–90 killed half the cattle in the Yakima Valley and nine out of ten animals in Big Bend.

What Did You Learn? ②

1. Describe the difficulties that faced early settlers.
2. Why did lumber, fishing, and whaling provide a better living in the Northwest than mining?
3. What enabled wheat and apples to become key crops in Washington?

Oregon Territory

Thousands of Americans as well as immigrants from foreign lands had settled in the Willamette Valley by the 1840s. They organized a temporary government in 1843 and asked the U.S. Congress for the creation of Oregon Territory. But the area was still claimed by both Britain and the United States. Both countries wanted the rich farmland in a mild climate and the natural harbors of Puget Sound.

Back East, James Polk used as his presidential campaign slogan the phrase "Fifty-four Forty or Fight." This meant that the United States wanted land north of today's present boundary, all the way to the 54th latitude line, the southern border of Alaska. *Expansionists*, or people who supported expanding the size of the United States, wanted Polk to win the election.

Treaties Settle Boundaries

In order for the nation to achieve its expansionist goals, it was necessary to reach some agreements with Great Britain and Spain. When Britain and the United States signed the treaty ending the War of 1812, they never fully agreed on a boundary separating British Canada from the United States.

To resolve that issue, the two nations signed an agreement to jointly occupy Oregon Territory. By the 1840s, many more Americans had settled in the territory and relations between American and British settlers were shaky. Some Americans were so determined to take over all of Oregon Territory that they were willing to go to war with the British for a third time! Fortunately, cooler heads prevailed and the two sides chose diplomacy over war to settle their differences. *Diplomacy* is a discussion between nations with the goal of reaching an agreement.

They did so with the 1846 Treaty of Oregon in which Britain agreed to give up its claims to the land below the 49th parallel. As a result, the border between the United States and Canada today is at the 49th parallel.

KEY IDEAS

- Treaties with Britain and Spain settled boundary issues.
- A belief in Manifest Destiny fueled the desire for western expansion.
- Washington Territory was created in 1853 when settlers asked to be separated from Oregon Territory.

KEY TERMS

diplomacy
expansionist
legislature
Manifest Destiny
mediate
survey

Oregon Territory (1848–1853)

0   100 miles

Oregon Territory

Continental Divide

Unorganized

The new Oregon Territory included both present-day Washington, Oregon, Idaho, and parts of Montana and Wyoming.

This famous painting illustrating the idea of Manifest Destiny hangs in the U.S. Capitol. **What symbols of the West did the artist use?**

Manifest Destiny

The fervor (enthusiasm) over expansion in the Northwest in the early 1800s was part of a growing belief in "manifest destiny." *Manifest Destiny* was the belief that it was the divine mission of Americans to spread their political and religious values to others. Supporters of Manifest Destiny not only wanted control of Oregon Territory but also expansion from Texas to California.

In the same year that the Treaty of Oregon was signed, the United States declared war on Mexico. The United States gained a lot of land as a result of the Mexican War. The new territory included what would eventually become the states of New Mexico, Arizona, Utah, Nevada and California.

What to do with all the new territory contributed to many disagreements among politicians in Washington, D.C. At issue was whether or not slavery would be allowed in the new territories. The question raised intense anger on both sides and helped to drive a wedge between the North and the South, leading to the Civil War.

It is America's right to stretch from sea to shining sea. Not only do we have a responsibility to our citizens to gain valuable natural resources we also have a responsibility to civilize this beautiful land.

—Admiral Alfred Thayer Mahan

The Slavery Question

In Washington, D.C., there was a great deal of discussion about Oregon Territory. Senator Stephen Douglas of Illinois had already proposed that Oregon be admitted as a free territory— free of slavery. Southern senators opposed this because it would upset the even balance in Congress between free states in the North with slave states in the South. Anti-slavery Northerners would have greater representation in Congress, Southerners argued. They feared that this would result in the abolition of slavery. The arguments continued as the nation drifted toward civil war.

Finally, on the last day that Congress was in session, President Polk created Oregon Territory. It was August, 1848. Salem, Oregon, became the capital. A young man from Illinois, Abraham Lincoln, was offered the job as governor of the territory, but he turned down the job.

Treaties Determine Boundaries

- **Convention of 1818**
  Great Britain and the United States agree to joint occupation of Oregon Country.

- **Adams-Onis Treaty, 1819**
  Spain gives its claims to land in Oregon Country to the United States.

- **Oregon Treaty, 1846**
  Great Britain retreats northward. International boundary is drawn at the 49th parallel. Oregon Country is finally owned by the United States.

Washington Breaks from Oregon

It wasn't long before settlers living north of the Columbia River wanted to separate from Oregon Territory and form their own government. They thought the government leaders in Oregon were too far away and that the territory was too big. After several requests, Congress passed the Organic Act, a law that allowed for the creation of Washington Territory in 1853.

The people wanted the territory to be named Columbia, but Congress changed the name so there would be no confusion with the District of Columbia. It was a huge piece of land and had only 4,000 American settlers and 17,000 Native Americans. Soon there would be conflict.

What Is a Territory?

Territories were different from states. The people in a territory could vote for representatives to send to Congress in Washington, D.C. However, the representative did not have a vote in Congress. They could only try to persuade Congress to make laws that were favorable to the people in the territory. Territorial officials and judges were appointed by the president and approved by Congress. The people in the territory did not elect them. The first governor of Washington Territory, for example, was appointed by the president.

The First Governor

President Franklin Pierce appointed Isaac Stevens to be the first territorial governor of Washington. He was also named Secretary of Indian Affairs. Stevens was born in Massachusetts. He was smart and ambitious. Because of his wish to bring the railroad to Washington Territory, he volunteered to *survey* (study or examine) a potential route on his way to the Northwest.

Once in Olympia, the territorial capital, he worked to organize the first legislature and create laws and schools. The *legislature* is the lawmaking body of a government.

Washington Territory was created in 1853 and included parts of present-day Idaho and Montana.

The Civil War Touches the Northwest

During the 1860s, the United States was bitterly divided by the Civil War. That conflict reached the Pacific Northwest, too. There were rumors that a Confederate ship was attacking Union ships off the Pacific Coast. Union troops were stationed at Fort Vancouver and several smaller posts to protect the coast.

After serving as territorial governor, Isaac Stevens fought for the Union Army and was killed in Virginia at the Battle of Chantilly. His son, Hazard, was wounded in the battle.

Before becoming commander of the Union Army, General Ulysses Grant and General Philip Sheridan both served at Fort Vancouver. Confederate General George Pickett, who had been stationed on San Juan Island during the Pig War, also went east to fight. He is famous for the bloody "Pickett's Charge" at the Battle of Gettysburg where he ordered his troops to charge into Union lines. The strategic move broke the Union lines but cost Pickett more than half his men.

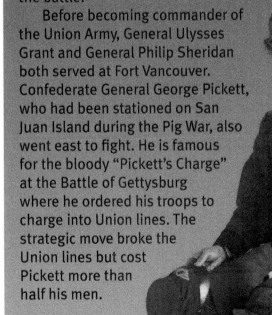

Isaac Stevens was appointed Washington's first territorial governor. He later was killed in Virginia during the Civil War.

Pig War

The 1846 treaty between Britain and the United States left one thing unclear: Who owned the San Juan Islands? By 1859, only 18 Americans lived there and they were a thorn in the side of the British settlers there. Each side complained that the other was trespassing.

Tempers were short when a British neighbor's pig got into an American farmer's garden and ruined the potato patch. The farmer shot the pig. This set off a fight between the Americans and British on the island. Sixty-six American soldiers took a position near the wharf.

The British were furious and sent three British warships to remove the men without firing on them. They refused to budge. Eventually five British warships and over 2,000 soldiers came. Americans, with 155 men stationed behind earthen walls, waited it out.

When news reached Washington, D.C., President James Buchanan sent General Winfield Scott to resolve the situation. The British retreated to one end of the island and the Americans to the other. It stayed that way for 12 years, until a German leader was asked to *mediate* (to step in and settle a dispute or disagreement). He declared that the islands belonged to the United States.

The "Pig War" was settled. The only casualty? One pig.

"It would be a shocking event if . . . two nations should be precipitated into a war respecting the possession of a small island . . ."

—From the instructions sent to General Scott

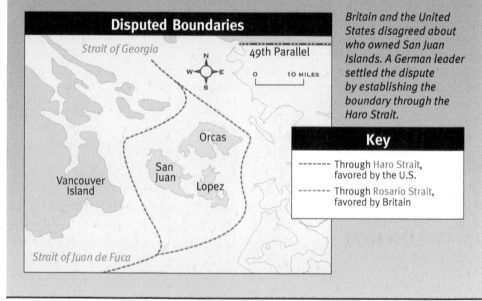

Disputed Boundaries

Strait of Georgia

49th Parallel

0   10 MILES

Orcas

San Juan

Vancouver Island

Lopez

Strait of Juan de Fuca

Key

------- Through Haro Strait, favored by the U.S.

------- Through Rosario Strait, favored by Britain

Britain and the United States disagreed about who owned San Juan Islands. A German leader settled the dispute by establishing the boundary through the Haro Strait.

What Did You Learn? ③

1. What was the Treaty of Oregon?
2. Why were Americans so interested in westward expansion?
3. Why was Washington Territory created?

Go to the Source

Life in the New Territory

These are excerpts from a letter Isaac N. Ebey wrote to his brother, Winfield S. Ebey, on May 20, 1853.

Dear Brother,

This letter leaves us all well, I have little or no news to write. You perhaps knew long before I did of the organization of our new Territory. The organization took place sooner by one year than we expected, but so much the better. We have now a separate political existence which will give new impulse for good to every thing connected with our Country. I am expecting the appointment of the Collectorship for the District of Puget's Sound. I think I shall get it, it will be worth about twenty five hundred dollars per annum, which I think I can get increased at the next session of Congress to three thousand besides the fees which would be worth another Thousand. If I should get that appointment it will be better for me than any other office I could hold as I could be at home most of the time and be improving my farm which would be worth several Thousand Dollars a year besides.

My name is spoken of freely as Delegate to Congress and I some times think I would like to have it mainly because I would see you all this comeing fall. However I will let things take there natural course. If I should accept the Delegate ship it will come with out any effort on my part.

Our season is very forward. Crops look very promising. Our Island is progressing more rapidly than our most sanguine (hopeful) expectations led us to believe. We have methodist preaching at our house about every two weeks, and we are to have a Camp meeting in about two hundred yards of our house on the 11th of July next.

I have a little to write about . . . except to keep my promise of writing on the 20th of each month. Before I write again, Rebecca will have been confined. I trust and hope her trial will not be a hard one yet I fear and tremble at the result. She is quite weak, yet not sick but is getting weaker as her time of confinement approaches. We have a good physician close at hand which is a good thing.

Observe

- List words or phrases that are new to you.
- Identify the topics Isaac tells his brother about.
- Who is Rebecca?
- What are Isaac's concerns about Rebecca?

Evaluate

- Why is Isaac pleased about Washington's new status as a territory?
- Why do you think Isaac might recommend that his brother or others move to Washington? Give three specific reasons.

Conclude

- What can you conclude about the economy, religion, health care, and government in the new territory?

Analyzing a Cartoon

Have you ever heard the saying "a picture is worth a thousand words"? Pictures and other images allow people to learn about a topic without reading many or any words. Political cartoons do the same thing. Political cartoons often use funny or exaggerated images to make a point. Political cartoons also encourage interest in a topic.

Cartoonists Use Different Techniques

Cartoonists often use different techniques to help make a point. Two common techniques are symbolism and exaggeration. Symbols are used to stress an idea. For example, a dove or an olive branch usually symbolizes peace. An image of the American flag or Uncle Sam symbolizes the United States. Death is sometimes symbolized with a skull and bones or a vulture. Exaggeration can be funny and emphasize a point. The cartoonist might exaggerate a physical feature or habit such as a large nose or ears, bushy eyebrows, baldness, or clothing style. A cartoonist may also use a caption or a title.

Steps for Analyzing a Cartoon

1. Identify the people or objects in the cartoon.
2. Identify any symbols used and what they mean.
3. Describe the action taking place in the cartoon.
4. Does the cartoon use exaggeration? How so?
5. Explain how the caption, title, or both, fit the action taking place and the symbols used.
6. If there is no caption or title with the cartoon, what might be fitting?
7. Identify the event or issue that may have inspired the cartoon.
8. Describe the cartoonist's view of the event or issue.
9. Can the cartoon be interpreted in more than one way? If so, how?
10. Use these observations to explain the message of the cartoon.

The Great White Father

Your Turn

The cartoon pictured here is of President Andrew Jackson in the 1830s. Examine the cartoon and answer the questions listed above. Also answer the question: What do you think the cartoon's message is regarding President Jackson's relationship with Native Americans?

Chapter Review Questions

1. List the main reasons people had for moving west.
2. Create a land claim advertisement for your new homestead in Oregon Country.
3. Identify five industries in which settlers were able to make a living.
4. How did the issue of slavery and the Civil War affect the Northwest?
5. Give two examples of how the United States and Britain settled differences over land ownership.
6. Describe the land and population of Washington when it became a territory.
7. Identify at least two differences between a territory and a state.

Becoming a Better Reader

Making Connections

Good readers connect the text to themselves. They connect the text to things they already know or to personal experiences they have had. Use this strategy to make a connection with yourself and the text. Write a paragraph about a connection you had with this chapter. Perhaps you can write about how pioneer life compares with your life or how your ancestors settled in the Northwest or somewhere else.

You Are the Geographer

1. Using the map of the Oregon Trail on page 60, calculate the distance pioneers had to travel from Independence, Missouri to Fort Vancouver. Through what present-day states did pioneers have to travel?
2. Give an example of how proximity to natural resources contributed to the growth of at least one town or city and at least one industry.
3. Using the maps of Oregon and Washington territories on pages 73 and 75, identify the natural landforms that formed boundaries for the two territories. (Remember that landforms include land and water.)

"*Civilization is a method of living, an attitude of equal respect for all men.*"

—Jane Addams, Progressive reformer and suffragist

Men made makeshift trucks with automobile engines. The trucks replaced horse-drawn wagons for hauling logs. Since lumber was plentiful, it was used to make a road for the trucks in the early 1920s. **What were the likely difficulties of traveling on such a "road"?**

Washington
Takes Shape

Question ?

Why were treaties made
with Native Americans,
and what was the impact
of this treaty-making
period?

Timeline of Events

1853
Isaac Stevens is
appointed governor of
Washington Territory as
well as Superintendent
of Indian Affairs.

1858
Nisqually
Chief Leschi is
executed.

1845   1850   1855

1848–1850
Cayuse War

1847
The Whitmans
are killed by
Cayuse Indians.

1854–1856
• Governor Stevens
signs 10 treaties
with Indians, who
then give up tribal
lands and move to
reservations.

• Yakama War

From Treaties to Statehood

Chapter 4

In 1854, Territorial Governor Isaac Stevens embarked on a tour of Washington Territory to meet with representatives of more than 10,000 native peoples who called Washington Territory their home. The treaty councils he held resulted in 10 treaties that forced the Indians to give up their land and move to reservations.

When Indians resisted the changes, war erupted, beginning a bloody chapter in Washington's path to statehood.

Flathead Indians gather for a treaty council with Governor Isaac Stevens. **What symbol of the United States is displayed?**

1875
The Indian Homestead Act gives individual Indians the opportunity to own their own land.

1877
Nez Perce War

1878
The first state constitutional convention is held at Walla Walla.

1883
The territorial legislature gives women the right to vote.

1887
The Dawes Act breaks up reservations and seeks to assimilate Native Americans into white society.

1888
The women's suffrage law is overturned.

1889
- A second state constitutional convention is held in Olympia.
- Washington becomes the 42nd state.

1875 1880 1885 1900

CONSTITUTION
of the
STATE OF WASHINGTON

Preamble.

Article 1.

KEY IDEAS

- The need for land for white settlement prompted treaty negotiations with Indians.
- The Stevens Treaties required Indians to give up their lands and move to reservations.
- Misunderstandings of Indian culture and the American belief in white superiority led to many problems.

KEY TERMS

assimilation
council
infringe
paternal
relinquish
reservation
sovereign
stipulate
superiority
treaty

A Changing Relationship

When sea traders, fur trappers, and missionaries first came to the Pacific Northwest, Indians were willing to trade with them, and most got along well. Indians worked for the fur companies and helped missionaries build homes and churches. As you read in chapter 2, Native Americans helped Lewis and Clark in their journey through the Northwest. However, as thousands of settlers came west on the Oregon Trail, relations between Indians and whites changed.

As pioneers moved west, thousands of oxen, mules, and horses followed, grazing their way west. They often spread out for a mile or more beside the wagons. So many animals passed through each summer that watering holes were drained by heavy use. Natural grasslands were depleted, so wild animals had trouble finding food. Always looking for fresh meat, the travelers hunted along the way. This meant that the supply of deer, elk, and buffalo that Indians relied on for food dwindled.

Pioneers observed Indians and wrote about them in diaries. A woman named Catherine Washburn observed: "Indians ketch crickets and dry them, pound to powder, mix with berries, and bake it for bread."

The dwindling food resources as well as disease took a toll on the Indian population. And, as more whites settled in the territory, there was conflict over land ownership. The changes brought by settlers and the increasing conflict sparked an era of warfare that lasted 30 years.

The painting shows the Battle of Seattle during the Yakama War. The artist, Emily Inez Denny, was three years old at the time of the battle. **How would you describe the activity and emotions in the painting?**

Cultural Conflict

Why were there so many problems? Why couldn't both groups live side by side in the vast territory?

- Indians and settlers had different ways of getting food. In some parts of North America, Indians had farmed before Columbus arrived, but not in the Pacific Northwest. Native people here lived by hunting, fishing, and gathering plant foods. White settlers expected native people to settle down on one spot of land, grow crops, and raise livestock.

- Land ownership meant different things to each group. American Indians had hunting and fishing grounds within tribal boundaries but did not own land individually. They used the natural resources on the land to provide food and shelter. They were satisfied with the ways they used the land. The settlers, however, wanted to own pieces of land. They wanted to grow crops on the land. They also wanted to make money by mining, cutting down trees to sell, and raising food and cattle to sell to others. They needed buildings, roads, railroads, and shipping harbors. They didn't mind changing the land so they could make a living.

- Language was another problem. When people spoke different languages, there was miscommunication.

- Leadership ideas were different. Settlers chose leaders to speak for them and make rules and laws. Native Americans had tribal *councils* that made decisions. The Indian chief had to get the support of the council regarding all decisions.

- The concept of white *superiority* gave settlers the belief that "good" meant "civilized our way." They did not respect the cultures of the native people. The settlers thought the Indians should eat, dress, work and worship like the white people.

The Cayuse War

The Whitman Massacre marked the beginning of a bloody period in relations between white settlers and native peoples. The murder of Dr. Whitman, his wife, and 12 others at the Waiilatpu mission sparked the Cayuse War. Settlers organized a volunteer militia and asked for assistance from Washington, D.C. Over the next several years, Cayuse Indians battled with local militia and U.S. troops.

In an effort to end the violence, a Cayuse chief ordered five warriors to surrender to U.S. troops for the murder of the Whitmans. The warriors were hanged, but the violence continued. By 1855, the Cayuse were defeated. Those who survived were placed on a *reservation* (land set aside for Native Americans).

What Do You Think?

White settlers and Native Americans were both guilty of savage cruelty. Some history books, however, have presented a skewed account of the conflicts. When whites slaughtered Indians, the conflict was usually a "battle," but when Indians slaughtered whites, it was a "massacre." What do you think is the reasoning behind these word choices?

A medicine man attends to a sick Indian. The Cayuse thought Dr. Whitman had deliberately infected them with measles.

In this painting, Chiefs at Dinner at the Walla Walla Council, *Governor Stevens and General Joel Palmer are serving food at each end of the banquet.* **What appears to be the mood of the dinner? How might the atmosphere help with treaty discussions?**

The Stevens Treaties

The murders of the Whitmans sparked the Cayuse War between the Cayuse people and white settlers backed by the U.S. Army. It would not be the only war, however.

In an effort to address the increasing tension between white settlers and native peoples, Washington's newly appointed governor, Isaac Stevens, embarked on a tour of the territory and held meetings with representatives of the largest Indian groups. In just over a year, Stevens signed 10 *treaties* (agreements between two or more independent nations) that resulted in the *relinquishing* (giving up) of Indian lands. By signing the treaties, Indians agreed to move to reservations. On the reservations, native groups would be concentrated in much smaller and less desirable lands.

The treaties also specified that on some reservations free agricultural and industrial schools would be established to teach Indian children the values and practices of white society. On the reservation, Indians also would have free access to health care. These benefits would be available for up to 20 years in most cases.

The treaties that Stevens negotiated were an example of the mindset of many Americans at the time. They reflected a belief in manifest destiny as well as the *paternal* (fatherly) attitude that many Americans had toward the Indians. The government thought that moving the Indians to reservations would protect them from white settlement and encourage them to adopt the beliefs and habits of white society.

> [T]he great end to be looked to is the gradual civilization of the Indians, and their ultimate incorporation with the people of the Territory. —Governor Isaac Stevens

The idea of *assimilation* (the act of accepting a new culture) was the cornerstone of Indian policy throughout the 19th century. Native Americans

What Is a Treaty?

A treaty is a written agreement between two states or *sovereigns* (independent nations). The federal government considered native groups living in the United States and its territories to be sovereign nations. According to the U.S. Constitution, the federal government has the responsibility of negotiating treaties with other nations. As an agent of the U.S. government, that's exactly what Governor Stevens was doing—negotiating agreements with Indian nations.

The United States signed about 800 treaties with Native Americans between 1789 and 1871, although less than half were approved by Congress. This made treaty enforcement difficult. All of the Stevens Treaties, however, were among those approved by Congress. Nevertheless, misunderstandings and disagreements over treaty terms continue to this day.

paid a heavy price for this policy, as it not only took away their land, but it chipped away at their cultural traditions and practices.

Broken Promises

The treaties made some promises to the native peoples, but often the terms of the treaties were either broken or only partially fulfilled. Additionally, treaty terms were open to interpretation and revised when the needs of white settlers changed.

Although the Indians were to be paid for their land, they were often paid very little and sometimes not at all. The money that was promised would be divided into payments spread over a period of years. The president of the United States would retain the right to dispense the money as he saw fit.

For example, the Treaty of Point No Point promised to pay natives of "said tribes and bands the sum of sixty thousand dollars" over a period of 20 years. The treaty further *stipulated* that:

> *All which said sums of money shall be applied to the use and benefit of the said Indians under the direction of the President of the United States, who may from time to time determine at his discretion upon what beneficial objects to expend the same.*

False Assumptions

The languages of the negotiations and the treaties could be confusing. Stevens and other U.S. officials did not speak native languages, and the natives spoke little or no English. The language used was something in between called Chinook Jargon. It had only 500 words, which made negotiating more difficult. Despite the trouble communicating, Stevens made his message clear: U.S. government officials wanted Indian land for settlers, and they wanted the Indians to live on smaller areas of land called reservations.

Not only did the Indians have to give up their lands, but some were also assigned to share reservations with other tribes that were their enemies. Government representatives ignored this

A group of Native Americans pose for a photo in front of a teepee at the Colville Indian Reservation in Northern Washington. **In what ways do they appear more American than Indian?**

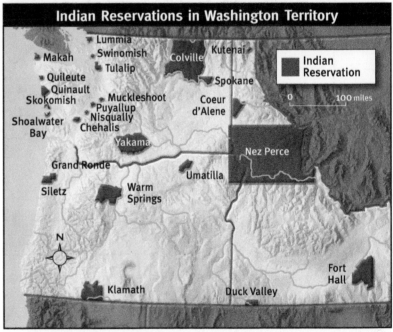

The Stevens Treaties required that Indians move to confined reservations that were much smaller than the lands they gave up. **Which reservations are the largest? Why do you think some tribes got more land?**

issue. What's more, officials did not recognize that the changes they wanted would be harder on some tribes than on others. Coastal Indians would be able to continue living and fishing on the coast, so their way of life would not change very much. But Indians who lived inland on the plateau were faced with significant changes to the way they lived. They needed plenty of space to hunt animals and gather seasonal plants. This would not be possible on the small reservations.

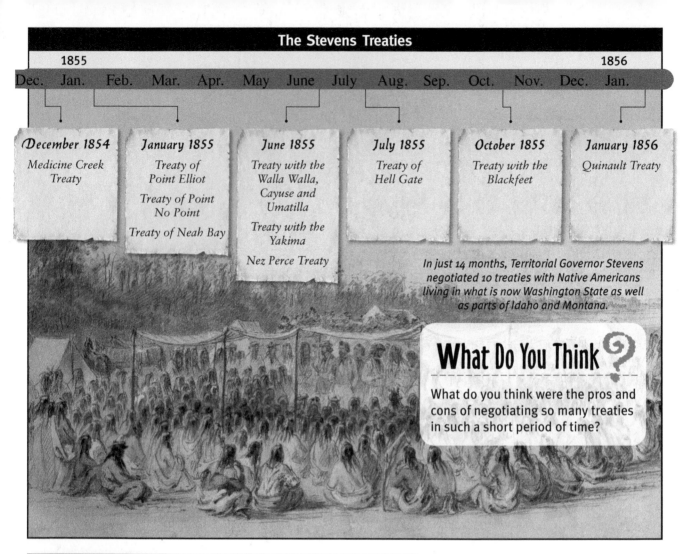

The Stevens Treaties

1855 — Dec. Jan. Feb. Mar. Apr. May June July Aug. Sep. Oct. Nov. Dec. **1856** — Jan.

December 1854
Medicine Creek Treaty

January 1855
Treaty of Point Elliot

Treaty of Point No Point

Treaty of Neah Bay

June 1855
Treaty with the Walla Walla, Cayuse and Umatilla

Treaty with the Yakima

Nez Perce Treaty

July 1855
Treaty of Hell Gate

October 1855
Treaty with the Blackfeet

January 1856
Quinault Treaty

In just 14 months, Territorial Governor Stevens negotiated 10 treaties with Native Americans living in what is now Washington State as well as parts of Idaho and Montana.

What Do You Think?

What do you think were the pros and cons of negotiating so many treaties in such a short period of time?

Treaties allowed Indians to retain tribal sovereignty. Here, an Indian chief leads a tribal council among his people. **What do you imagine the chief is telling his people? How would you describe the chief's role in the council?**

Tribal Sovereignty

One important concept that the treaties were to uphold was the idea of tribal sovereignty. Tribal sovereignty refers to the right of Native Americans to govern themselves. Although the treaties required native peoples to give up land and move onto reservations, the Indians would retain the right to govern themselves.

Today, this right of self-government, however, does have limits. While Indians can govern themselves according to tribal law and custom within Indian reservations, federal law is still considered supreme. This means the U.S. government can overrule tribal laws and even overrule decisions made by tribal courts.

By the turn of the century, fishing had become an important economic activity for Indians and whites. **How does the photo justify concerns about overfishing?**

Fishing Rights

Since fishing was a source of food and trade, and because it was significant to Indian values and customs, most of the treaties included fishing rights. Indians would be allowed to continue to fish in "usual and accustomed" places even if those places were not on the reservation.

Initially, granting these tribes fishing rights off the reservation was not a problem. Most white settlers were interested in other economic activities such as farming and logging. Indian fishing rights posed no threat to those activities. However, by the turn of the century, commercial fishing was a significant livelihood for many Americans. This led to competition—and conflict—with Indians when they continued to fish on land considered to be private property outside of the reservation.

Besides fueling conflict, the competition started to make a noticeable dent in the fish supply. This sparked fears that some fish,

Linking the Past to the Present

Disputes over fishing rights led Indian activists to stage "fish-ins" in the 1960s and '70s to protest state regulations that undermined treaty rights promised them 100 years earlier. Indian activists modeled their protests after those of black Civil Rights activists who staged sit-ins, wade-ins, and other "ins" to protest segregation in public facilities, including restaurants, movie theaters, swimming pools, beaches, and schools.

Tribal groups repeatedly challenged state laws throughout the 20th century and finally succeeded in securing their rights in a 1974 Supreme Court ruling known as the "Boldt Decision."

According to the ruling, treaty tribes could continue to fish in traditional places outside of reservations. Further, the Court ruled that treaty and non-treaty fishermen would have an equal share of the harvestable fish.

like salmon, would disappear if there was too much fishing. State officials responded to the fears by setting size limits on fish catches. Native Americans saw these regulations as *infringing* on their treaty rights.

What Did You Learn? ①

1. What was the purpose of the treaties between the United States government and the Indians?
2. What problems resulted from broken promises and false assumptions?
3. Explain how the treaties represented American attitudes about Indians at the time.

KEY IDEAS

- Anger over treaty terms and violations triggered war between Indians and white settlers.

- War devastated the native peoples and forced survivors onto reservations.

- The Dawes Act broke up reservations and attempted to Americanize Indians.

KEY TERMS

allotment
coerce
encroach
fraud
humane
intruder
retaliate
slaughter
trespass
truce

The Yakama People

Governor Stevens met with 5,000 Indians at Walla Walla to discuss the division of land on the Columbia Plateau. Nez Perce, Cayuse, Walla Walla, Umatilla, and Yakama people gathered for the meeting.

Until the meeting, the Yakama people were not considered a tribe. Fourteen related bands who spoke the same language, shared hunting grounds, and intermarried were grouped into the new tribe by Governor Stevens.

At the recommendation of a Catholic priest who had worked among the scattered bands and had come as an interpreter, Stevens appointed Kamiakin, a respected Indian man, to be the leader of the group. He was to sign the treaty for all of them. Kamiakin was named "head chief" of what became known as the Yakama Nation. Men from other bands were named as "subchiefs."

Chief Kamiakin was a proud man who did not talk much. He had not wanted to come to the council at all. When the subject of a reservation for the newly formed Yakama Nation was brought up, he responded:

The forest knows me; he knows my heart. He knows I do not desire a great many goods. All that I wish for is a [government] agent, a good agent, who will pity the good and bad of us and take care of us. I have nothing to talk long about. I am tired. I am anxious to get back to my garden. That is all I have to say.

At the large meeting, where English, Chinook Jargon, and various Indian languages were all spoken, interpreters tried to negotiate between Governor Stevens and Indian leaders. Stevens agreed to give the larger tribes—the Nez Perce and Yakama—large reservations in their homelands. Smaller groups, who did not have much bargaining power, were forced to agree to this arrangement.

Hostilities Begin

Only a few years after the treaty agreements, something happened that changed everything—gold was discovered along the upper Columbia River. Gold seekers rushed into the area, *trespassing* on lands given to the Yakamas in the treaty. The Indians were angry. Stevens ordered whites not to enter Yakama lands, but they came anyway. Angry bands of Yakamas

Nez Perce Indians arrive at a treaty negotiation site with Governor Stevens. Stevens and other government officials stand in the center. **How might you feel if you were standing with Stevens as the Indians arrived?**

sought revenge and started killing white *intruders*. The U.S. Army stepped in and captured Chief Kamiakin and his followers. This ended the fighting, at least for a while.

At almost the same time, Seattle, still a village, was attacked by neighboring Indians. It seemed as if the entire region was at war. An army was sent from Fort Walla Walla to look over the situation, but as they reached the open grasslands near Rosalia, they were surrounded by Indian warriors from several tribes. During the night, soldiers escaped and retreated to their fort, abandoning weapons, horses, and several soldiers who had been killed.

The army sent a group of 600 soldiers to punish the tribes. They captured and *slaughtered* 700 Indian horses and hanged 24 of the Indian leaders. They also forced the Indians to sign peace treaties, which ended the Yakama War.

Chief Kamiakin was given a chance to return to the reservation, but he would not. He spent the rest of his life alone in remote parts of Washington and Canada.

In this painting, white settlers seek safety from Indian attack.
What do you think was the artist's view of Indians?

Native Leaders React to White Settlements

Chief Moses

Chief Moses, of the Columbia-Sinkiuse Indians, was forced to take his people to the Yakama Reservation. In an 1879 letter, he told how the settlers created problems for Indian survival:

There are white men living in my country. Some can stay forever and some must go. . . . People who raise hogs in my country must go with their hogs, because they kill out the young camas, and to kill that is to starve us. It is our bread and we cannot eat earth. . . . We must fish and hunt and our squaws must dig camas and other roots, and when you touch us on any of these points, then we carry our rifles on the right and left of us.

Chief Sealth

Chief Sealth was leader of the Duwamish. He welcomed the protection of the federal government against local Indian enemies. Wanting peace for his people, Chief Sealth tried to help the white settlers. When it was time to move to a reservation, he encouraged his people to go peacefully.

Here is part of a famous speech he gave to Governor Stevens:

The White Chief says that Big Chief in Washington sends us greetings. . . . His people are many. They are like the grass that covers vast prairies. My people are few. . . . They are ebbing away like a rapidly receding tide that will never return. . . . Let us hope that hostilities between us never return. We would have everything to lose and nothing to gain. My people will retire to the reservation you offer them. Then we will dwell apart in peace.

The Nez Perce War

One band of Nez Perce Indians was led by *Hin-maton-Yal-a-kit*, which meant Thunder Traveling to Loftier Mountain Heights. The white settlers called him Chief Joseph. Like his father, whose tribe had assisted Lewis and Clark, Joseph had worked peacefully with fur traders and missionaries. Many of the tribe had become Christian. They had made an art of breeding horses and grazed them on rich grasslands. They signed the treaty at Walla Walla and lived peacefully on a reservation until gold was discovered there.

The government responded by opening some reservation land for mining and white settlement and forced the native people to move yet again. Then, a few young men whose fathers had been killed by white settlers killed four white men in revenge. When Chief Joseph found out, he knew the U.S. Army would *retaliate*. He prepared a band of 200 young men, some older men, and nearly 600 women and children for flight. Chief Joseph was 36 years old.

The U.S. Army caught up to the Nez Perce, who sent out a small party under a *truce* flag (a flag of surrender).

Chief Joseph

However, a battle broke out when someone fired a gun.

This began a series of battles that were recorded by journalists. Readers in the East followed the stories in the papers, and the Nez Perce War and Chief Joseph became famous. Unlike in other wars, many more soldiers were killed than Indians.

Nez Perce Tactics

One reason for the success of the Nez Perce was that they did not fight in traditional Indian ways. They took higher ground, dug rifle pits, and surrounded a force six times their size. They used bows and arrows, shotguns, and rifles. They outshot and outrode the U.S. Army.

The Nez Perce fled east and into Montana, but they were caught by a surprise attack. Again they fought back. Warriors pinned the soldiers down with rifle fire while the rest of the Nez Perce gathered their wounded and dead and escaped into the hills.

What Do You Think ?

Do you think it was morally right for the settlers to assume that they could take, or buy, land already occupied by Native Americans on the reservations?

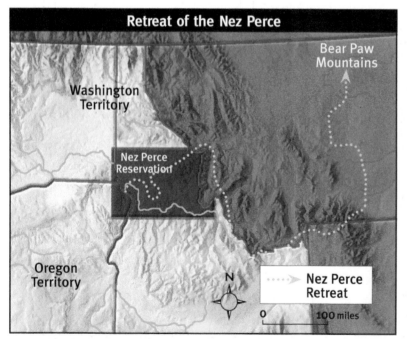

Retreat of the Nez Perce

Bear Paw Mountains

Washington Territory

Nez Perce Reservation

Oregon Territory

N

Nez Perce Retreat

0   100 miles

*The Nez Perce fled their reservation and were pursued by the U.S. Army until Chief Joseph surrendered at the Battle of Bear Paw in Montana. **About how many miles did the Nez Perce travel before surrendering?***

The Washington Journey

Chief Joseph Surrenders

Finally, the army sent about 600 men to overtake the Nez Perce, who were resting along a creek close to the Canadian border. The combat was fierce, with hand-to-hand fighting between the soldiers and the Indians. The battle went on until nightfall. Many Indians were dead. Chief Joseph knew that his people could not keep fighting.

The next day a snowstorm blew in, adding to the misery. Heartsick, freezing, and hungry, Chief Joseph and his people had little choice but to surrender. The surrender took place at Bear Paw Mountain in the Big Hole Valley of Montana.

Chief Joseph's surrender speech shows the strong feelings of a leader for his people:

> *Our chiefs are killed. . . . It is cold and we have no blankets. The little children are freezing to death. My people, some of them, have run away to the hills and have no blankets, no food. . . . Hear me, my chiefs, I am tired. My heart is sick and sad. From where the sun now stands, I will fight no more forever.*

The army moved the band to a reservation in Oklahoma. Later, they were returned to Washington to live on the Colville Reservation.

Erskine Wood and Chief Joseph

A white teenaged boy spent summers living with Chief Joseph on the Colville Reservation. His name was Erskine Wood. His father had met Chief Joseph when they were negotiating treaties, and admired him greatly.

In his diary, Erskine described the way the Indian families combined 10 teepees into one long lodge during the winter. Fresh venison strips were hung on racks over the fires in the center of the lodge and smoked to make jerky. He also wrote that Chief Joseph refused to accept the overalls distributed by the Indian agency, wanting to wear the traditional style of leather leggings.

When Erskine was preparing to go home to Portland, he asked Chief Joseph if there was any gift that his father could give to repay his kindness. Chief Joseph thought about it and then asked for a horse. To young Erskine, that did not seem like much of a gift —Chief Joseph already had many horses. "I did not know what the gift of a horse was," Erskine recalled.

Years later, Erskine Wood's family purchased a fine Appaloosa and gave it to Chief Joseph's 250 descendants on the Colville Reservation.

Erskine Wood

"I will fight no more forever," were the words spoken by Nez Perce Chief Joseph as he and his followers surrendered to U.S. troops.

93

White Support of Indians

John James was a boy when his three older brothers were asked to join volunteers to fight Indians. The James family was against fighting the Indians. This aggravated their neighbors. The neighbors thought everyone should join together to get rid of Indian problems.

An Indian was lured to the James' property and then murdered by neighbors. The neighbors thought that if Indians retaliated against the James family for the murder, the James family would join the volunteer forces in fighting the Indian wars. However, there was no Indian retaliation against the James family, though, and they still refused to fight the Indians. White neighbors frequently looted their farm, and their sheep and butter were stolen.

My father thought we should not have to fight the Indians . . . as there were no settlements over there . . . with the exception of one or two army posts. This created considerable feeling among the families that wanted to [fight the Indians] . . . I am satisfied it takes just as much nerve and courage to oppose a war as actual participation in the fighting.

—John James

Aftermath of Wars

War and the continuing flood of settlers overwhelmed the Indian people. Indian tribes were crowded out of their homelands, and most were assigned to reservations. And, as you read, when gold was discovered, white settlers began *encroaching* on the reservations. Indians were hopeful that the federal government would protect their treaty rights and their land titles.

The Indian Homestead Act

In an effort to protect Indian rights and encourage individual ownership of land, the U.S. Congress passed the Indian Homestead Act. It gave individual Indians the right to own a piece of property. However, Indians did not value land ownership in the same way as did white settlers. This difference in values led to more problems.

For example, the laws included loopholes. When whites wanted Indian land, they would *coerce* (persuade) the Indian owner into selling it to them, or use *fraud* (dishonest or unlawful behavior). Indian people were at a loss when it came to defending their rights in the legal system.

Linking the Past to the Present

Nisqually Chief Leschi was hanged for the murder of a U.S. soldier during the Indian wars. Chief Leschi was not alone in objecting to the terms of the Medicine Creek Treaty that he felt forced to sign. The treaty stripped his people of tribal lands and assigned them to a reservation that had no access to the Nisqually River. His people had lived and fished on that river for many generations.

The war that followed resulted in the death of many on both sides. Chief Leschi argued that the soldier's death was the result of war, not murder.

I do not know anything about your laws. I have supposed that the killing of armed men in wartime was not murder; if it was, the soldiers who killed Indians are guilty of murder too. . . .

More than 150 years later, a Historical Court of Justice agreed with Chief Leschi's statement and ruled that the execution was unjust. The ruling stated that Chief Leschi should never have been charged because he fought during a time of war.

Nisqually Chief Leschi was executed for the murder of a U.S. soldier during wartime. In 2004, a court ruled that the execution was unjust.

The Dawes Act

Finally, in an attempt to be *humane* to Indians and reverse the damage done by the reservation system, Congress passed the General Allotment Act. Often called the Dawes Act, the law divided reservation land into individual *allotments*, or portions of land (usually 160 acres), and encouraged Indians to become farmers.

Although it was hoped that the new law would help improve the lives of Native Americans, in many cases it did not. Much of the land assigned to Indians was dry and unsuitable for farming.

According to the new law, individual Indians could apply for citizenship once they got title to a plot of land. However, Indians were required to break tribal ties in order to gain citizenship. As a result, tribal authority and Indian culture were weakened.

Similar to previous laws, the Dawes Act caused problems. It was repealed in 1934 and replaced by a new policy intended to restore tribal authority and culture. The new policy helped restore unity among Native Americans. This restored unity fueled the Indian Rights Movement later in the century.

The Dawes Act opened land from Indian reservations to settlement by Indians and whites. What Indians did not claim was available to whites. **What are the selling points in the advertisement that might appeal to homesteaders?**

An Indian confronts a miner who is illegally mining on land belonging to Indians according to treaty terms. **What do you suppose each man is thinking? Describe the emotions they might be experiencing.**

Carrie Anderson, Annie Dawson, and Sarah Walker were the new names given to these girls on their arrival at the Hampton Normal and Agricultural Institute in Virginia. The photograph below was taken 14 months later to show the successful Americanization of the girls. **Compare the two photos. In what ways did the lives of the girls change?**

Boarding Schools

Another aspect of the Dawes Act was the establishment of Indian boarding schools. Policies at the schools were based upon the idea that there was nothing of value in Indian culture. The majority of whites thought that it was in the best interest of Indians to abandon their old ways and adopt the ways of the white culture.

As a result, Indian children were taken from their families on the reservations and sent far away to boarding schools. Children from Northwest reservations were often sent to Oklahoma. Most did not see their parents again for many years.

The boarding school experience was a culture shock. Indian students had their long hair cut short. They were dressed in uniforms and given new names. They were punished if they spoke their native language. The students washed their own clothes in tubs of water and kept their dormitory rooms clean. They helped prepare and clean up after meals.

Boys and girls were taught English, reading, spelling, geography, and arithmetic. The course of study for older children emphasized job and housekeeping skills. Boys learned carpentry and to run machines. Girls learned how to make clothes on sewing machines.

Sid Bird was sent to the Genoa School in Nebraska when he was six years old. Returning years later, he found that he could not talk to his grandmother:

> *My own language had been beaten out of me. I was no longer an Indian. I guess I was an imitation white man.*

What Do You Think ?

In an 1892 speech explaining the purpose of educating Indians, Captain Richard C. Pratt said, "Kill the Indian in him, save the man." What do you think he meant by his words? Was he a "friend to the Indians," as he described himself? Why or why not?

A Century of Dishonor

In 1881, Helen Hunt Jackson sent a copy of her new book, *A Century of Dishonor*, to every member of Congress in Washington, D.C. The book was a harsh criticism of U.S. policy and treatment of Native Americans from colonial times through the 1870s. Jackson hoped that by reading her book, the nation's lawmakers would change their attitudes about Indians and perhaps pursue more humane policies.

It makes little difference, however, where one opens the record of the history of the Indians; every page and every year has its dark stain. The story of one tribe is the story of all, varied only by differences of time and place; but neither time nor place makes any difference in the main facts. . . . [T]he United States Government breaks promises now as deftly [skillfully] as then, and with an added ingenuity [creativity] from long practice.

Cheating, robbing, breaking promises—these three are clearly things which must cease to be done. One more thing, also, and that is the refusal of the protection of the law to the Indian's rights of property, "of life, liberty, and the pursuit of happiness."

Her book did impress some members of Congress who took it into account when they wrote the Dawes Act. The intention of the new law was to correct the injustices of the Indian reservations.

Although the new policy was well-intentioned, it actually contributed to the destruction of native culture by breaking up reservations. The law provided for individual Indians to own land carved out of the reservation. Additionally, Indians could become U.S. citizens but only by breaking their tribal ties.

Helen Hunt Jackson's book, A Century of Dishonor, *was influential in the passage of the Dawes Act in 1887.*

What Did You Learn? ②

1. Why did white settlers disregard treaty terms?
2. What was the result of the Indian wars?
3. How did white cultural values influence new policies?

KEY IDEAS

- It took Washington more than 30 years to become a state despite several requests to Congress.

- Washington's constitution reflects the basic principles of liberty and justice found in the U.S. Constitution.

KEY TERMS

census
delegate
franchise
jurisdiction
ratification
sectarian
speculate
suffrage

Road to Statehood

As you read in chapter 3, Washington Territory was created in 1853, when it was separated from Oregon Territory. It would take 36 years for Washington to transform from a territory to a state. The wait finally ended on November 11, 1889, when it was admitted to the Union along with Montana, North Dakota, and South Dakota. Why did it take so long?

First, the population of the territory needed to be at least 60,000. Then, the territorial legislature had to draft a state constitution. The state constitution was required to uphold the principles of the U.S. Constitution and the Declaration of Independence. Further, the constitution would have to guarantee basic civil rights for its citizens, including free speech and freedom of religion.

The new state would also have to establish a public school system, "which shall be open to all the children of said States, and free from sectarian control." *Sectarian* refers to a person or group connected to a particular religion or set of beliefs. Once all these conditions were met, application could be made to the U.S. Congress for statehood.

A Constitutional Convention

By 1878, Washington's population exceeded the minimum necessary to apply for statehood. In the summer of that year, territorial officials convened a constitutional convention in Walla Walla and began work on a state constitution.

The issue of voting rights for women resulted in some heated discussions among the *delegates* in Walla Walla. Abigail Scott Duniway addressed the convention, asking the delegates to make Washington the first state to give women *suffrage*, or the right to vote. The proposal was turned down, as were other proposals that would have abolished the Indian reservation system and established segregated schools for black children.

Eligible voters (men aged 21 and over) approved the constitution later that year, and it was sent to Congress for approval. However, Congress failed to approve it and grant statehood to Washington. Some historians *speculate* that the Democratic majority in Congress was concerned that admitting Washington and other western territories to the Union would tip the balance of power to Republicans who

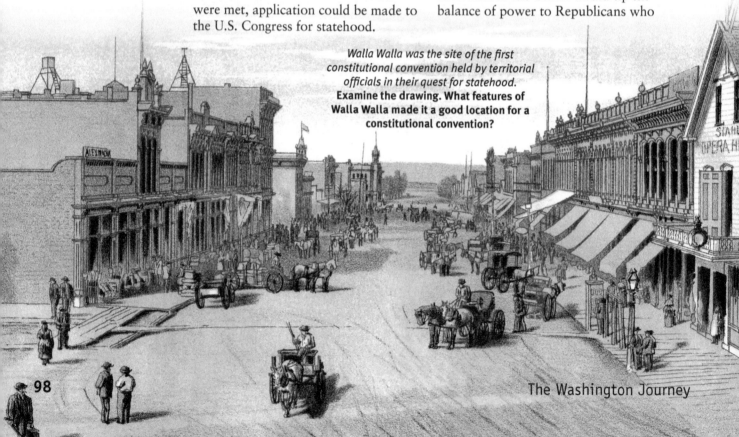

Walla Walla was the site of the first constitutional convention held by territorial officials in their quest for statehood.
Examine the drawing. What features of Walla Walla made it a good location for a constitutional convention?

outnumbered Democrats in the western territories.

For the next 11 years, territorial leaders made several applications to Congress for statehood. Every application was rejected. Finally, in 1889, Congress approved the Enabling Act. This was a law to "enable" Washington, along with the territories of North Dakota, South Dakota, and Montana to become states.

Once again territorial officials gathered to draft a state constitution. This time they met at the territorial capital in Olympia. An amendment (proposed addition) to grant voting rights to women and another amendment to ban the manufacture and sale of alcohol (known as Prohibition) were both rejected by delegates. The territory's male citizens overwhelmingly approved of the constitution, and it was sent again to Congress for *ratification* (formal approval). This time, Congress gave the green light, and Washington was admitted as the 42nd state. Republican Elisha P. Ferry was elected as the state's first governor.

*Washington officials received a telegram from the president of the United States. **To whom is it addressed and what does it say?***

Territorial Growth

The first *census* of Washington was recorded when it was designated as a territory in 1853. A census is an official count of the population. At that time the white population was 3,985. The Native American population was not included in the territory's census although Native Americans greatly outnumbered white settlers.

Following the initial territorial census, Washington's population was included in the national government census. The national government began taking a census in 1790. The national census is updated every 10 years.

As you can see, Washington's population grew rapidly. In fact, the population more than doubled every 10 years until 1900, when the growth rate began to slow.

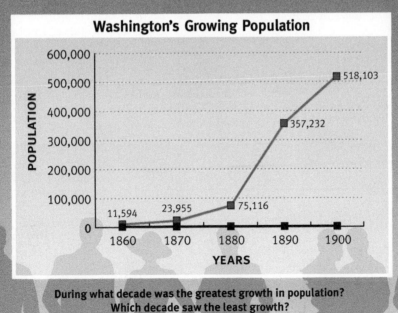

Washington's Growing Population

During what decade was the greatest growth in population? Which decade saw the least growth?

From Treaties to Statehood

Washington PORTRAIT

Elisha P. Ferry
(1825–1895)

When Washington became a state in 1889, voters elected Elisha Peyre Ferry as their first governor. Up until then, the president of the United States had always appointed the territorial governor. Ferry served two terms as territorial governor. As territorial governor, Ferry encouraged the creation of laws that would regulate banking, railroads, education, and agriculture.

At one time, he called out the militia to help restore order during a strike of Northern Pacific Railroad workers. He also traveled to Eastern Washington during the Nez Perce War to "try and quiet matters," as one historian wrote in a biography of Ferry.

After serving two terms as territorial governor, Ferry served as the vice president of Puget Sound National Bank and practiced law in Seattle.

Washington's quest for statehood brought Ferry back to the political scene as the Republican candidate for governor. He served one term before he died.

Washington's Constitution

Although our state's official constitution was written and adopted in 1889, territorial officials had adopted an earlier version in 1878. The delegates who wrote the 1889 constitution used lots of the ideas from the first constitution. Much like the men who wrote the U.S. Constitution, they were all white males. They were men of property and high social standing—mostly lawyers, bankers, businessmen, and well-to-do farmers.

The new state constitution shows clearly that the constitution is a product of its time. The framers of the constitution feared giving too much power to lawmakers who might be influenced by special-interest groups, such as farmers, laborers, or big business, so they gave the governor broad veto powers. As a result, the governor can veto a whole bill or entire sections of any bill.

Rights and Freedoms

As required by the U.S. Congress, our state constitution upholds the basic freedoms and principles of liberty and justice that are included in the first 10 amendments—the Bill of Rights—of the U.S. Constitution. However, Washington's constitution clarifies rights that were either not addressed or were vaguely worded in the U.S. Constitution. For example, Article 1, Section 7 of our state constitution ensures that citizens of Washington have a right to privacy. No such right is stated in the U.S. Constitution.

Our state constitution also includes specific requirements for establishing a system of public education. Article 9 of the Washington constitution states that it is "the paramount duty of the state to make ample provision for the education of all children" in the state.

Additionally, Washington's constitution is more specific in establishing a citizen's right to bear arms. It states that an individual has a right to bear arms "in defense of himself, or the state." The constitution, however, does not allow "individuals or corporations to organize, maintain or employ an armed body of men." Constitutional scholars have pointed out that the framers likely included this limitation in response to some of the violent labor strikes that had occurred in the country and in Washington in the late 1800s. During some of these strikes, business owners hired their own private armies to control striking workers. You will read more about labor unrest in a later chapter.

Status of Indian Rights

Article 26 of the Washington constitution specifies that Indian land and the native people living there fall under the *jurisdiction* (power or authority) of the federal government, not the state government. As you read in the last lesson, Indian tribes do have tribal sovereignty (the right to self-government). Federal law, however, is the supreme law of the land. Therefore, tribal law, as well as individual state laws, can be overruled by federal law.

How Our Constitution Compares to the U.S. Constitution		
	Washington State Constitution	U.S. Constitution
Pages	70	9
Articles	31	7
Times amended since adoption	98	27

Washington's constitution was written just over 100 years after the U.S. Constitution. How do the two documents compare? **Why do you think our constitution is longer?**

This is an image of the first page of Washington's 1889 constitution.

Washington residents gather in front of the statehouse in Olympia for the inauguration of Governor Elisha P. Ferry. **Can you estimate the number of people in attendance?**

101

Voting Rights for Women

The road was long for women who fought for the right to vote, both nationally and in Washington. Women began lobbying (petitioning) for suffrage in 1848 when national suffrage leaders met at Seneca Falls, New York, and issued a Declaration of Sentiments modeled after the Declaration of Independence. Nationally, women would not get the vote until 1920 with the ratification of the 19th Amendment. Women in Washington finally won the right to vote in 1910.

Repeatedly, from the time that Washington was designated as a territory, women had asked for voting rights. Their requests were continually denied, with one exception. In 1883, the territorial legislature approved a suffrage bill, granting women the right to vote. And vote they did—at least until 1888, when the law was overturned. During the five years when they could vote, women typically supported "law and order" issues by voting in favor of laws restricting alcohol and prostitution.

Although attempts were made to include suffrage in the new state constitution, women did not regain voting rights until 1910, when male voters agreed to give them the *franchise*. Franchise means the right or privilege to vote. Washington became the fifth state, behind Wyoming, Utah, Colorado, and Idaho, to grant voting rights to women.

LINCOLN SAID

Seventy-five years ago Abraham Lincoln said: "I go for all sharing the privileges of government who assist in bearing its burdens, by no means excluding women."

WOMEN SHOULD VOTE

Women's suffrage supporters hang signs urging approval of a voting rights bill for Washington women. **How were Lincoln's words used to promote women's suffrage?**

What Did You Learn? ③

1. List the steps Washington needed to meet before it could become a state.
2. How does Washington's constitution compare to the U.S. Constitution?
3. How were women affected by Washington's quest for statehood?

Go to the Source

Examine a Treaty

The Treaty of Point Elliott was one of the 10 treaties Governor Isaac Stevens negotiated with the native peoples of Washington Territory. The governor, as well as other U.S. officials, signed each treaty, as did all Indian chiefs and representatives present at a treaty council. The image below shows just a few of the signatures of Indian chiefs who represented the more than 20 tribal groups at the Point Elliott treaty council.

Examine the treaty and answer the questions using specific reference to the image as well as your understanding of events from chapter 4.

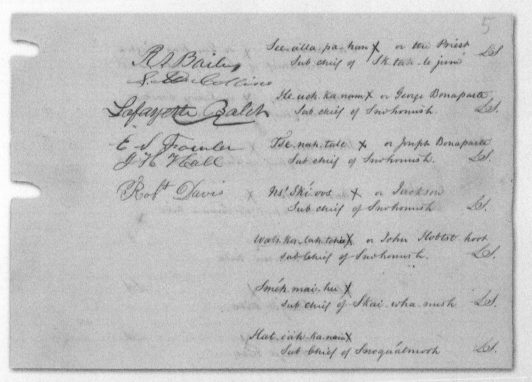

Observe	Evaluate	Conclude
• What do you notice about the treaty's signatures?	• What does the X tell you about the chiefs' understanding of the treaty and the significance of a signature?	• What can you conclude about the difficulties in negotiating treaties? • How did such difficulties contribute to warfare?

Analyzing Sources

Historians use primary sources and secondary sources to study events and people from the past. A primary source is a document such as a letter, diary, newspaper article, or image written or created during the time under study. A secondary source interprets and analyzes one or more primary sources.

One of the keys to studying sources is being able to judge their reliability. Much like a detective sorts through evidence to solve a crime, historians must critically sort through sources to piece together an event from the past.

Questions to Consider When Analyzing a Source

1. When and where was the source created? *The closer in time and place a source was created to an event, the more reliable the source is considered to be.*

2. Who created the source, and why? *All sources are biased in some way. As a result, the source can shape the way we view the event. Therefore, sources should be critically evaluated with the creator's point of view considered.*

   Consider these questions when testing for bias:
   - Was the source created during the event or after?
   - Did the author of the source have opinions or interests that might have influenced what was written (or painted, etc.)?
   - Was the source meant to inform or persuade others?

Your Turn

Examine the two documents below. Are they primary or secondary sources? What topic from the chapter are they connected to? Using brief quotes from each document, write a short paragraph expressing your own thoughts on the significance of the documents in understanding the impact of Indian policies on whites and natives.

The School Days of an Indian Girl, from an *Atlantic Monthly* article written in 1900 by Zitkala Sa, or Gertrude Bonnin.

Letter from W. C. Chattin, a teacher at the Skokomish Indian School in Washington Territory, to an official of the federal Indian Bureau.

Late in the morning, my friend Judewin gave me a terrible warning. Judewin knew a few words of English; and she had overheard the paleface woman talk about cutting our long, heavy hair. Our mothers had taught us that only unskilled warriors who were captured had their hair shingled by the enemy. Among our people, short hair was worn by mourners, and shingled hair by cowards! . . . I cried aloud, shaking my head all the while until I felt the cold blades of the scissors against my neck, and heard them gnaw off one of my thick braids. Then I lost my spirit.

June 30, 1867
I . . . endeavor to persuade them to abandon their evil practices and to become industrious, moral, and good. My experience as teacher . . . has established my faith in the power of the gospel, with right surroundings, to elevate this race to a far better humanity and a glorious immortality, and I believe that the only reason why it has not to a greater extent been accomplished on this coast is because of the infidelity of those whose business it should be to labor for such elevation instead of their extermination, the prevailing opinion being . . . the sooner they are out of the way the better.

Chapter Review Questions

1. Why did the U.S. government negotiate treaties with Native Americans in Washington Territory?

2. Identify factors that contributed to the outbreak of war between Indians and white settlers.

3. List the needs of the white settlers and the needs of the Native Americans. Use your list to create a treaty that would address the needs of both white settlers and Native Americans.

4. Draw a picture illustrating Washington's path to statehood that includes milestones and roadblocks. What conclusions can you draw about why it took so long for Washington to become a state?

Becoming a Better Reader

Visualizing the Text

Effective readers "see" the story in their heads as they read. It's like going to the movies in your head every time you open a book. Picturing the story in your head helps you make the connections needed to understand. We call this reading strategy visualizing the text. *The Washington Journey* is full of stories of exciting people and events. Choose one person or one event from this chapter and describe the person or event using your imagination and senses to provide interesting details.

You Are the Geographer

Compare Maps

Compare the map on page 87 of Indian Reservations in Washington Territory with a current map of Indian reservations found on the Web Site of the Governor's Office of Indian Affairs: http://www.goia.wa.gov/Tribal-Information/Map.htm. Click on "Map of Reservations."

1. Compare and contrast the number and location of Indian reservations. What similarities and differences do you notice?

2. What do you think happened to some of the reservations that were created during Washington's territorial period?

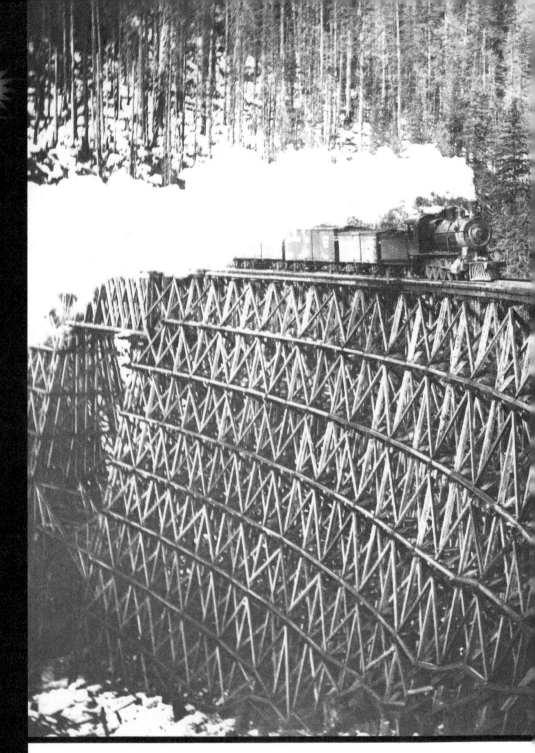

Essential Question ?

How did Washington's economy and population change in the era following statehood?

Timeline of Events

1869
The first transcontinental railroad is completed.

1870

1882
The Chinese Exclusion Act bans immigration from China.

1880

1883
Washington becomes part of transcontinental railroad when the final rails of the Northern Pacific are joined.

1886
The world's largest sawmill is built in Tacoma.

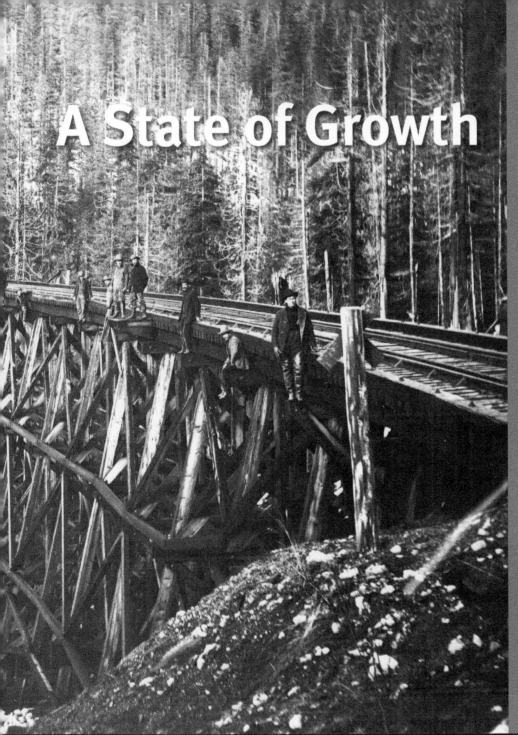

A State of Growth

In the late 1800s, the United States experienced incredible growth. The nation's economy and population were growing by leaps and bounds. Much of the growth was due to the construction of railroads that stitched together the country, connecting city to city and coast to coast.

The construction of railroads in Washington fueled the state's lumber and coal industries, and brought thousands of immigrants to the countryside and rapidly growing cities.

A steam train crosses a recently completed railroad bridge. **How does this bridge differ from those that are built today?**

1880–1910
Waves of immigrants come to Washington and the Pacific Northwest.

1893
The Great Northern Railroad is completed.

1906
Union Depot opens in Seattle.

1910
Seattle is the largest city in the Pacific Northwest.

1890

1900

1910

1889
• Washington becomes a state.
• Fire destroys Seattle's business district.

1897
Gold is discovered in the Klondike region of Canada's Yukon Territory.

107

KEY IDEAS

- The Northern Pacific Railroad and the Great Northern Railroad connect Washington to the rest of the country.

- The U.S. government provided generous loans and land grants to build the transcontinental railroads.

- The growth of the railroads contributed to the economic development of the state and the nation.

KEY TERMS

bankrupt
corporation
corruption
distribution network
solvent
stock
subsidy
transcontinental

Exploring a Northern Route

When Isaac Stevens was appointed as Washington's first territorial governor, his responsibilities were many. As you read in the last chapter, one of his duties was to negotiate treaties with Native Americans to open up Indian lands for white settlement. The land gained by the treaties was not just for homesteads. There were also plans to build a railroad through the new territory.

In the same year that Washington became a territory, Congress passed the Pacific Railroad Survey Bill. This bill authorized the exploration of a potential route for the nation's first *transcontinental* railroad. It would stretch across the continent, connecting the Atlantic Coast with the Pacific Coast. Because the Mexican War added so much new territory to the United States, there were at least four possible routes to explore. Governor Stevens was asked to explore a northern route that would connect the Great Lakes to Puget Sound.

Because there was so much terrain to consider for a potential railroad route, Stevens shared the surveying duties with Captain George B. McClellan. (McClellan would later be appointed commander of the Union army during the Civil War. President Abraham Lincoln fired him from that position. McClellan then challenged Lincoln in the 1864 presidential election.) McClellan's party traveled from the West in search of a practical route through the Cascades. Stevens' party traveled from the East following the Missouri River to the mouth of the Yellowstone River at Fort Union.

Stevens concluded that there were at least two possible routes over the Cascades. However, the U.S. government decided to build the first transcontinental railroad farther south than Washington. The route chosen would start in Omaha, Nebraska, and run through the present-day states of Nebraska, Wyoming, Utah, Nevada, and California. This first transcontinental line was completed in 1869. It eventually stretched from San Francisco to Chicago and on to eastern railroad lines that connected to the Atlantic seaboard.

The Northern Pacific Railroad

Washington became part of the transcontinental system when the tracks of the Northern Pacific's rail line from the Great Lakes to Puget Sound were joined in 1883. Now a journey that once took three to five months could be made in only five days—or even less.

An article in the *Spokane Falls Chronicle* described the excitement surrounding the arrival of the first passenger train of the Northern Pacific:

Governor Stevens receives a message from McClellan's surveying party. **Where do you think Stevens is in the illustration?**

About half past 6 o'clock in the evening, Graham's band struck up a lively tune, and then almost the entire population of the town left homes, stores, shops, and offices, and hastened to the depot. At 7:14 the train came into view . . . the crowd cheered, the band played, and greetings were extended to those who came to Spokane by rail.

The Northern Pacific Railroad was a very important corporation in the state's history. A *corporation* is a business owned by a group of people who own stock in the company. Additionally, the company can sell *stock*, meaning a share in the company, to the public to raise money that helps finance the business. If the business makes money, so do all the stockholders. No other business had a greater influence on Washington's settlement and economic development than the Northern Pacific Railroad.

In general, railroads boosted economic development throughout the country because the railroads were connected to so many other industries. For example, railroad construction consumed between 20 and 50 percent of annual timber production in the United States, most of it from the West. Sawmills cut the timber into lumber, which was used for railroad ties, bridges, train stations, tunnels, and fences. Additionally, the railroad contributed to the growth of the coal industry since trains were fueled by coal. It took thousands of tons of coal to run train engines. This encouraged the development of western coal mines.

Once established, the railroads provided a *distribution network*,

Railroad officials celebrate the completion of the Northern Pacific Railroad. **Who else attended the celebration?**

What Do You Think ?

Consider the impact of railroads on the national economy. The influence the railroad had on the national economy is much like the influence the computer and the Internet have on today's economy. What jobs and businesses do you think were helped by the growth of the computer and Internet?

which transported people and products throughout the country. This new method of distribution was fast and inexpensive. Farmers and ranchers used the railroads to get their crops and livestock to markets in the Midwest and East. Coal mines relied on the railroads to get the machinery and tools they needed in the mines from manufacturers in the East. Lumber companies used the railroads to ship their product not only to other parts of the United States but also to markets in Europe and Asia.

Locomotives are pictured at a roundhouse in Lester. Roundhouses are where trains are maintained and stored. They are usually located near railroad turntables.

Henry Villard
(1835–1900)

The individual most responsible for the completion of the Northern Pacific was a man of remarkable talent and energy. Henry Villard came from Germany to the United States when he was 18 years old. He worked as a journalist, reporting the Lincoln-Douglas debates, Lincoln's election, and the Civil War.

During a visit to Europe to recover from overwork, Villard met a group of German men who were interested in investing money in American railroads. They persuaded him to handle their financial affairs in the states. Villard, in turn, persuaded them to invest $16 million in American railroads.

Villard used the money to form the Oregon Railway and Navigation Company. The company built tracks along the Columbia River to where they met the tracks of the Northern Pacific Railroad in 1883. Then Villard bought the Northern Pacific and directed the completion of the tracks through Idaho and Montana.

Land Grants, Loans, and Labor

Railroad construction was an expensive undertaking that required lots of land, money, and workers. It was clear that funding was needed from either a very large and wealthy company or the national government.

The vast unsettled nature of the land was a stark reality. There were deep gullies, raging rivers, thick forests, and steep mountains to cross. Indians would likely resent railroad tracks crossing their hunting grounds, as this could violate treaty rights. Land had to be cleared, bridges built, and tunnels blasted. Teams of wagons were needed to deliver heavy steel rails, lumber, and supplies to construction sites. Thousands of workers were hired.

Chinese and Irish Workers

In order to get enough workers to build the railroads, the government and the railroad companies encouraged immigration from Europe and Asia. In particular, immigrants from China and Ireland provided most of the labor. The Chinese and the Irish were paid much less than American-born workers for this very dangerous work. As a result, many American-born workers resented these two immigrant groups for taking the railroad jobs.

The federal government helped fund construction costs through loans and land grants. At one time, the federal government owned all of the land in the West. However, to encourage settlement, the government distributed the land to farmers, ranchers, timber companies, and railroads. Policies like the Homestead Act, the Timber Culture Act, and the Pacific Railway Act enabled distribution of the land.

Huge amounts of land were given to the railroad companies to lay track. Railroad companies set aside land for track construction and sold the remaining land to settlers. This provided more funding for construction. Additionally, the government provided loans for each mile of track laid. The harsher the condition of the land, the higher the loan amounts.

Construction of the Northern Pacific was made possible through a federal land grant subsidy of 40 million acres (an area about the size of the state of Washington). A *subsidy* is a contribution of money, or in the case of the railroads, land from the government. Without land grants, it would have been almost impossible for private companies to build transcontinental railroads.

Railroad workers for the Great Northern Railroad build a train tunnel in Seattle. **Describe the work done here to build the tunnel.**

Abusive Practices

One downside to the loan practices and land grant system was fraud. Because railroad owners worked closely with the government, this often led to corruption. *Corruption* is dishonest practices in business or politics. During the Age of Railroads, corruption included politicians taking bribes to support laws favorable to the railroads. Corrupt railroad owners often lied about their expenses in order to get larger loans. And, sometimes they offered stock in their company that was worth far less than the price paid for it.

A State of Growth

The nation's sixth transcontinental railroad was built by the Great Northern Railroad Company. The Great Northern lived up to its name by building rails that skirted the Canadian border and ran westward through the Dakotas and Montana to the Pacific Coast at its terminus in Seattle. A terminus is the last stop, or the end, of the line for a railroad.

The president of the Great Northern Railroad, James Hill, is credited with fueling the economic growth of Seattle and the Northwest. Hill built a railroading empire by using his money wisely and promoting his railroad effectively. His business was described as an empire because of its large size and economic influence.

Unlike his competition, Hill did not get financial help from the federal government. Instead, he financed his railroad by selling land to homesteaders and real estate developers.

Beating the Competition

Once the Great Northern was complete, Hill went after his biggest competitor—the Northern Pacific. A ride from St. Paul, Minnesota, to Seattle on the Great Northern was almost half the price of the same trip on the Northern Pacific. Freight charges (cost for shipping goods and other materials) were also less expensive. Such pricing policies helped fuel the growth of one of Washington's most significant industries—timber.

In addition to charging lower ticket prices and freight rates, Hill also helped spur the growth of agriculture and ranching in the Northwest. He was a student of agricultural science and used what he knew to introduce new farming methods as well as new breeds of cattle and hogs to the region. For example, farmers could board his trains at stops throughout the West to speak with experts about new methods for increasing wheat harvests. These happy and more productive farmers then took advantage of Hill's reduced rates to get their crop to market.

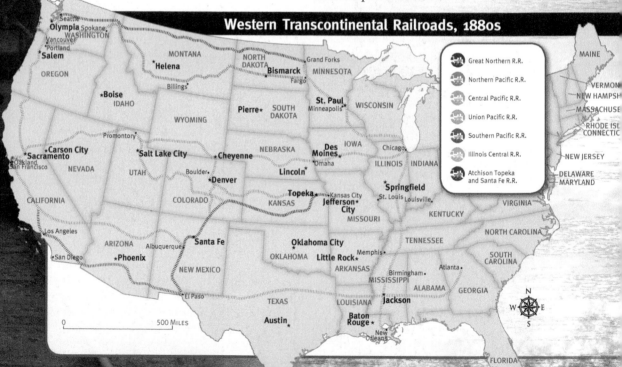

Western Transcontinental Railroads, 1880s

Great Northern R.R.

Northern Pacific R.R.

Central Pacific R.R.

Union Pacific R.R.

Southern Pacific R.R.

Illinois Central R.R.

Atchison Topeka and Santa Fe R.R.

Weyerhaeuser Company

One of James Hill's neighbors in St. Paul, Minnesota, happened to be Frederick Weyerhaeuser. At the time he moved next door to Hill, Weyerhaeuser was head of a timber company in the Midwest. His company had logged most of the forests of the Great Lakes region. Weyerhaeuser was in search of more trees to harvest.

When Hill purchased the Northern Pacific railroad, he became owner not just of rail lines and railcars but also about 44 million acres of land. This land was rich with timber. In what historians describe as one of the "largest single land transfers" in American history, these two businessmen made a deal. Hill agreed to sell his neighbor 900,000 acres for $5.4 million. This worked out to about six dollars an acre. As part of the deal, Hill agreed to charge Weyerhaeuser very low shipping rates for his timber.

Lumberjacks attach the choker (chains) to cut trees. The chokers will enable them to drag logs to the lumberyard.

Hill's methods were so successful that when the other major transcontinental lines went **bankrupt** (unable to pay debts), the Great Northern remained **solvent** (had enough money). In fact, the Great Northern used its financial weight to purchase the Northern Pacific.

A Transportation Network

The construction of the transcontinental railroad transformed the country by creating a network of transportation that moved people and products from coast to coast. The railroads made trade with foreign countries easier, too. The Northern Pacific and the Great Northern railroads helped fuel the rapid economic growth of Washington and the Northwest. And, the railroads brought thousands of immigrants from Europe and Asia to Washington.

Boxes of fruit are stacked on the railroad platform in Wenatchee, waiting to be loaded on a Great Northern boxcar. **How was the fruit transported to the railroad?**

A portrait of James J. Hill, owner of the Great Northern Railway company.

What Did You Learn? ①

1. What two railroads eventually connected to Washington?
2. How did railroad companies get land and money to build the railroads?
3. Identify three industries that either contributed to or benefited from the growth of the railroads.

KEY IDEAS

- The government and the railroads encouraged immigration from Europe and Asia.

- The largest population of immigrants in Washington came from Scandinavian countries.

- Some immigrant groups faced discrimination from "native-born" Americans.

KEY TERMS

anti-Semitic
backlash
discrimination
emigrate
fjord
incentive
menial
nativist
quota
revenue

Early Immigration

The story of Washington's growth is a story of immigrants. They came from many parts of the world, bringing their culture with them. Their many voices and ideas created a diverse society. Sometimes different groups got along. Other times, *discrimination*, or treating people unfairly because of race, age, or gender, made life miserable.

Some of the first immigrants to Washington were not British or American. They came from Hawaii, Ireland, China, and Japan.

Hawaiian Kanakas

Hawaiian men, called Kanakas, had agreed to work for the Hudson's Bay Company for a period of years. They worked as fur trappers, boatmen, cooks, and laborers. After the company moved its fur trade into Canada, many of the Kanakas returned to Hawaii, while some remained in Washington Territory. Some Kanakas married Indian women and blended into the local Indian communities.

Irish Immigrants

In the 1840s, a terrible disaster hit Ireland, where most people existed on a diet of potatoes. A fungus infected the potato crop, causing them to turn black and shrivel up. Men and women took their starving children and moved away to the "Promised Land" of America. Most Irish immigrants settled in eastern cities like Boston, New York, and Philadelphia where they usually lived in poverty.

However, California's gold rush inspired some Irish men to move west. When the gold rush failed to make them rich, many left California and headed north to Washington. They settled first in Walla Walla. Many ran for government offices. Some of the Walla Walla Irish moved farther north, where they started the first agricultural communities in the Columbia Basin. Other Irish came as laborers on the railroads. The Irish also worked as housemaids, mill hands, miners, or soldiers in the U.S. army.

Irish immigrants prepare to board a ship leaving for the United States. **What details do you notice in the image?**

Chinese workers clear snow from railroad tracks.

Chinese Laborers

In the mid-1800s, China's government seemed ready to collapse. There was war, flooding, and famine. People were desperate to find jobs to provide for their families.

Chinese men came to work in the mining camps of the Pacific Northwest. By 1870, there were twice as many Chinese miners in eastern Washington as white miners. Chinese men were also hired at low wages to build the transcontinental railroad. Both Chinese and Irish laborers were largely responsible for construction of the first transcontinental railroad.

Chinese laborers were not given full rights. They could not vote or testify in court cases involving whites. They were paid much less than white men for the same work. They did menial labor such as washing clothes and cooking. *Menial* labor is work that is considered to be shameful or humiliating. They also did the most dangerous and difficult jobs on the railroads and in the mines.

Japanese Workers

Japanese men and boys also came to find jobs. Here is one story from a boy who came to work on the railroad:

My work was to cut down trees or to dig and fill in land in the mountains. I was only a boy of 15, having just graduated from grade school. When I worked ten or twelve hours a day, the next morning I couldn't open my hands. I dipped them in hot water in order to stretch the fingers back to normal and sometimes I secretly cried.

My pay was $1.75 for ten hours. I had good reason to work my hardest, gritting my teeth, for when I left Japan, I had promised my mother, whose health was not good, "I'll surely come back to Japan in a year."

Many Asian laborers worked for timber companies in Washington.

Railroads Boost Immigration

Besides hiring Irish and Chinese laborers to build the transcontinental railroads, railroad companies sold American land to people overseas. Although their motivation was to earn *revenue*, or income, for the railroad, the effect was a flood of immigration. Many immigrants came to the Northwest, and Washington in particular. Railroad-sponsored migration was the principal cause of the state's growth after 1880.

Railroads hired land agents to sell excess land to businessmen and settlers. Northern Pacific land agents spread out across the United States, the British Isles, and northern Europe. They distributed advertisements for cheap land and job opportunities at weekly farmers' markets. Brochures were published in English, French, Swedish, Norwegian, and other languages.

Washington's Melting Pot

By providing *incentive* (motivation to do something) and a fast way to travel to the Northwest, the railroads were largely responsible for the ethnic mix of the state. In the late 1800s and early 1900s, mostly Canadian, English, German, and Scandinavian immigrants came. People also came from many other countries.

By 1910, 46 percent of Washington's population was either born in another country or their parents were. These new immigrants joined the Chinese and Irish already here.

Scandinavian Immigrants

Scandinavians were attracted to Puget Sound because its wet climate, high mountains, and many ocean inlets reminded them of home. Norwegians started a settlement at Poulsbo on the Olympic Peninsula because it looked like their native fjord in Norway. A *fjord* is a long, narrow body of water between steep cliffs. Poulsbo is located just inland of the narrow Liberty Bay (also called Dogfish Bay at one time) in the Puget Sound region.

Other Scandinavian immigrants also contributed to the Washington economy by working in key industries. Swedes worked for logging companies, doing work that was familiar to them in their homeland. For example, Carl Hanson and his sons founded the White River Lumber and Shingle Company in Enumclaw. Their company became known for its high-quality finished lumber, which was transported by railroad to every state. Within a decade of opening, the company employed 500 people, eventually becoming one of the largest employers in the region. White River eventually merged with the Weyerhaeuser Company, which was the largest employer in the region.

Like Norwegians and Swedes, the Finns and Danes were attracted to industries familiar to them in Finland and Denmark. Finns were drawn to fishing, while Danes were drawn to dairy farming.

Scandinavian families working together on a farm in the 1860s. **What kind of farm do you think it was?**

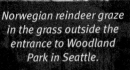
Norwegian reindeer graze in the grass outside the entrance to Woodland Park in Seattle.

POULSBO:
Washington's "Little Norway"

By the 1880s, the number of Norwegians coming to Washington was noticeable. By the early 1900s, more than 7,000 Norwegians lived and worked in the state. They significantly outnumbered other Scandinavian groups. While many Norwegians settled in Seattle, it was the little fishing town on Liberty Bay across the sound that became known as "Little Norway."

At least until after World War II, the majority (up to 90 percent) of Poulsbo residents were Norwegian. They came from nearly every region of Norway except the southern areas near Oslo. Not surprising, Poulsbo residents spoke Norwegian as much, if not more, than English.

Before the Norwegians arrived, Poulsbo was the site of a logging camp and a dogfish oil operation. Dogfish oil was used as a lubricant, or grease, that helps make the movement of heavy objects easier. The first Norwegian to settle in Poulsbo was Ole Stubb, whose Norwegian name was Ole Anderson Stubbhaug. He and his family arrived in 1875 and were joined by fellow countrymen in the 1880s. These first Norwegians worked as farmers and loggers, and some worked for the railroads. But it was fishing that eventually became the town's major industry.

By the turn of the century, there was a large influx of Norwegians from Norland, an area of Norway near the Arctic Circle. Many had made a living in Norway as fishermen and reindeer herders (a person who raises reindeer). In fact, some of them came to America to deliver reindeer to Alaska and decided to settle in Poulsbo after delivering the animals.

Some of these immigrants became part of a group of men who created the Pacific Coast Codfish Company. The company's processing plant was located in Poulsbo. Company fishermen caught cod off the coast of Alaska. They usually sailed north to the cod banks in April and then returned to Poulsbo in September. Their catch typically netted between 100,000 and 600,000 cod. Workers salted and canned the fish at the Poulsbo plant, and sold the finished product under the brand name "Icicle."

Today, residents of Poulsbo still make a living from fishing, farming, and logging, as well as running small businesses.

Sami herdsmen from Norway wait for a ship to take them and their reindeer to Alaska.

Norwegian immigrants, Ole and Elmer Moen, pose for a photo on their front porch. Little sister, Agnes, is peeking through the window.

• Little Norway

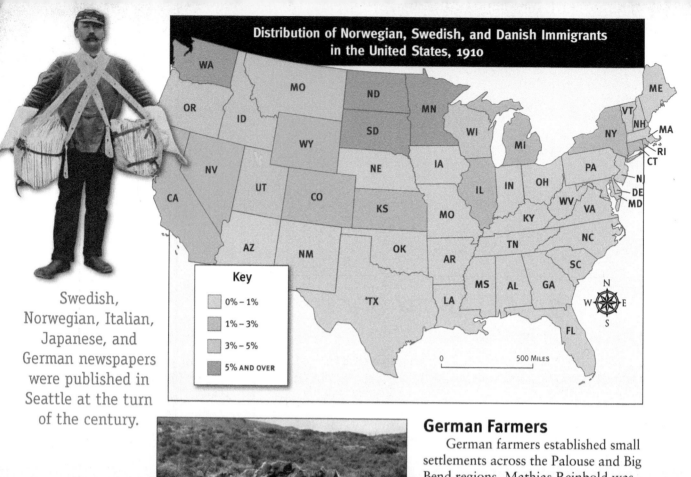

Distribution of Norwegian, Swedish, and Danish Immigrants in the United States, 1910

Key
- 0% – 1%
- 1% – 3%
- 3% – 5%
- 5% AND OVER

0   500 MILES

Swedish, Norwegian, Italian, Japanese, and German newspapers were published in Seattle at the turn of the century.

This pile of rocks is actually an oven built by Italian railroad workers.

German families built round barns. This barn actually has twelve sides.

German Farmers

German farmers established small settlements across the Palouse and Big Bend regions. Mathias Reinbold was so impressed by the railroad's message in Germany that he persuaded nine of his 14 children to emigrate. *Emigrate* means to leave one's own country and settle in another. Today their descendants live in Lincoln County.

Italians Helped Build Cities

Just as the railroad brought Irish and Chinese immigrants, it also brought Italians to Washington as part of construction crews. Others came as skilled stonemasons to help rebuild Spokane, Ellensburg, and Seattle after the terrible fires of 1889. Italian farmers located in the Walla Walla Valley, where they became famous in later years for their sweet onions.

Linking the Past to the Present

Today, Seattle's international district remains a thriving reminder of the city's diversity. It is also a stronghold of Asian and Pacific Island cultures.

The fire that engulfed businesses and homes in Seattle started by accident. **What limitations do these firefighters have in putting out the flames?**

Fire!

In 1889, the same year Washington became a state, people living in Seattle, Ellensburg, and Spokane had to deal with the devastation of huge fires.

In Seattle, a craftsman was heating glue in his shop when the pan boiled over. When the glue hit the hot stove, it caught fire. Soon entire blocks of wooden buildings were burning. Flames were jumping from roof to roof and even across dirt streets. By evening, the entire business district was in ruins. Soon people were doing business from tents.

Italian, Chinese, and other workers helped rebuild the cities—this time with fireproof brick and cement.

The fire destroyed the Occidental Hotel shown here at the corner of James Street and Yesler Way.

Anger Over Immigration

Along with the flood of immigration to Washington and other parts of the United States came reaction from nativists. *Nativists* were white, Protestant Americans born in the United States who did not like seeing so many immigrants come to the country. In particular, nativists disliked those who looked, spoke, and worshipped differently from them. They were often anti-Catholic, *anti-Semitic*, meaning they disliked Jewish people, and anti-Asian. Many nativists held racist views.

Nativists objected to immigration for a number of reasons. One reason was job competition. Nativists feared that they would lose their job to an immigrant willing to work for less money. Also, some feared that foreigners weakened American culture and values. Their fears were increased by the belief that foreigners would never adopt American culture and customs.

GREAT

ANTI-CHINESE

Mass Meeting!

WEDNESDAY EVENING, JUNE 3rd, 1885,

8 O'CLOCK P. M.

AT ALPHA OPERA HOUSE.

ABLE SPEAKERS

Will address the citizens of Tacoma on the Chinese question. Also the Committee on the habits and modes of living of the Chinese will make a full report of their labor, and submit a plan of organization for the action of the citizens.

The time has come for action. Delay is weakness, unpardonable sin against ours lives, our families, society and mankind. Action, decided action, redemption, salvation. Therefore come all, come everyone, and protest against this life and soul-destroying curse. This will be the people's meeting, who should not be fiddling whilst Rome is burning.

Nativists attack a group of Chinese men during a riot in Seattle. **Is anyone helping the Chinese?**

The Anti-Chinese Committee in Tacoma used this poster to call a meeting to address the "Chinese question." **What else does the committee plan to address?**

The Gentlemen's Agreement

The Chinese were not the only Asian group subject to anti-immigrant feelings. Many Americans also felt threatened by Japanese immigration. Concern over the growing population of Japanese in California resulted in the Gentlemen's Agreement between the United States and Japan. In the agreement, the United States promised to combat anti-Japanese discrimination if the Japanese government restricted the number of Japanese farm workers coming to America.

Chinese Immigrants Targeted

One of the first groups to experience the nativist **backlash** (meaning a reaction, usually negative) was the Chinese. Nativists were alarmed that too many Chinese were coming into the country and taking jobs. As a result, Congress passed the Chinese Exclusion Act. It stopped Chinese laborers from entering the country.

A few years later, when many white workers were jobless, they turned their anger against Chinese residents. Violent riots erupted in Issaquah, Tacoma, and Seattle. More than 1,000 Chinese people were expelled from Washington. Their homes and businesses were burned. White residents attacked Chinese men in Walla Walla and Pasco.

"There is a wash house occupying a prominent position among business houses and hotels. This is not a credit to our town. If Chinese must come, let no man encourage them to locate where their presence will make white residents uncomfortable."

—Spokane Falls Review

Immigration Quotas

The anti-immigrant movement came to a head in the early 20th century. At that time, Congress passed laws that sought to cut immigration through strict quotas. A *quota* is a part or percentage of a whole. The quotas restricted immigration based on an immigrant's country of birth. In other words, the laws placed a limit on the number of people who could come to the United States from any one country. The laws placed higher restrictions on immigrants from eastern and southern Europe than those from northern and western Europe. Northern and western Europeans were not as threatening to white Americans since they had similar physical features and were mostly Protestant. In contrast, eastern and southern Europeans had darker skin and practiced Catholicism or Judaism.

The Pledge of Allegiance was first written in response to the flood of immigration. It was hoped that the pledge would strengthen American values.

The caption on this cartoon from the 1880s reads: "The Anti-Chinese Wall." The wall is being built by other immigrants. On each brick is a reason why the Chinese were not welcome in this country. **How does the cartoonist seem to view other immigrants? What words can you make out on the bricks?**

Linking the Past to the Present

Today, immigrants represent between 8 and 9 percent of the total population of the United States. Although the number of immigrants coming to the country is less than it was in the 19th century, nativist fears still exist. Asians and Latinos (people from Central and South America) are often the focus of criticism. Nativists argue that immigrants take jobs from "real" Americans and they are a drain on our system of health care and public education. Do you think the United States should tighten restrictions on immigration? Why or why not?

Immigration to the United States, 1860–1900

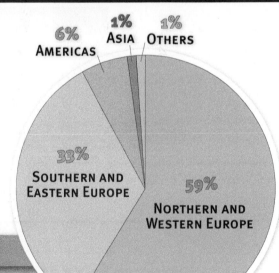

6% AMERICAS
1% ASIA
1% OTHERS
33% SOUTHERN AND EASTERN EUROPE
59% NORTHERN AND WESTERN EUROPE

What Did You Learn? ②

1. What role did the railroads play in bringing immigrants to the United States and to Washington?

2. Identify five countries from which immigrants came and settled in Washington.

3. Why did nativists dislike immigrants?

KEY IDEAS

- Washington cities saw rapid population and economic growth in the late 19th and early 20th centuries.
- Cities with train stations and seaports grew the fastest.
- Construction of the railroad and the Klondike gold rush helped make Seattle the largest city in the state.

KEY TERMS

booster
exploit
rival
rural
urban
urbanization

The famous writer Rudyard Kipling visited Tacoma in 1889 and noted that on the city's muddy streets "men were babbling about money, town lots and again money."

Urbanization

The years from 1880 to 1910 were a time of spectacular population growth in the Pacific Northwest. Some places that were inhabited by Indians and an occasional trapper were transformed within a generation. They changed from small *rural* (having characteristics of the countryside) communities into *urban* areas, or bustling cities, with brick buildings, paved streets, trolley cars, and electric lights! In all of American history, there had been nothing quite like this. Nowhere was urbanization as rapid as it was in the state of Washington. *Urbanization* refers to the transformation of small communities into cities.

Most of the urban population was found in the region's four largest communities—Portland, Seattle, Tacoma, and Spokane. By 1910, these four cities contained almost one-third of the entire population of Washington, Oregon, and Idaho.

Population Growth
Washington State 1880–1910

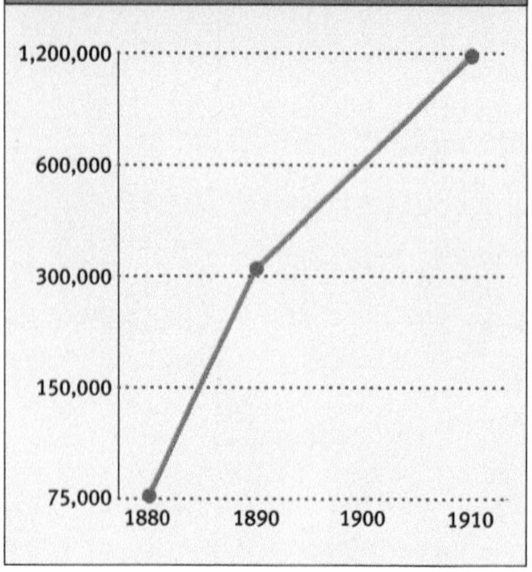

1,200,000	
600,000	
300,000	
150,000	
75,000	
1880 1890 1900 1910	

This is a view of the Tacoma waterfront in 1901. **What features shown here would make Tacoma a good candidate for growth?**

Tacoma and the Northern Pacific

Leaders of the Northern Pacific Railroad planned to run tracks from St. Paul, Minnesota, all the way to the harbors of Puget Sound. Company officers planned the route, knowing that wherever the tracks ended there would be tremendous growth and new business for cities along the route.

Cities were often built up around train stations, especially cities that also had a seaport. Goods and raw materials such as coal, iron ore, lumber, and grain could be shipped from mines, mills, and factories across the country by rail, and then shipped to other countries and cities on the East Coast by sea. People who rode the trains started businesses near train terminals.

When Tacoma was chosen for a railroad terminal, the railroad company bought land cheaply, had it surveyed, and drew land plots. Tacoma's growth rate in the 1880s boomed.

The world's largest sawmill was built there in 1886. Then growth slowed down. An economic slump in the 1890s was especially hard on Tacoma, and opened the way for its rival, Seattle, to become the largest city in the state. A *rival* is a competitor or opponent. At this time, Seattle and Tacoma were intense rivals.

Population Growth		
Washington's Cities 1880–1890		
City	1880	1890
Tacoma	1,098	36,006
Seattle	3,553	42,837
Spokane	350	20,000

Powerful water cannons shot out streams of water to slice away the steep hills of Seattle. Leveling out many hills was a huge engineering project. **What other work would need to be done to finish the job?**

Seattle

Seattle was one of a number of port cities on Puget Sound under consideration for a railroad terminal. However, the Cascades cut it off from the interior of the region. City residents fought hard to overcome such obstacles and bring the railroad to Seattle.

At the time, Seattle's population was less than 1,200 people and it was competing against larger, more established cities. Nevertheless, officials were confident their city would win. Toward that end, Seattle offered the Northern Pacific generous loan and land grants, including a 30-foot-wide strip along the waterfront on which to build a train station. To the dismay of city officials, the Northern Pacific chose to build the terminus in Tacoma.

Eventually, Seattle *boosters* (energetic or enthusiastic supporters) were able to convince James Hill to build a train station in Seattle. At first, he was reluctant, saying that "it was more important to Seattle to have goods delivered to it cheaply, than to have a fancy depot." But, after he bought the bankrupt Northern Pacific (which by then had built a small station on Railroad Avenue), he agreed to build a station.

The new King Street Station—called Union Depot at the time—opened in 1906. Five years later, the Union Pacific Railroad built its own station—Union Station. The two stations are about a block apart.

Although the two stations made Seattle residents proud, the city's crowning achievement became its successful promotion as the only gateway to the gold of the Klondike. The Klondike is an area in Canada's Yukon Territory, just east of Alaska, where gold was discovered in 1897.

In addition to building the two train stations, several ambitious engineering projects further contributed to the development of Seattle. An electric power system was created, a sewer system was constructed, and a water system suitable for a much larger city was developed. City leaders spent millions of dollars lowering Seattle's steep hills and leveling out land in the downtown area to facilitate growth and better transportation. Today you can take an "underground tour" in the Pioneer Square area to see a bit of the old Seattle.

Urban rivalries pitted city against city because the stakes were high. Growth meant more railroad and steamship connections, higher land values, and more business. All of these meant more money.

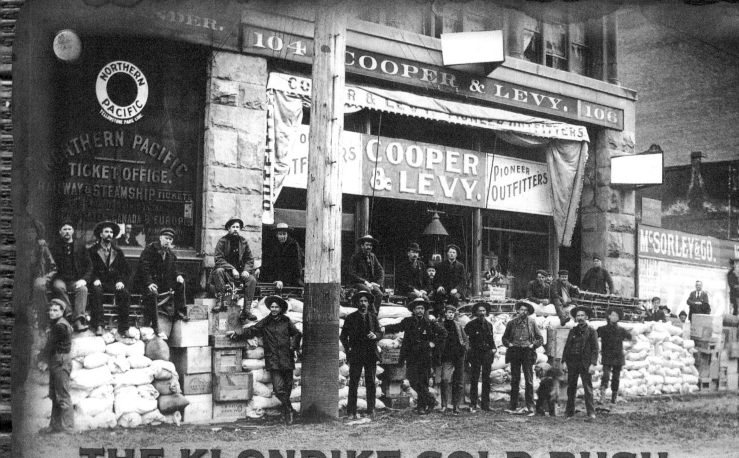

THE KLONDIKE GOLD RUSH

Expecting large crowds, outfitters stacked supplies on the sidewalks in front of stores. **What businesses are pictured here?**

The discovery of gold in the Klondike region of Canada's Yukon Territory was an important event in Seattle's history. The city *exploited* (took advantage of) the Klondike rush to gain the advantage over all of its rival cities.

No American port was closer to Alaska and the main trails that led from there to the Klondike. When gold was discovered, about 1,500 people fled north on the first ship to Alaska, with nine other ships crowded in the harbor waiting to follow them. Even the mayor of Seattle quit his job and went to the gold fields.

Stores ordered in so many provisions that the merchandise was stacked ten feet high in downtown Seattle. Each miner had to take about a ton of supplies with him, including tents, cooking pots, tools, winter clothes, and over 1,000 pounds of food. All the provisions were called an "outfit." Outfits were sold in Seattle. So were hotel rooms, restaurant meals, and many forms of entertainment. Shipyards bustled with construction. All this meant a booming business for Seattle.

Erastus Brainerd of the city's Chamber of Commerce was directed to promote Seattle as the gateway to the Klondike. And he did! Brainerd let loose on the United States and foreign countries a flood of advertisements and articles in magazines and newspapers. He wrote letters to government leaders, all promoting Seattle as a place for miners to buy their provisions and as the nearest seaport where miners could board a ship for Alaska and Canada.

The frenzied result was a stampede. In fact, the crazed gold seekers were actually called stampeders. Stampeders took gunnysacks (a woven bag) to carry back the gold nuggets they assumed were just lying all around. The truth was that less than half of the 100,000 people who left for the Klondike actually got there. The extreme cold and isolation of the Klondike was scary.

Waterways froze solid. Miners faced blizzards, hikes across glaciers, and falls into crevasses or off icy cliffs.

In the warmer months, deep mud holes, floods, and mosquitoes made life miserable for man and beast. When men reached the tops of icy peaks with part of their provisions, they had to go down again to bring up another load. They repeated this process as much as 30 times.

Finally, the town of Dawson City welcomed them at the edge of the gold fields. Anxious to begin finding gold, miners would often find that the best claims were already staked. They sold their provisions to other miners for a fraction of what they had paid and made the long journey home.

A newspaper correspondent described the arrival of the stampeders in Dawson:

> It is a motley throng—every degree of person gathered from every corner of the earth and from every state of the Union— weather-beaten, sunburned, . . . Australians with upturned sleeves and a swagger, young Englishmen in golf stockings and tweeds; would-be miners in mackinaws [raincoats] and rubber boots or heavy highlaced shoes; Japanese, Negroes—and women, too, everywhere.

Some successful stampeders who returned to Seattle invested in local businesses. John Nordstrom invested $13,000 of his gold into a shoe store. A man he had met in the Klondike owned the store. That modest start was the beginning of the Nordstrom department store chain. Edward Nordoff, a Seattle merchant who profited from the Klondike rush, turned his small store into the Bon Marché stores.

The gold rush was not good for many miners, but it was very good for Seattle businessmen. New businesses meant more growth. By 1910, Seattle was the largest city of the Pacific Northwest.

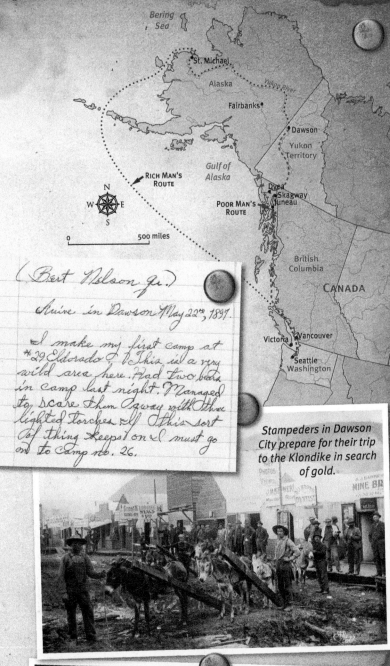

(Bert Nelson jr.)

Arrive in Dawson May 22nd 1897.

I make my first camp at #29 Eldorado. This is a very wild area here. Had two bears in camp last night. Managed to scare them away with the lighted torches. If this sort of thing keeps on I must go on to camp no. 26.

Stampeders in Dawson City prepare for their trip to the Klondike in search of gold.

John Nordstrom posed for a photo in front of his new shoe store in Seattle.

Spokane

Spokane, first called Spokane Falls, was built next to the waterfalls of the Spokane River, so the city's first advantage was water power. The water power was used to run a sawmill and a flour mill to grind grain into flour. Then the water power produced Spokane's first electricity.

After both the Northern Pacific and Great Northern railroad lines came through, the city's growth seemed assured. Its location made it a transportation hub. Soon branch rail lines linked Spokane to mining, timber, and agricultural areas.

Spokane reaped the benefit when silver was discovered in Idaho's Coeur d'Alene region in the 1880s. People brought their new wealth from the mines and settled in Spokane. Silver from mines in Idaho and British Columbia provided the money to build many of the mansions in Spokane.

Spokane grew rapidly into one of Washington's largest cities thanks to the railroad. **What modern conveniences does this photo show?**

Newspapers reported the rapid growth of Spokane and its impact on businesses and residents:

I am today selling four times the quantity of merchandise [to miners] of which I disposed one year ago. I can scarcely order goods rapidly enough to meet the daily requirements.
—Spokane Review, *1890*

My next stop was Spokane Falls, where I was greatly surprised to find the improvements that have been made there within two years. Electric lights, telephones, and other metropolitan conveniences are available. Every face expresses vitality, every voice is cheerful, and everyone has a little money.
—The Morning Review, *1886*

Spokane Falls is well supplied with churches. It is a sure sign of peace and prosperity. . . . People in the East always locate in a place where there are good influences, whether they follow them or not.
—R.P. Elliot,
Spokane Falls Review, *1890*

The Next Step

Like the rest of the country, Washington's population increased as a result of this period of urbanization that was fueled by the railroads and immigration. Many of the new immigrants went on to play a large role in organizing labor unions and encouraging economic and political reforms—a topic you will learn about in the next chapter.

What Did You Learn? ③

1. When did Washington cities experience their greatest growth?
2. What factors contributed to the growth of cities?
3. What impact did the Klondike gold rush have on Seattle's population and economy?

Go to the Source

Analyzing a Cartoon

This cartoon, drawn by artist Joseph Keppler, was published in *Puck Magazine* in 1893. The caption of the cartoon is: "Looking Backward." *Puck Magazine* started as a German language weekly in 1877. An English version of the magazine was published a year later. By the 1880s, more than 80,000 copies of the magazine were sold per week.

"Looking Backward"

Go to the Source

Observe	Evaluate	Conclude
• Describe the people pictured in the cartoon. • Describe the action taking place in the cartoon.	• About what issue do you think the cartoonist was commenting?	• What do you think is the cartoonist's message about the issue portrayed in the cartoon? • What is your opinion of the cartoonist's message?

Developing a Research Question

Construction of the transcontinental railroad was very important to the economic growth of Washington and the entire nation. Railroad construction required a lot of resources, such as lumber, iron, coal, and labor. When construction was completed, many of the industries that helped to build the railroad could now transport their goods to market much faster and for less money. The railroads helped move people and products all over the country.

Think about some part of the Age of Railroads that interests you. Maybe you would like to learn more about a particular company, person, immigrant group, or industry that was affected by construction of the transcontinental railroads.

In order to develop a good research question, consider the following steps:

1. Pick a topic that interests you and write it at the top of a piece of paper.

2. Create two columns under the topic and label them "What I already know" and "What I want to learn"?

3. Jot down some notes and ideas in each column.

4. Using your notes, brainstorm a list of questions you would like answered about the topic.

5. Evaluate your list and eliminate questions that are either too broad or too narrow.

   • Too broad: A question that is too broad is one that would be impossible to answer in a one-page paper. For example: What was the impact of the railroad on economic growth in the United States? That is just too big a question. It would take a lot more than one or two pages to answer!

   • Too narrow: A question that is too narrow is one that could be answered in just a few words. For example: When was the Great Northern Railroad completed? That can be answered with the year that the railroad was completed, 1893.

   • Just right: How did construction of the Great Northern Railroad contribute to population growth in Seattle? This question is specific but can be answered with some detail in a page or two.

6. Circle the best question from your list.

7. Develop a list of at least three sources to answer your question.

Chapter 5 Review

Chapter Review Questions

1. Describe the role of land grants and loans in building the transcontinental railroad.
2. List three reasons why the Great Northern Railroad was more successful than the Northern Pacific.
3. Make a chart identifying the immigrant groups that came to Washington in the 1800s along with where they settled, what they did for a living, and how other Americans treated them.
4. Compare and contrast the growth of Washington's three biggest cities.
5. Write a letter home from the point of view of a stampeder describing your experience during the time of the Klondike gold rush.

Becoming a Better Reader

Find the Main Idea

When reading nonfiction information, good readers always keep in mind the main idea of what they are reading. Thinking about the main idea helps good readers organize the new information they gather as they read. Main ideas can be found in chapter and lesson titles and in main and subheads. What is the main idea of this chapter? Write a paragraph stating the main idea and three supporting ideas using the titles of the chapter and lessons to help you.

You Are the Geographer

Use the map of the transcontinental railroads on page 112 to answer the following questions.

1. Which railroad line(s) could you take if you wanted to travel from Chicago to Seattle?
2. Which railroad line(s) could you take if you wanted to travel from Seattle to New Orleans?
3. Calculate the distance to travel from Seattle to Grand Forks on the Great Northern Railroad.
4. Which states appear to lack rail lines?

An Era of Reform

Timeline of Events

1891
A coal mine in Franklin hires black strikebreakers.

1896
John Rogers is elected governor.

1900
Seattle has at least 40 labor unions.

1890

1900

1893
Seattle's treasurer steals $125,000 in city funds.

1905
Industrial Workers of the World is founded.

◄———— **1865–1900** ————
Gilded Age

The late 1800s and early 1900s were a time of great change for Washington and the nation. Increased wealth along with increased corruption was a sign of the times. Reformers began demanding changes to working conditions, business and government practices, and social conditions.

World War I marked a turning point for our state's economy and ushered in a period of prosperity for most people.

A procedure of cars carries workers in Seattle's 1905 Labor Day parade. **Workers from what unions are shown here?**

1909
IWW organizes a free speech campaign in Spokane.

1914
Prohibition is adopted in Washington.

1910

1910
Washington approves women's suffrage.

1914–1918
World War I

1916
• Everett Massacre
• Boeing Company is founded

1917
The United States enters the war.

1920

1919
• Seattle General Strike
• Centralia Massacre
• 18th Amendment (Prohibition) is ratified

1920
The 19th Amendment (Women's Suffrage) is ratified.

1924
The KKK holds rally in Seattle.

1930

1928
Herbert Hoover is elected president.

U.S. MARINES
SERVICE ON LAND AND SEA

131

KEY IDEAS

- Many workers had jobs with low wages and dangerous working conditions.

- Labor unions worked to improve conditions, but they were not always successful.

- Violent strikes and fear of extreme ideas made many Americans distrustful of labor unions.

KEY TERMS

blacklist
capitalism
capitalist
dignity
harass
hostility
labor union
radical
reformer
sabotage
strike
vigilante

Working Conditions

As you read in the last chapter, many immigrants came to Washington to work for the railroads as well as the lumber, fishing, mining, and other industries. As with workers throughout the country, many of Washington's workers were subject to low wages, long hours, and dangerous working conditions. Wages were as low as $1 a day in some industries, and workers were expected to work at least 12 hours a day, six days a week.

Many jobs were very dangerous. For example, miners and railroad construction crews used dynamite to clear mines and blast tunnels. If the dynamite blew up at the wrong time, workers nearby could be seriously injured or killed. In sawmills, gigantic saws cut through logs. Men had to stand close to the saws to feed the logs through. Sometimes this resulted in a worker losing fingers, a hand, or even an arm. If a worker was injured, he often lost his job. There were no laws to protect workers, and businesses did not have to help workers who were hurt on the job.

Because most work in Washington was in mines, logging camps, lumber mills, farms, and orchards, the workers were typically young, single men. However, women and children also worked. Poor families could not survive if both parents and the children didn't work. Because women and children were considered weaker than men, they were paid less. Women and children worked in jobs that were just as dangerous as those done by men.

Coal miners are lowered underground at the Franklin Mine. **How are they being lowered into the shaft?**

A procession of women from the Laundry Workers Union march in Seattle's 1917 Labor Day parade. **According to their banner, what common interest do these women share?**

As a result, many workers felt helpless. There was a constant fear of job loss. Workers were easy to replace. Immigrants, women, children, and African Americans could easily replace a white male worker. This caused division among workers. If workers could unify, they might be able to increase wages, reduce hours, and improve job safety. However, discrimination against immigrants and blacks often made unity difficult.

Labor Unions

One way for workers to unify was through the creation of a labor union. A *labor union* is an organization of workers whose goal is to improve working conditions. The idea behind organizing is that a group of workers has more power than one worker. There is "strength in numbers," as the saying goes. In the 1800s, workers formed labor unions so they could demand better pay, shorter hours, and safer working conditions.

Different unions allowed different people to join. Some unions allowed only men to join. Others allowed people of a certain race or immigrant group. Still others limited their membership to workers with certain skills.

Washington Labor Unions

By the turn of the century, there were at least 40 labor unions in the Seattle area. Many of the unions attended the first annual ball hosted by the Barber's Union in 1901. Here is a list of some of the unions who attended.

- Bricklayers
- Butchers
- Cigar Makers
- Electrical Workers
- Newsboys
- Stone Cutters
- Waitresses

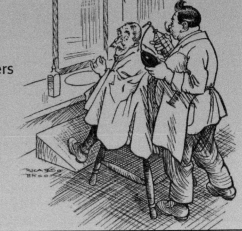

What Do You Think ?

Why do you think some unions only allowed certain workers to join? What advantages do you think these unions had over those that accepted any worker?

Striking for Better Conditions

In an effort to increase pay and improve working conditions, workers sometimes went on strike. In a **strike**, workers refuse to work until the company grants their demands. However, rather than giving into the demands of workers, company officials often fired the striking workers. The company replaced the striking workers with "strikebreakers." Oftentimes, the strikebreakers were new immigrants or African Americans. The fired workers called these strikebreakers "scabs."

Such action on the part of company officials did little to help workers unify. In fact, the anger that resulted contributed to discrimination and violence toward immigrants and blacks. For example, owners of the coal mines in Franklin offered a free train ride and good pay to black coal miners from other states who were willing to come and work in Franklin's mines. The black miners did not know that they were being used to replace striking workers until they arrived in Franklin. **Hostility**,

or a feeling of anger and resentment, between the two groups lasted for years. When miners first organized a labor union, they denied membership to black miners.

In addition to firing striking workers and hiring "scabs," company management used other methods to prevent workers from unifying. Sometimes company officials **blacklisted** labor leaders. This meant they considered the labor leader a troublemaker who should not be hired. The blacklist was passed around to other companies, making it difficult, if not impossible, for a blacklisted worker to get a job.

To make matters worse, the government often sided with companies during labor strikes. At times, state and federal troops were sent to the site of strikes to prevent violence. But the presence of troops often contributed to bloodshed. One infamous example of this occurred in Homestead, Pennsylvania, during a strike of steel workers in the 1890s.

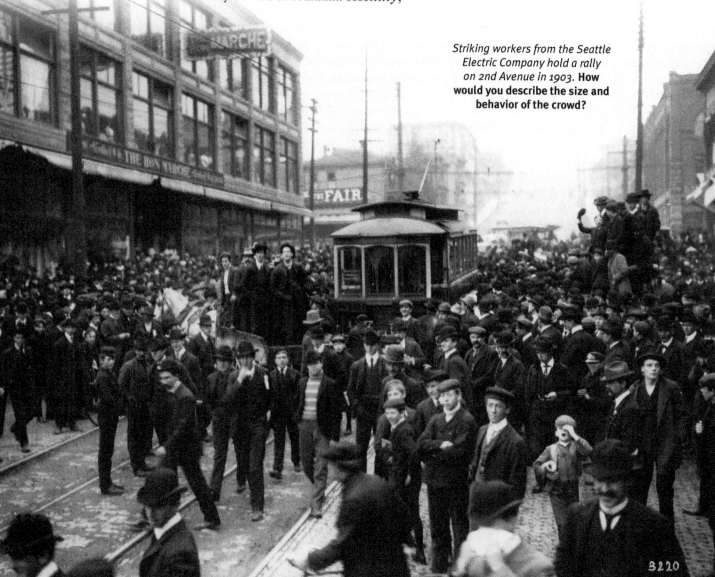

Striking workers from the Seattle Electric Company hold a rally on 2nd Avenue in 1903. **How would you describe the size and behavior of the crowd?**

IWW members are gathered for a picnic in 1919. **What can you read in the banner? What is IWW's message?**

Fear of Unions

Many Americans did not like labor unions. They feared that unions were *radical*, or extreme. Their fear was based on concern that radical labor unions threatened to overthrow capitalism—the economic system of the United States. *Capitalism* is private ownership of land, property, and business. Instead of the government owning and operating businesses, individuals have the freedom to own and run them. The fear was that poor workers would unite to overthrow rich *capitalists*, or business owners, in a class war. A class war is a war between the rich and the poor.

Industrial Workers of the World

One of the most well known labor unions was the Industrial Workers of the World (IWW). From its creation in the early 1900s, the IWW championed the concept of "One Big Union" and the overthrow of capitalism. Unlike other unions, the IWW did not discriminate against immigrants, blacks, or women. The union welcomed all workers. Also, it gave dignity to unskilled workers who were barred from other unions. *Dignity* is self-respect or pride in oneself.

Called "Wobblies," members of the IWW wanted radical change. They agreed to strike if necessary. Workers fought for the right to speak in public to get safer working conditions and higher wages. Wobblies who spoke on street corners and in parks were sometimes arrested. While some people were sympathetic to the Wobblies, others were fearful. After all, the IWW supported *sabotage*, or the deliberate destruction, of company property.

What Do You Think?

A flyer written by the IWW's Seattle branch stated:

> There will be insecurity and hunger among those who toil [work] for as long as there is an employing class which benefits from low wages and evil working conditions. The IWW holds that there can be no solution . . . until the . . . system itself is abolished.

What do you think made this message scary to Americans?

Washington PORTRAIT

Elizabeth Gurley Flynn
(1890–1964)

One of the most popular IWW free-speech fighters was Elizabeth Gurley Flynn. As an 18-year-old girl, she led a free speech rally in Spokane. Speaking on Wobbly philosophy on the city's street corners, she and several hundred IWW members were arrested for disturbing the peace.

Flynn spent one night in jail, but it was long enough for her to see criminal activity. The city's chief of police knew what was going on and did nothing to stop it. Flynn's account, printed in the next edition of *The Industrial Worker*, provoked outrage across the country.

Flynn was the inspiration for the popular IWW ballad "The Rebel Girl."

The Everett Massacre

While fears about IWW ideas were reasonable, the record shows that Wobblies suffered more violence then they started themselves. A tragic example is the Everett Massacre. In Everett, Wobblies gathered to support striking shingle mill workers. They gave speeches criticizing mill owners and capitalism. Many were arrested and then repeatedly beaten by police and vigilantes. *Vigilantes* are people who take it upon themselves to punish criminals.

In support of their union brothers, a boatload of nearly 300 Wobblies landed at Everett. As they sang union songs and tried to get off the ship, they were met with gunfire. Five mill workers and two vigilantes were killed.

More than 70 Wobblies were charged with murder. After a trial, the defense showed that no one could tell who fired the first shot, and no guns were found on the ship. The Wobblies were freed.

Read this IWW memorial poster remembering the Everett Massacre. **Why should the Wobblies who died be remembered?**

The Seattle General Strike

Probably the most well-known labor strike in Washington occurred in Seattle just after World War I. (You will read more about World War I in lesson 3.) At the end of the war, Seattle shipyard workers struck for wage increases that had been suspended during the war. Other unions voted to go on strike to show their support. Since members from many different unions and industries were on strike, it was called a general strike. The city almost shut down. People could not get a ride on a streetcar or a meal in a restaurant.

The strikers wanted to prove to people that workers, not just business owners, could run things. Therefore, strikers made sure that food was brought into the city and that hospitals kept running. The Seattle General Strike was headline news across the country.

People were afraid that the strike was the beginning of a revolution. It certainly looked like a revolution was expected. Soldiers were posted outside of the city and the mayor recruited college students to serve as "special deputies." The students carried clubs. Some even carried guns. Machine guns were placed around the city. Fortunately, the strike was peaceful. Within five days the strike was over.

Rather than strengthening the unions, the strike actually weakened them. Most of the striking workers only wanted better wages, not revolution. The public saw it differently. They saw unions as unpatriotic and disloyal to the nation. As a result, the public became more suspicious of labor unions.

Striking workers gather at the corner of 9th Avenue and Pike Street in Seattle. **How would you describe the crowd? Is there cause for alarm?**

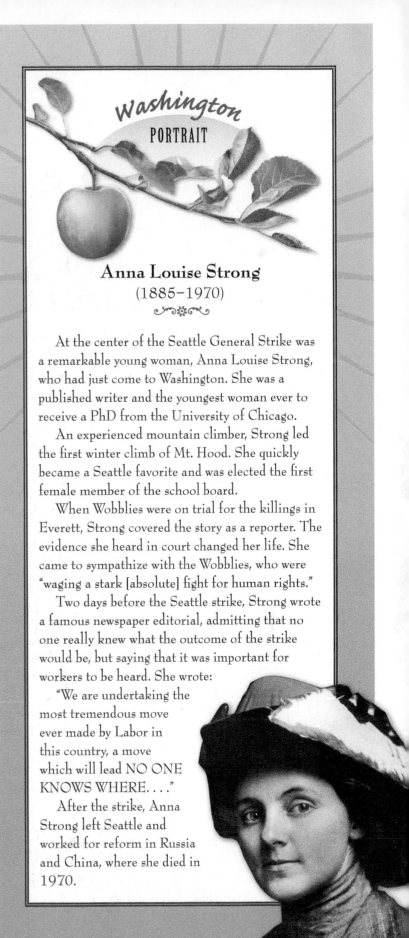

Washington PORTRAIT

Anna Louise Strong
(1885–1970)

At the center of the Seattle General Strike was a remarkable young woman, Anna Louise Strong, who had just come to Washington. She was a published writer and the youngest woman ever to receive a PhD from the University of Chicago.

An experienced mountain climber, Strong led the first winter climb of Mt. Hood. She quickly became a Seattle favorite and was elected the first female member of the school board.

When Wobblies were on trial for the killings in Everett, Strong covered the story as a reporter. The evidence she heard in court changed her life. She came to sympathize with the Wobblies, who were "waging a stark [absolute] fight for human rights."

Two days before the Seattle strike, Strong wrote a famous newspaper editorial, admitting that no one really knew what the outcome of the strike would be, but saying that it was important for workers to be heard. She wrote:

"We are undertaking the most tremendous move ever made by Labor in this country, a move which will lead NO ONE KNOWS WHERE. . . ."

After the strike, Anna Strong left Seattle and worked for reform in Russia and China, where she died in 1970.

Seven Centralia defendants who were tried for murdering Legionnaires.

The Centralia Massacre

Another event that hurt union efforts occurred in Centralia, a lumber mill town south of Olympia. Mill owners were in a dispute with the IWW. The mill owners had recruited World War I veterans called Legionnaires to harass local Wobblies. To *harass* someone is to bother or attack them.

The Legionnaires were tricked into thinking the Wobblies were a real threat to America. After marching in a parade celebrating the end of the war, the Legionnaires went on to attack the IWW meeting hall. The Wobblies were warned about the attack and so armed themselves. The Legionnaires were met with gunfire, and three were killed.

Wesley Everest, a Wobbly, shot into the crowd, killed a man, and ran. He was caught and taken to jail. Other Wobblies were also arrested.

•Centralia

IWW member Wesley Everest was pictured on a postcard in remembrance of Centralia. The caption on the postcard read: "Tell the boys I did my best."

That night, an angry mob of more than 1,000 men kidnapped Everest from jail. They hanged him on a bridge outside of town. Mobs harassed Wobblies throughout the state for days.

No one was ever charged with the murder of Wesley Everest, but eight Wobblies went to jail for murdering Legionnaires. They were given long prison sentences, though no one could prove who shot first. The events at Centralia further fueled the public's fear of labor unions.

Gains for Labor

Despite the violence of Everett and Centralia, workers in Washington and the rest of the nation did improve wages and working conditions. By the turn of the century, the nation's workers had the attention of reformers. *Reformers* are people who seek to address social, economic, and/or political problems by bringing about positive change. Reformers saw the need not only to address the problems faced by the nation's workers but also to tackle other big problems of the day.

What Did You Learn? ①

1. What hardships did workers endure?
2. Why was it hard for unions to improve wages and working conditions?
3. Why were many Americans afraid of unions?

Growing Pains

In the late 1800s, Washington experienced tremendous growth. The railroads brought immigrants from Europe and Asia to the state, and also connected the state's biggest industries to the rest of the nation. Immigration added to the state's increasing population.

Many people were settling in Washington's cities. Although all this growth was good for Washington, it did create some problems. Among the problems created were corruption in business and government, poor working conditions, poverty, and child labor.

The Gilded Age

All of this growth and the resulting problems occurred during a time period that historians call the *Gilded Age*. The word *gilded* means covered in gold. During this time period, the growth of industry made many Americans very wealthy. When people thought of America, they thought of the wealth they saw. The country had an image of being covered in gold. However, beneath the country's gold cover, there were problems.

KEY IDEAS

- Corruption in business and government as well as economic hard times sparked a desire for reform.

- Reformers worked to address the nation's biggest problems and make the government more responsive to the needs of the public.

KEY TERMS

Gilded Age
initiative
monopoly
political machine
poverty line
progressive
recall
referendum
repeal
spoils system

Young boys working as "breakers" in a Pennsylvania coal mine. Breaker boys also worked in the coal mines of Washington. **What hazards do you think boys such as these faced working in a coal mine?**

The caption of this 1882 Thomas Nast cartoon reads: "The people fill it, and Congress empties it. The law-makers relieve the Treasury, but not the people." **How do the people and actions in the cartoon connect to the caption?**

Corruption in Business

Big business and the government often worked together. As you learned in chapter 5, the railroads worked closely with the government to get land grants and loans. Sometimes railroad and government officials abused this relationship. Many large companies (in addition to the railroad) wanted to do work for the government. They wanted contracts to build bridges, roads, and buildings. Companies were sometimes willing to bribe, or make an illegal payment, to government officials in order to get a contract. Once they got the contract, company officials charged larger fees for the work than the work was worth.

Other companies wanted to control certain industries so that they would not have any competition for business. When one company controls an industry, it is called a *monopoly*. Because it has no competition, a monopoly can charge whatever price it wants and force smaller companies out of business. At this time, there were no laws to prevent big companies from becoming monopolies. Business leaders wanted to keep it this way.

Corruption in Politics

Similar to big business, government was sometimes controlled by a handful of powerful people, called a *political machine*. These groups were called machines because all the members of the group worked together, like machine parts, to stay in power. The political machines were powerful enough to put down anyone who challenged them. The machines used their power to control politics and business. Rather than serving the public, machine politicians were often motivated by the money they could make.

Political machines did do good things at times, such as helping people find jobs or housing, but they often abused their power. In exchange for helping people or businesses, machine politicians expected votes or money, or both. Loyal voters were rewarded with jobs in the government. The practice of giving a loyal supporter a government job was called the *spoils system*.

What Do You Think?

What do you think were the negative consequences of the spoils system? What examples can you think of to support the idea that a spoils system exists today?

Tough Times for Many

Another problem of the Gilded Age was the growing gap between the rich and poor. The wealth of the country was in the hands of very few people. About 5 percent of Americans controlled most of the nation's wealth. The average yearly earnings of most Americans fell below the poverty line. The *poverty line* is a level of income below which a person or family is considered poor.

In the late 1800s, the United States experienced economic hard times. During these hard times, businesses and

Seattle Treasurer Steals $125,000

Within months after Adolph Krug was elected treasurer of Seattle, he skipped town along with about $125,000 in city funds. Six days after he fled Seattle, he was arrested in Minnesota about to board a train to New York. He and five leading Seattle businessmen were charged with "using public money in a manner not authorized by law."

Krug was found guilty and sentenced to seven years of hard labor. He served only two years of his sentence and was released. Krug returned to Seattle, where he purchased a saloon. Krug and the five businessmen eventually repaid the city treasury.

The Washington Journey

banks ran out of money. Thousands of Americans lost their jobs and their savings. Tough economic times left many people with a feeling of distrust for those with power and wealth. Some people wanted to deal with what they believed were the causes of these problems. The result was a period of reform, or change.

The Progressive Movement

The Progressive Movement was a collection of many different reforms. Supporters of the movement were called *progressives*. They wanted to end corruption, address economic problems, and improve society. Progressives brought about change in cities and states. They also made changes to the whole nation. Four amendments were added to the U.S. Constitution, including voting rights for women, a federal income tax, prohibition of alcohol, and the direct election of U.S. senators.

Prohibition

One way that progressives wanted to improve society was by banning alcohol. Women headed the efforts. They wanted to make alcohol illegal. They said alcohol was responsible for violence against women and children. They also thought alcohol contributed to most crimes. They said buying alcohol wasted money a family needed for food.

The 18th Amendment to the U.S. Constitution made alcohol illegal all over America. However, Washington was still very "wet" because "rumrunners" smuggled liquor from Canada into the state. The rumrunners could legally buy it north of the border. They brought the illegal alcohol to private clubs or roadhouses called "blind pigs."

Millions of Americans seemed willing to break the law if it interfered with having a good time. Violations became so widespread that local police stopped enforcing Prohibition in many cities. Bribery of the police to ignore the selling of alcoholic drinks was so

Tacoma police seize a still used to make illegal alcohol during Prohibition. **Where in the house does it look like the still was located? Why?**

Linking the Past to the Present

How does Prohibition compare with today's illegal drug trade?

A reformer uses an axe to destroy a barrel of illegal alcohol.

common that one Spokane man said years later that it was a shock to find an honest law officer.

Prohibition was finally repealed in 1933. To *repeal* a law is to cancel or overturn it. The attempt to ban alcohol throughout the nation was seen as a failed experiment.

An Era of Reform

Political Reform

Progressives also worked to stop the corrupt practices of political machines. They wanted the government to be more responsible. Progressives demanded that the government should work for the people. In Seattle, reformers created the Municipal League. One of the league's goals was to end the spoils system. The league wanted to be sure that all government officials were qualified to do their jobs. As a result, the league looked into the work experience of government employees.

Citizens in many states, including Washington, adopted three major reforms: the initiative, the referendum, and the recall. These reforms gave voters a greater say in the laws. They also let citizens remove government officials from office.

- The *initiative* let citizens propose laws themselves by gaining enough signatures on a petition. The public then voted on the law at the next election.

- The *referendum* allowed citizens to vote for or against laws already passed by their state's lawmakers.

- The *recall* allowed citizens to remove an elected official from office if they did not like how he was doing his job.

Voters Recall Hiram Gill

From the moment he was elected mayor of Seattle in 1910, Hiram Gill's opponents looked to remove him from office. The list of complaints against him was long. He was accused of voter fraud right after his election. Critics claimed that Gill brought thousands of jobless and homeless men into the city to vote for him. The city did see its largest election turnout ever, which only raised the suspicions about Gill.

Following his election, Gill appointed Charles Wappenstein as chief of police. The previous mayor had fired Wappenstein for corruption. As Gill's chief of police, Wappenstein resumed his criminal behavior.

Seattle Voters recalled Mayor Hiram Gill from office in 1911.

According to a newspaper reporter, "cigar stores and barbershops did a lively business in crap-shooting [a dice game] and race-track gambling, drawing their patronage [customers] largely from school boys and department-store girls."

When the list of complaints against Gill and his followers stacked up, voters petitioned to recall Gill. They succeeded with the help of women voters, who had just won the right to vote the year before the recall.

Surprisingly, Gill ran for reelection several years later as a reform candidate and won!

Washington PORTRAIT

John Rogers
(1838–1901)

John Rogers was a leading reformer in Washington and was twice elected governor. As governor, Rogers fought against the spoils system by appointing capable and trustworthy men to government jobs. He fired unqualified and corrupt government workers.

Rogers also supported education and signed the "Barefoot Schoolboy" law. It provided money so that all children could go to school. He also supported free school books for school children, lower railroad rates, a decrease in the salaries of elected officials, and voting rights for Washington women.

School buses line up outside a public school in Enumclaw. More children were able to attend school because of the Barefoot Schoolboy law signed by Governor Rogers.

An Era of Reform

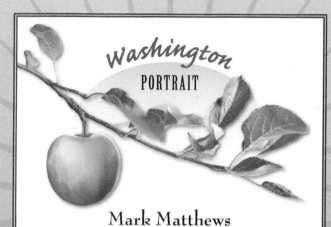

Washington PORTRAIT

Mark Matthews
(1867–1940)

Much of the Progressive Movement in Seattle revolved around Reverend Mark Matthews. Matthews came to Seattle from the South in 1902. A tall, slender man, he was a powerful speaker and a dynamic leader. Matthews turned Seattle's First Presbyterian Church into an instrument of social change. His congregation worked to create public hospitals, parks, and playgrounds, as well as a juvenile court system.

Matthews said, "It is cheaper to establish schools, parks, . . . and places of refinement, culture and morality, than it is to support hundreds of policemen, jails . . . and asylums for [alcoholics]."

Matthews fought against the "moral evils of liquor, gambling, and prostitution." He was particularly angered by political corruption in city government. He directed the campaign to recall Mayor Hiram Gill from office.

Controlling Business

As part of the Progressive Movement, the government started to take greater control of businesses that had too much power. Reformers wanted to control monopolies that charged high prices and put smaller companies out of business. Railroad companies and utilities (companies that provide water, gas, and electricity) were seen as the worst offenders. In Seattle and other cities throughout the United States reformers took over utility companies.

Following the devastating fire in Seattle, voters supported a plan for the city to take over the water system. The company that operated the system did not provide firefighters with enough water to battle the flames of the fire. Voters did not want that to happen again. They supported government ownership of the utility. This was the beginning of the Seattle Water Department. The department went on to build a modern water system that still supplies most of King County.

Help for Workers

Reformers also passed laws to shorten the workday to eight hours. They passed laws banning child labor in mines. Children were required to go to school. Laws that would end child labor in all industries took a little longer.

Two young boys who worked for the Coast Fish Company in Anacortes are surrounded by hundreds of cans of fish.

144

ELECTION—DAY

The artist of this cartoon did not support women's suffrage. **What images or words in the cartoon show this view?**

Women's Rights

Washington's most significant victory was voting rights for women. The state constitution had denied women both the right to vote and to serve on a jury. Women were leaders in all areas of Progressive reform, and they understood how much more effective they would be with the right to vote and hold office. Across the state, women's groups campaigned for political rights.

Finally, a state constitutional amendment gave women the right to vote in state and local elections, hold public office, and serve on juries. Washington was the fifth state to do this, 10 years before the 19th Amendment to the U.S. Constitution gave all women in the nation the right to vote.

Washington PORTRAIT

May Arkwright Hutton
(1860–1915)

A colorful and energetic campaigner for women's suffrage was May Arkwright Hutton. She was a former mining camp cook who had struck it rich in the silver mines in Idaho. May was always on the side of striking miners. She spoke bluntly. Her language often embarrassed both men and women, but her speeches were effective. "Criminals and idiots can't vote," she said, "and neither can women."

Hutton enjoyed being driven to her many social and political activities in Spokane by a chauffeur in a fire-engine-red car. She loved to wear scarlet dresses, a tiger-striped coat, and a hat with billowing ostrich plumes.

After her death, her husband, Levi, opened the Hutton Settlement, an orphanage in her memory. As an orphan himself, Hutton wanted to create a home where orphaned and needy children could be raised in a happy environment.

What Did You Learn? ②

1. Why did people see a need for reform during this time?
2. Why was Seattle Mayor Hiram Gill recalled from office?
3. What were some of the successes of progressive reformers?

KEY IDEAS

- Washington contributed to the nation's World War I efforts by providing men and materials.

- The 1920s was a decade of hardship for some but also a period of change marked by new inventions, attitudes, and overall prosperity.

- The need for cheap electricity and water to irrigate dry lands influenced plans to build the Grand Coulee Dam.

KEY TERMS

consumer
credit
hydropower
interest
intolerance
irrigation
neutral
vandalize

World War I

The Great War, as it was called at the time, raged in Europe from 1914 to 1917 before the United States became involved.

On one side were the Central Powers of Germany, Austria-Hungary, and Turkey. On the other side were the Allied Powers of England, France, Italy, and Russia. Many American businesses sold weapons, supplies, and food to England and France. The companies made enormous profits.

Many Americans did not want the United States to get involved in the war. When the war started, President Woodrow Wilson declared the United States to be neutral. To be *neutral* means to not take a side or participate in a war or dispute between countries. But neutrality proved difficult. Many Americans came from countries involved in the war, so it was hard not to choose sides. Making it more difficult was the fact that Germany had a new weapon—submarines. Germans called them U-boats, short for *unterseeboats*. ("under the sea" boats). They attacked without warning, sinking all kinds of ships, including passenger ships with Americans on board.

When the Germans sunk a ship that was carrying American tourists off the coast of England, U.S. citizens were outraged. Still President Wilson tried to keep the nation out of the war. Later, when more ships were attacked, and more Americans killed, the United States entered the war. It joined the Allied Powers.

Men were asked to join the war effort. When not enough men signed up, Congress passed the Selective Service Act. It required all men between 21 and 30 years of age to sign up for military service. They called it "being drafted." About 75,000 Washington men fought in the war.

Officials draw names of men to draft into military service for World War I.
How would you describe the process taking place here? Why do you think so many people were involved in selecting names?

An American Army field hospital set up inside the ruins of a church in France in 1918. **What challenges do the doctors, nurses, and patients face in this environment?**

A World War I recruitment poster shows a marine in dress uniform. **What else is pictured and where can interested men sign up?**

U.S. MARINES

SERVICE ON LAND AND SEA

ENLIST AT
203½ West Holly Street, Bellingham, Wash.

Fear on the Homefront

All of the fighting was in Europe, and Germans were the enemy. Back in the United States, Americans grew suspicious of German Americans. They feared that German Americans were disloyal or even enemies of the United States. As a result, some Americans beat up German Americans and vandalized their farms and businesses. To *vandalize* is to damage or destroy something on purpose. Many schools stopped teaching the German language. Americans renamed popular foods that had German names. Frankfurters (hot dogs) became "liberty sausages"; sauerkraut became "liberty cabbage."

More than 5,000 soldiers trained during World War I at the University of Washington's U.S. Navy training station on the shores of Lake Union. The men in this image appear to be learning how to sight and position deck guns. **How would you describe what they are doing?**

Soldiers conducting drills at the University of Washington's U.S. Navy training station.

Elizabeth Gurley Flynn addresses an IWW free speech rally during World War I. **What new law was she likely violating with her speech?**

Wobblies Criticize War

Members of the Industrial Workers of the World did not support American participation in the war. They claimed the war was being fought to enrich big businesses. Many American businesses profited from selling war supplies to the Allies. The Wobblies organized strikes against companies that supplied tanks, guns, uniforms, and other war materials. They gave angry speeches against those who profited from war.

At one point during the war, the IWW organized a strike of lumber workers. They demanded an eight-hour workday. Because lumber was needed for the war effort, the U.S. government stepped in to settle the strike. The government forced lumber company officials to accept the workers' demands. To the IWW, it was a great accomplishment.

Free Speech Challenged

Since the Wobblies and many other Americans were against the war, Congress made laws to stop people from criticizing the war in public. The laws made it illegal for anyone to write or say anything critical of the war effort, the military, the government, the flag, or the Constitution. Many Wobblies were arrested for breaking these laws. Despite the arrests, the Wobblies continued to speak out against the war.

"If we have to suppress everything we don't like to hear, this country is resting on a pretty wabbly basis."

—Historian Charles Beard in 1917

What Do You Think?

Do you think it was a good idea for the U.S. government to limit the exercise of free speech during World War I? Why or why not?

Linking the Past to the Present

The Espionage and Sedition acts passed during World War I made it illegal for Americans to say or write anything critical of the U.S. war effort. The laws even allowed the post office to read mail searching for violations.

Following the terrorist attacks in New York City and Washington, D.C., in 2001, Congress passed the Patriot Act. The Patriot Act has been criticized for preventing free speech and violating other rights.

Look up the Patriot Act on the Internet and get some opinions from people you know. In what ways is the Patriot Act similar to or different from the laws passed during World War I?

Washington's Economy Booms

The war created many new jobs. Washington industries and workers benefited from the demand for war supplies. Workers used lumber to build ships, airplanes, and new houses. The federal government sent army men to help the lumber industry meet production demands. Since there was a shortage of food in Europe, Washington's crops were shipped overseas. To increase production, farmers found new ways of using machines to grow and harvest more food for everyone.

Men too old to be drafted, who had a hard time finding good jobs before the war, found better jobs once the soldiers left for Europe. Many workers came from other states to work in Washington's industries. Women took the jobs of the men who were fighting in Europe. Women became factory workers, auto mechanics, printers, and farmers. Some even worked in lumber camps. Everyone hated the horrors of war, but business was booming.

Before the war, there was only one shipbuilding company in the United States. By the end of the war, there were more than 25. The war also fueled the new airplane industry. For Washington, the war helped to create a company that became the state's largest industrial employer—the Boeing Company.

More than two million women joined the workforce for the first time during World War I. Here, women work in a factory making guns.

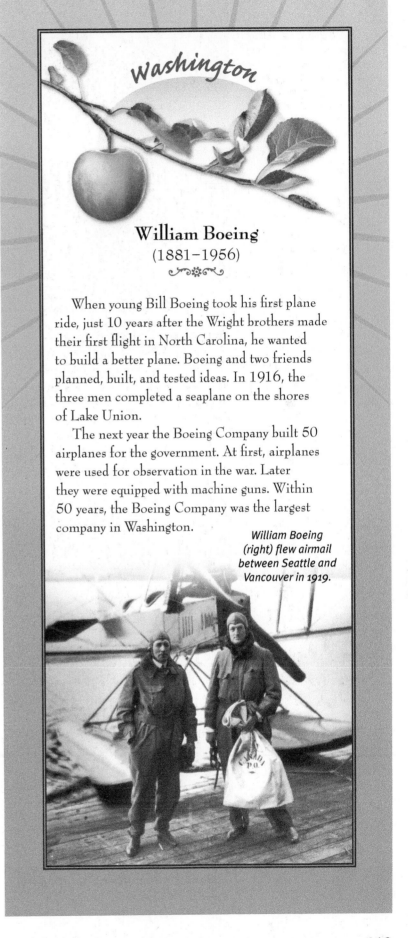

Washington

William Boeing
(1881–1956)

When young Bill Boeing took his first plane ride, just 10 years after the Wright brothers made their first flight in North Carolina, he wanted to build a better plane. Boeing and two friends planned, built, and tested ideas. In 1916, the three men completed a seaplane on the shores of Lake Union.

The next year the Boeing Company built 50 airplanes for the government. At first, airplanes were used for observation in the war. Later they were equipped with machine guns. Within 50 years, the Boeing Company was the largest company in Washington.

William Boeing (right) flew airmail between Seattle and Vancouver in 1919.

Children in Puyallup organized their own parade to celebrate the end of the war in 1918. The poster on the wagon reads: "Hurray! The war is over!! Father and brother are coming home. To hell with the Kaiser that's where he belongs!"

The War Ends

Finally, peace came to America once more. For lucky families, Washington's soldiers and nurses came home. For those whose sons and husbands were killed or injured, there was relief, at least, that the killing had stopped. Life in America might now return to normal.

After the war, many African Americans migrated from the South in search of jobs in northern and western cities.

Postwar Pains

A sharp drop in the economy followed the economic boom of the war years. The government no longer needed businesses to make guns, ammunition, ships, airplanes, and uniforms. Unemployment soared. Millions of people left their homes in search of work. In particular, many African Americans left the South and moved to northern and western cities in what became known as the Great Migration.

Washington farmers and workers also suffered right after the war. Europe no longer bought as much food from Washington. Because there was too much food to sell locally, farmers had to drop their prices. This hurt their income and a lot of farmers went bankrupt. Shipyards suddenly had no orders and were forced to cut their workforce. Lumber mills no longer needed to supply wood for ships and planes, so they closed their doors. Weyerhaeuser lumber sales dropped 50 percent. Many smaller mills went out of business. Men talked in quiet voices of their fears about feeding their families.

Anger increased once again toward immigrants and blacks who competed with white workers for scarce jobs. Women were forced out of work and told that they should stay home and give jobs to men.

Race Relations

After the war, there was much *intolerance*. Many people were not willing to accept different cultures, races, or ideas. One example was the rebirth of the Ku Klux Klan (KKK). The KKK was a group created in the South after the Civil War. The Klan terrorized blacks to prevent them from gaining political power. By the late 1800s, the KKK had all but disappeared. However, the growth of labor unions, increased immigration, and World War I renewed the fears many Americans had about non-whites and foreigners. These fears helped bring about a rebirth of the Klan. The new Klan extended its hatred to Catholics, Jews, immigrants, and labor unions.

It also extended its reach from the South to other parts of the country, including Washington. In the 1920s, the Seattle chapter of the KKK held several rallies that attracted between 20,000 and 70,000 people. KKK members threatened union members and Japanese farmers in Yakima Valley and elsewhere. They burned crosses to scare people. Members also proposed an initiative to ban Catholic schools. Washington voters did not support the initiative.

An unidentified klansmen salutes members at a rally. **What is threatening about his appearance?**

Washington PORTRAIT

Horace and Susie Cayton
(c. 1860–1940) (1870–1943)

Horace Cayton and his wife, Susie, were well-known African Americans who worked for political reform and racial equality in Seattle. Horace was born into slavery on a plantation in Mississippi. After slavery ended, he moved to Washington where he started his own newspaper, *The Seattle Republican.*

Susie was the daughter of Hiram Revels, the first black elected to the U.S. Senate. She helped her husband with the newspaper and wrote many articles addressing race. In one of her editorials, she wrote about the lack of black dolls available for children. She urged African American mothers to make their own.

Susie was involved in charitable activities. She raised money and organized Christmas toy drives to help the poorest of Seattle's black community.

The Caytons' influence in the black community was so great that several important black leaders, including Booker T. Washington, visited their home in Seattle's wealthy Capitol Hill neighborhood. Despite their standing in the community, their white neighbors did not like having blacks in the neighborhood. In a lawsuit, the neighbors claimed that the presence of the Caytons decreased the value of the homes in the area. The Caytons defended themselves successfully, and continued to live in the neighborhood for some time.

Lingo of the 1920s

The decade of the 1920s is often called the "Roaring Twenties," the "Jazz Age," and the "Age of Nonsense." Young people had a lot more freedom than their parents did. A generation gap was noticeable. Young people even created their own slang. Here's a short list of some of the words and phrases from the 1920s.

applesauce—an exclamation such as "nonsense!"

bee's knees—an extraordinary person, thing, or idea

big cheese—the most important person; the boss

bootleg—illegal liquor

cat's meow and cat's pajamas—something splendid or stylish; similar to the bee's knees

dogs—feet

dumb Dora—a stupid female

flapper—a stylish, loud, wild, young woman who wears short skirts, short hair, and makeup

heebie-jeebies—the jitters or the creeps

jalopy—old car

joe—coffee

pill—an unlikeable person

pinch—to arrest

swell—wonderful

The Roaring Twenties

Despite some of the troubles that immediately followed the end of the war, the 1920s are remembered by many as a time of prosperity and fun. Many Americans were ready to let go after years of sacrifice and loss. New inventions and new ways to spend money transformed America. Americans became *consumers*, or buyers, of goods and services. Instead of saving money, people in the 1920s spent it!

Less of a family's income went to buying necessities and more went to entertainment, recreation, and new products. Automobiles, which were introduced at the turn of the century, became more affordable. The number of roads and highways increased. The automobile gave Americans, especially young people, independence.

The automobile helped to connect the countryside to the city. Farm families could drive to major cities to shop, attend concerts, and see movies. The price of Henry Ford's Model T dropped from $850 in 1908 to under $300 by the mid-twenties. Auto ownership was within the reach of many Americans.

The Charleston was a fun and popular dance in the 1920s. Dance competitions drew large crowds in many cities. The contestants of a Charleston contest at Tacoma's Winthrop Hotel pose for a snapshot.

The engine that powered automobiles was also used in farm machinery, logging trucks, freight trucks, and school buses. School districts replaced one-room schools with larger ones since children could now ride buses many miles from their farm homes to schools in town.

Electricity was becoming commonplace. Most American homes had electricity. This created new industries for electric appliances, telephones, and radios. New appliances such as toasters, refrigerators, vacuum cleaners, and washing machines saved time and improved family life.

Buying on Credit

Most families had only one income. In order to pay for all of these new things, people began to rely on credit. *Credit* allowed people to pay for their purchases a little bit at a time. However, buying on credit cost more in the long run because businesses charged interest on the amount owed. *Interest* is the fee that must be paid for borrowing money.

What Do You Think?

What do you think are the advantages and disadvantages of using credit to buy things?

New Fashions

For the first time, women cut their hair short and wore skirts above the ankle. They hung long bead necklaces around their necks, colored their cheeks with rouge, and wore nylon stockings with seams down the back. Women who wore the new fashions were called "flappers." In an effort to look as stylish as the flappers, men adopted new fashions. They wore wide ties and black-and-white shoes, and they slicked back their hair.

Women model the latest 1920s fashions. **How do their outfits represent the fashion of the time?**

A Seattle telephone operator uses a telephone switchboard to connect calls. All phone calls were made individually by an operator at a switchboard. This was a popular job for women.

In the late 1920s, the government approved construction of the Grand Coulee Dam. Here is the completed dam.

Help from Hydropower

Because electricity was essential to run the new inventions, producing hydropower became important. *Hydropower* refers to the use of water as a source of power. The Pacific Northwest had about 40 percent of the nation's hydropower potential. The state's abundant rivers could be used to produce electricity. Business and political leaders wanted the state to benefit.

The Campaign for Grand Coulee Dam

Farm families of the Columbia Basin had a hard time making a living in the 1920s. Their income dropped after the war, and to make matters worse, a drought made it hard to grow crops. Farmers wanted a dam to help them cope with the effects of the drought. Water from a dam could be used to irrigate the basin's dry lands. *Irrigation* is a way to supply water to crops by redirecting it from another location.

Supporters of a dam at Grand Coulee were called "pumpers." A dam across the Columbia River would have many benefits. It would provide a source for hydroelectricity, or water-powered electricity. Enough electricity would be generated to pump water uphill to a reservoir. The water stored there could then be released as needed to the dry farmland below.

In the late 1920s, the government finally approved of the plan to build the dam. Construction of the massive project, however, did not start until years later. The Columbia Basin Reclamation Project was the largest project of its kind in U.S. history. You will read more about it in chapter 7.

Construction of the dam required people to move from their homes. In some cases, the homes were also moved, but that was rare. **What difficulties do you see in moving an entire home?**

What Did You Learn? ③

1. What contributions did Washington make to the nation's World War I efforts?

2. Describe two positive and two negative events of the 1920s.

3. What was the strongest argument for building a dam on the Columbia River?

Go to the Source

The IWW's View of Capitalism

This 1911 IWW poster takes a critical look at the capitalist system. The IWW saw capitalism as an enemy to the working class. Look closely at the image and answer the questions.

Observe —— Evaluate —— Conclude

- How does each level of the pyramid differ? Describe the people you see.
- Where is the working class in the pyramid? How do you know?
- Which level do you think represents the capitalist, or wealthy, class? How do you know?

- What is the significance of the statements connected with each level?
- Why do you think the bag of money at the top is so far from the people at the bottom of the pyramid?

- Do you think this poster is a fair criticism of capitalism? Why or why not?
- What impact do you think this poster had on public opinion? How might it have added to the public's fears of labor unions?

An Era of Reform

How to Cite Sources

The purpose of citing sources is to identify the resources you used in conducting your research. Citing your sources gives credit to the person(s) whose ideas or words you used. A List of Works Cited also helps your readers find the sources that you used in case they want to find more information.

There are many different types of sources that must be included in a List of Works Cited. A list might include the following:

- Printed material such as books, magazines, and newspapers
- Web Sites
- Primary documents such as letters, diaries, audio, video, or film recordings
- Government documents

Knowing the proper way to cite your sources is an important skill. Here are some examples:

A Book with Two Authors

Author(s): Notice how they are organized   Place of Publication

Green, Michael K., and Laurie Winn Carlson. *The Washington Journey.* Layton, Utah: Gibbs Smith, Publisher, 2009.

Date of Publication

Title of Book (in italics)

Name of Publishing Company

A Web Site

Name of Web site

Date site was last updated

Seattle Civil Rights and Labor History Project. 20 Oct. 2008. The University of Washington. 22 Jan. 2009. <http://depts.washington.edu/civilr/>.

Group responsible for the site

Date you visited the site

Web address

A Primary Source from a Digital (online) Collection

Place where collection is stored

Author   Name of recipient   Date written   Name of Collection

Baumgartner, A. J. Letter to Pendleton Miller. March 25, 1899. Special Collections: University of Washington Libraries Digital Collections. 22 Jan. 2009. http://content.lib.washington.edu/cdm4/document.php?CISOROOT=/pioneerlife&CISOPTR=2701&REC=1

Date you visited the site

Web address

Your Turn

Choose a topic from the chapter you just completed. Visit your school library and gather three different sources for your topic. Create a List of Works Cited for the sources you found. Use the examples here to help you with proper format. Your completed list should be in alphabetical order by the author's last name.

Chapter 6 Review

Chapter Review Questions

1. Describe the difficulties of workers in trying to organize unions and improve working conditions.
2. Why did the Everett Massacre, the Seattle General Strike, and the Centralia Massacre fuel fears about labor unions?
3. What is meant by the term *Gilded Age*? List three examples of corruption during the Gilded Age.
4. What do you think were the three most significant reforms of the Progressive Movement?
5. How did World War I help the economy of the United States and Washington?
6. What happened to Washington's economy after the war ended?
7. Why did the KKK expand its membership after World War I?
8. What made life in the 1920s "roaring"? Give at least three examples.

Becoming a Better Reader

Finding Details

Good readers know how to read to find detail. Details provide more information and support the main idea. If books only had main ideas, readers would be left with lots of questions. When reading a textbook or a nonfiction book, heads and subheads give clues about where to find the details. Choose one of the main ideas of this chapter. Write four details you learned about one of these main ideas.

You Are the Geographer

Use an atlas, an encyclopedia, or search the Internet to find a map of World War I. Identify the Allied Powers and the Central Powers.

1. What geographic advantages and disadvantages did each side have?
2. Which side did the United States join?
3. What geographic advantages and disadvantages do you think the United States had?

"We have flown the air like birds and swum the seas like fishes, but have yet to learn the simple act of walking the earth like brothers."

—Martin Luther King Jr., Civil Rights leader

U.S. Astronaut John Young salutes the flag after landing on the moon in 1972. Young was the commander of the Apollo 16 mission. The Lunar Module, Orion, is parked next to the flag. Boeing helped create the lunar module. **What other details do you see in this image?**

Challenging Times

Essential Question ?

How did the people of Washington respond to the economic, social, and political challenges of the Great Depression and World War II?

Timeline of Events

1932
- Franklin D. Roosevelt is elected president.
- The New Deal begins.

1934
The Indian Reorganization Act is passed.

1936
Roosevelt is reelected.

1930

1935

1929
- The New York Stock Market crashes.
- The Great Depression begins.

1933
- Construction of the Bonneville and Grand Coulee dams begin.
- The Civilian Conservation Corps (CCC) is created.

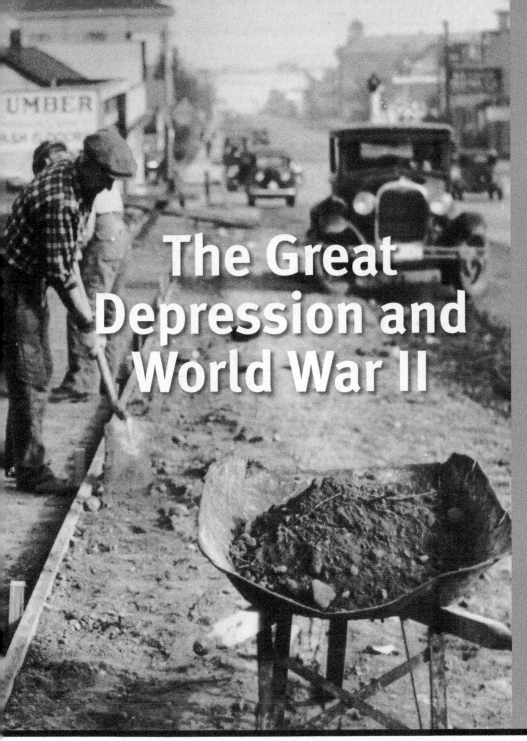

Chapter 7

The Great Depression and World War II

The Great Depression of the 1930s brought hard times to the nation and to Washington. New Deal projects like the Columbia Basin Reclamation project helped get some Americans working again.

By the end of the decade World War II had started in Europe. The Japanese attack on Pearl Harbor forced the United States into the war. Washington's airplane, shipbuilding, and other industries helped supply the war effort.

Franklin Roosevelt's New Deal created jobs for many unemployed Americans. These men were working in Seattle for the Works Progress Administration. **What job are they doing?**

1939–1945
World War II

1940
Roosevelt is reelected.

1942
Japanese Americans in western states are ordered to "relocation" camps.

1944
Roosevelt is reelected

1940

1945

1938
The Bonneville Dam starts producing electricity.

1941
• The Grand Coulee Dam is completed.
• Japan attacks a U.S. naval base at Pearl Harbor.
• The United States enters WW II.

We Can Do It!

1945
• May: Germany surrenders
• August: United States drops two atomic bombs on Japan
• WW II ends.

161

From Boom to Bust

The 1920s was a time of prosperity (wealth) and change. Americans elected Herbert Hoover as president at the end of the decade. "I have no fears for the future of our country," Hoover announced as he took office. "It is bright with hope." Like people in most states, Washingtonians looked forward to a new decade of peace and prosperity.

All of this prosperity suddenly changed when a wave of panic spread over Wall Street—the nation's financial center—in New York City. On October 29, 1929, later called *Black Tuesday*, the largest selling day in the history of the New York Stock Exchange began. Since so many people were selling their stock, and few were buying, prices *plummeted*. That means they dropped suddenly and steeply. In just two months, the stock market lost 40 percent of its value.

Some people lost everything they had overnight. Many Americans, including some millionaires, went bankrupt. Although few believed it at the time, the country was about to fall into the worst economic depression in history. An *economic depression* is a period of time when the economy is suffering from mass unemployment, low business activity, and a weak stock market. The *optimism*, or confidence, of the 1920s was quickly replaced by gloom and fear.

What Caused the Great Depression?

Scholars today still disagree about what factors caused the Great Depression. Some say it was the growing gap between the rich and poor. Others claim that the *supply* of goods and services was higher than the *demand* for them. In other words, businesses and farms produced more than consumers could use. Still other scholars blame banks and the stock market. Neither was strictly supervised by the government. As a result, people who deposited their money in banks or invested in the stock market were not protected.

A crowd of people gather outside the New York Stock Exchange following the Crash of 1929. **What words would you use to describe the crowd?**

162

This Hooverville was built in Seattle just west of where the sports stadiums now stand. Some Hoovervilles elected their own mayor. **What would be the difficulties of living here?**

A Ripple Effect Begins

When the stock market crashed, a ripple effect began throughout the country. The banks closed first. Many banks had invested recklessly in stocks. When the stocks became worthless, the banks lost their money. People who had saved their money in the banks lost their entire savings. Soon many factories and businesses closed because no one had money to buy anything. Thousands of workers lost their jobs.

President Hoover did not have a workable plan to help end the depression. The public blamed him for not doing enough. Homeless people built housing developments out of scrap lumber, metal, and cardboard and called them "*Hoovervilles*."

Since people with little or no income could not pay their taxes, there was not enough tax money in government funds to help people. Washington counties maintained 24 shelters, or "poor farms," for homeless people, but the shelters were forced to turn away many.

A homeless man sits in front of his Hooverville shack in Seattle in 1931.

Linking the Past to the Present

Like the 1920s, the United States experienced an economic boom in the late 1990s into the early 2000s. By 2008, however, the economy started to slow beginning with the housing market. Trouble in the housing market spread to the stock market and banks. Many Americans were unable to afford to live in their homes, and businesses started to cut their work forces. Is it true that "history repeats itself"?

In the worst year of the Great Depression, national unemployment reached 25 percent. In Washington, unemployment varied between 11 and 26.5 percent. Almost every industry in Washington suffered. When shipping in and out of the Port of Seattle slowed, many dockworkers lost their jobs. Other workers lost their jobs in manufacturing, coal mining, lumber, fishing, and flour milling—all industries that had once thrived. For those people who did not lose their jobs, their pay and work hours were often reduced.

DEPRESSION CYCLE

- Factories produce less.
- People lose their jobs.
- People cannot buy things.
- Stores go out of business.
- Stores do not order from factories.
- Factories do not get orders.

How Hard Were the Hard Times?

Given the wealth that many Americans have today, it is difficult to imagine how much suffering people endured in the 1930s. Hunger, misery, fear, and anger were found in every community.

Four-year-old Angeline D'Ambrose died after eating poisonous weeds in her backyard. Her father, a Seattle shoemaker, had been out of work for a year. "I guess my baby was hungry," he sobbed. "We haven't had anything in the house to eat for two days."

In later years, people wrote what they remembered about their family's struggle during the Depression:

We wore clothes made out of material from old clothes. We put cardboard in our shoes, and when they wore out we wore any shoes that we could get our feet into. They hardly ever fit.

We shared an egg for breakfast, with bread.

We ate potatoes three times a day—fried for breakfast, mashed at noon, and in potato salad for dinner. My mother even learned how to make potato fudge.

This photograph, which was labeled "poor kid," was printed in a 1936 newspaper article.

Hardship and Opportunity

Just as occurred during World War I, many businesses asked married women to resign from their jobs so that a man could have the job. For example, the Seattle Library Board issued a new policy that read:

It shall be the policy of the Seattle Library Board not to employ a married woman whose husband is able to provide her a living. Any library employee marrying a husband able to provide a reasonable income will be required to tender [give] her resignation.

Besides losing their homes and their jobs, many Americans went hungry during the Depression. Americans in many cities took to the streets to

What Do You Think ?

It is not possible for a country to have an unemployment rate of 0 percent (or a 100 percent employment rate). Instead, economists say that a healthy economy typically has an unemployment rate of between 4 and 5 percent. Why do you think there will always be some unemployment, and why is that okay?

"With the help of 240 agencies and churches who helped with sewing, the Red Cross distributed 2,800 shirts."

—*Spokesman-Review,* January 11, 1932

*Men read the notices posted on the window outside of Seattle's Public Employment Office. **What are the notices for?***

demand relief. About 1,000 protestors marched to the capitol in Olympia. They demanded that the state provide help to the unemployed, free lunches and free water for children, and free or cheap electricity and gas to Washington citizens.

Although theirs was a peaceful demonstration, marchers were not always met with open arms. When they heard there might be as many as 50,000 protestors, Olympia officials beefed up the police force. A group of vigilantes vowed to help the police. Bad weather and the threat of violence must have discouraged the protesters because the march was cancelled.

One person's hardship could be another person's opportunity. There were bargains for those with ready cash. A long-time resident of Cheney remembers an entire block of 12 lots selling for $38. Farms, homes, and businesses sold for a fraction of their true value.

• Olympia

Children lined up with their pails for soup at a local soup kitchen. Soup was provided every night to the poor or homeless.

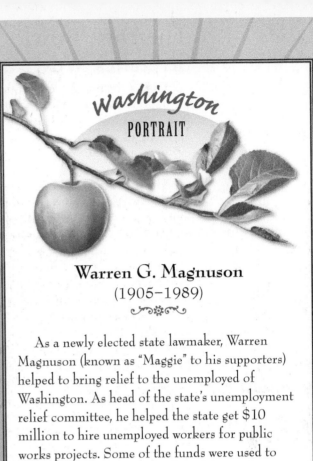

Washington PORTRAIT

Warren G. Magnuson
(1905–1989)

As a newly elected state lawmaker, Warren Magnuson (known as "Maggie" to his supporters) helped to bring relief to the unemployed of Washington. As head of the state's unemployment relief committee, he helped the state get $10 million to hire unemployed workers for public works projects. Some of the funds were used to build the Grand Coulee Dam and the Washington Park Arboretum in Seattle.

Before Magnuson's election to the state legislature, Washington politics was dominated by the Republican Party. Magnuson's election along with other Democrats marked a big change for the state. Washington was now truly a two-party state.

In addition to unemployment relief, Magnuson supported the repeal of the 18th Amendment—Prohibition.

Magnuson went on to become the King County prosecutor and a United States senator. He served 36 years in the Senate and was known for his support of laws protecting consumers and the environment.

The Great Depression and World War II

The Dust Bowl Stretches Westward

During the 1930s, companies that made home-canning jars were one of the few businesses that made money. People wanted to make sure they had food on their shelves. Within a 100-mile radius of Spokane, 18 million jars of fruit and vegetables were canned by women.

One of the most severe droughts in the nation's history came to the Great Plains states in 1928. It lasted in some areas for 12 years. Strong winds turned dry farming regions into a gigantic *dust bowl*.

The drought also reached the Pacific Northwest. Billowing clouds of topsoil from the Columbia Basin were visible to ships hundreds of miles off the Washington coast. Dust storms plagued the basin for years. One lady with a reputation for fastidious, or very thorough, housekeeping decided she could not keep up with the dust. "She just opened her front door and opened her back door and let the dust blow right through," reported a neighbor.

The dry, hot winds turned forests into a fire waiting to happen. In 1936, with drought conditions at their worst, the Forest Service reported that 450,000 acres of national forest in the Northwest had been destroyed by fire.

Dorothea Lange took this famous photo of a migrant mother in California. She told Lange that she and her seven children had been living on frozen vegetables and birds the children had killed. **What story does the mother's face tell?**

Starting Fires to Get a Job

Some unemployed men were so desperate for a job that they deliberately set fires. They hoped to get a job as a firefighter. During the summer of 1931, Idaho's Governor Ben Ross ordered the National Guard to prevent people from entering the forests.

Farmers Suffer

Suffering on the farm took many forms. Crops rotted in the fields because farmers could not get a good price for them. Crop prices were not high enough to cover the cost of harvesting and shipping the crops to market. In Oregon, thousands of sheep were slaughtered and fed to the buzzards and coyotes. Farmers there reasoned that the money they could get for the meat and wool was too low to make a profit. In Washington, some farmers burned fruit trees for fuel. It was cheaper than buying fuel.

Migrants Flock to the Northwest

Because of the drought and Dust Bowl, many farmers and their families fled the Great Plains states. They migrated west in search of work and a better life. Since so many of the migrants were from Oklahoma, they were nicknamed "Okies."

With such grim conditions, it was a shock to westerners that their region was regarded as a land of opportunity by people from the Great Plains. Most migrants traveled across country to California on Route 66, but many others "rattled down" Route 30 to Oregon and Washington.

With crops ruined and fearing his children were coming down with dust pneumonia, Jim Emmett joined the migration west. His grandfather had started for the Northwest over the Oregon Trail in 1849, but he had stayed in the Dakotas instead. Richard Neuberger, a prominent author of the time, observed a number of these Dust Bowl pilgrims. His description of the Emmett family is a touching word picture of hard times:

Jim headed the radiator cap of the automobile into the West. A thin roll of ten-dollar bills was tucked in his purse—the proceeds of the sale of his livestock. Martha sat at Jim's side in the front seat, holding the youngest child on her lap. The other three children shared the [torn up back seat] with pillows, books, pots, dishes, jars of preserves and pickles, irons, baskets and other articles of household equipment. From a trailer jolting along behind [stuck out] bedsprings, chairs, tables, lamps.

By 1940, more than 400,000 migrants had followed Jim Emmett to the Northwest. But not every migrant found a "promised land." Many migrants made barely enough money to live by working as fruit and vegetable pickers. This army of **transient**, or temporary, workers moved into the Yakima, Willamette, and Snake River Valleys during the harvest seasons. Living in crowded, unsanitary shack camps, these people received little attention until 1939. That year, a government program provided housing and medical clinics for migrant workers in the Northwest.

Voters Blame Hoover

The Great Depression was the worst and longest economic downturn in the nation's history. It lasted more than a decade. No one knew when it would end or how to fix it. Americans were becoming very discouraged. They grew increasingly upset and angry with the government. No one seemed to be helping the many people who were suffering. Although President Hoover did not cause the Depression, many Americans blamed him. So when it was time to elect a president, Americans rejected Hoover. To replace him they elected Franklin D. Roosevelt.

"We loaded up our jalopies [old run-down cars] and rattled down the highway never to come back again," said the words of a Woody Guthrie song.

Unemployed workers held a rally in Seattle's City Hall Park in 1931. One of the signs reads: "Free lunches for school children of the unemployed." **What do some of the other signs say?**

What Did You Learn? ①

1. Identify three factors that scholars claim caused the Great Depression.
2. Describe how the Depression affected workers and farmers in Washington.
3. For what reasons did farmers from the Great Plains migrate to the Northwest?

KEY IDEAS

- President Franklin D. Roosevelt's New Deal sought to end the Great Depression.

- New Deal projects like the Grand Coulee Dam created thousands of jobs for needy Americans.

- The Indian Reorganization Act tried to fix the problems created by earlier policies.

KEY TERMS

anthropologist
destitute
federal
longshoremen
reservoir
teamster

A New President

The Depression got worse in 1932. It was a presidential election year and the Democrats chose Franklin D. Roosevelt, governor of New York, as their candidate. Northwesterners were unsure of Roosevelt's views, but they were anxious for a change. FDR, as he was called, won the election. He promised a "New Deal" for the American people.

Alphabet Soup

FDR's New Deal created jobs to put people back to work. Many job programs were started. So many, in fact, that the programs were referred to as "alphabet soup" since most people identified them by their abbreviations. One of the most popular programs was the Civilian Conservation Corps, or CCC. Young men from every part of the nation were stationed in camps throughout the country. There were more than 200 camps in the Northwest. The men earned from $30 to $45 a month and received good food, education, and discipline. CCC camps were commanded by army officers. The program helped the young men of the CCC and their families, too. Each CCC worker was required to send $25 home to family each month.

Young men worked on soil conservation projects, provided labor at fish hatcheries and wildlife refuges, planted millions of trees on public lands, and fought forest fires. CCC workers also blazed trails in many state and national parks, including trails in the Grand Canyon in Arizona. They built the headquarters site for Olympic National Park.

An Indian division of the CCC, with headquarters in Spokane, worked on Indian reservations. They built trails, roads, and forest fire lookout towers.

Work for Everyone

There were also hundreds of smaller construction jobs funded by the New Deal. These provided much-needed employment. Workers built highways, bridges, school buildings, libraries, post offices, parks, and sewer and water systems.

1932 Election Results

- 57.4% Franklin D. Roosevelt (D)
- 39.6% Herbert C. Hoover (R)
- 3.0% Other

Men working on a Civil Works Administration project clear a swamp north of Seattle. **What does their work involve?**

One of the most well-known New Deal programs was the Works Progress Administration (WPA). In addition to hiring people for construction work, the WPA hired musicians, writers, historians, and artists. One of the WPA's most important projects was a collection of interviews with former slaves. Journalists traveled all over the country to speak with and record interviews with former slaves.

Also, histories of cities and states were written and published. Public buildings received a facelift. The WPA also hired artists to paint murals on the walls of libraries, hospitals, and government buildings.

The work of the WPA can be seen in Washington and around the country. In King County, for example, WPA projects included:

- Improvements to the King County airport

- Road construction in Auburn, Seattle, Mercer Island, and Vashon Island

- Construction of the Issaquah Fish Hatchery, as well as the Duvall Library, the Renton Fire Station, and Bothell City Hall

- New construction, improvements, and additions to school

- Housework and child-care services.

- Reader services for the elderly and blind

- Public art projects, including murals and sculptures in post offices, libraries, and hospitals

A New Deal for the Pacific Northwest

President Roosevelt viewed the Pacific Northwest, with its small population and abundant natural resources, as a "last frontier" of undeveloped places. He wanted people to use forests and rivers wisely. He was also willing to use federal money to help them. *Federal* money comes from the national government.

Men apply for jobs with the Works Progress Administration.

Women working as seamstresses for the Civil Works Administration press clothes in a Seattle sewing center.

Men clean used bricks as part of a project for the Civil Works Administration.

What Do You Think

Franklin D. Roosevelt was the nation's only president to be elected president not just two times, but four times. He won elections in 1932, 1936, 1940, and 1944. Why do you suppose Americans elected him so many times? Why might some Americans have been fearful to have the same person serve so many years as president?

THE GRAND COULEE DAM

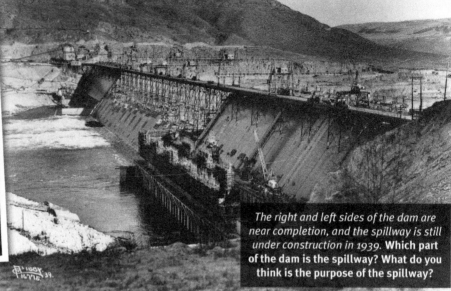

The right and left sides of the dam are near completion, and the spillway is still under construction in 1939. **Which part of the dam is the spillway? What do you think is the purpose of the spillway?**

A worker carries a 193-pound nut and bolt. It was one of 16 used to join sections of the generator shaft.

President Roosevelt and his wife, Eleanor (in the back seat of the car), toured the site of the Grand Coulee Dam where the president spoke to a crowd of 25,000.

This photo shows a panoramic view of the Grand Coulee Dam construction site in the 1930s.

The biggest New Deal project in Washington was the construction of the Grand Coulee Dam. As you read in chapter 6, the campaign to build a dam on the Columbia River began in the 1920s. The Columbia Basin region was a hot and dry region. Early explorers called it "the Great Columbia Desert." This arid region was made worse during the Great Depression by a drought that created a dust bowl like the one in the Great Plains states. At one point, a windstorm created a cloud of dust rising thousands of feet in the air. The dust swept across Washington to the Pacific Ocean. It was reported that a huge cloud of dust completely surrounded an ocean liner 600 miles off the coast of Seattle.

The severe drought and high unemployment led to approval of the Columbia Basin Reclamation Project. The project would include several other dams. President Roosevelt thought large-scale public works projects would provide immediate jobs for many of the *destitute*, or needy, Dust Bowl migrants. Construction on the dam began in 1933 and was finished in 1941.

Jobs for Thousands

More than 12,000 workers were hired during the time it took to build the dam. The pay was good by Great Depression standards. The average pay for unskilled labor was 85 cents an hour. Skilled workers could make up to $1.20 an hour. However, the work was not steady and could be dangerous. More than 70 workers died on the job, mostly from falling or from having something fall on them. There were frequent work shutdowns due to scheduling or cold weather. Although most of the workers were white, the project did employ blacks and Native Americans from the nearby Colville Reservation.

The dam, which has been called the "Eighth Wonder of the World" and "the mightiest thing ever built by man," was the largest concrete structure in the world. The reservoir created by the dam stretches 150 miles long and produces more electric power than any other dam in the United States. A *reservoir* is a natural or artificial pond or lake used for the storage and control of water.

Journalists covering this grand project described what they saw:

> *It will contain enough concrete to build a highway from Philadelphia to Seattle and back.*
>
> *Enough water will flow through the dam each year to provide New York City's drinking water for a hundred years.*
>
> *A surprising feature is the number of young men employed at Grand Coulee. I noticed dozens of tall lads wearing football sweaters from nearby universities.*
>
> *The work is dangerous and scarcely a day passes without someone's being injured. 54 men have already been killed.*

The Cost of Progress

Construction of the Grand Coulee Dam created thousands of jobs. It also brought water to dry land and cheap electricity to the region, and provided flood control on the Columbia River. However, this progress came at a high price. Between 3,000 and 4,000 people were forced out of their homes to make way for the dam. Their homes and farms were located in areas flooded by the dam.

The dam turned out to have devastating consequences for Native Americans. Construction of the dam submerged ancient villages, fishing spots, and burial grounds. Tribes were relocated once again. Most devastating, however, was the impact on salmon fishing. The Grand Coulee Dam destroyed wild salmon runs on the upper Columbia. A way of life for many of the Indian tribes in the region came to an end.

Songs Promote Electricity

Another of the major dams constructed in Washington during the Great Depression was the Bonneville Dam. The Bonneville Power Administration (BPA) was created to operate the dam and provide electric power to the region. To promote a wider use of electricity, the BPA hired famed folk singer Woody Guthrie to write songs praising the Columbia River projects. "Roll on, Columbia" became popular. It was made Washington's official folk song in 1987. Guthrie also wrote the well-known song "This Land Is Your Land."

ROLL ON, COLUMBIA
Roll on, Columbia, roll on,
Roll on, Columbia, roll on
Other great rivers add power to you
Yakima, Snake, and the Klickitat, too
Sandy Willamette and Hood River too
So roll on, Columbia, roll on
At Bonneville now there are ships in the locks
The waters have risen and cleared all the rocks
Shiploads of plenty will steam past the docks
So roll on, Columbia, roll on
And on up the river is Grand Coulee Dam
The mightiest thing ever built by a man
To run the great factories and water the land
So roll on, Columbia, roll on

Grand
Coulee Dam

When the government cut back funding for some New Deal programs in 1937, many workers lost their jobs. Former WPA workers held a rally in Seattle to protest the layoffs. **How might a protest like this call attention to their troubles?**

A group of WPA picketers marches outside the Seattle Chamber of Commerce at Third Avenue and Columbia Street. **Which signs do you think have the most effective message?**

Victory for Labor

Despite the progress made by many New Deal programs in creating jobs, many workers still suffered. Wages were low, work hours were long, and conditions were still dangerous for many workers. Many workers thought that the New Deal had not done enough. They wanted more.

They got their wish with the passage of the National Labor Relations Act. The law, also known as the Wagner Act, guaranteed workers the right to join unions and organize strikes. It would now be against the law for an employer to prevent workers from organizing or to punish them when they did. The law gave workers a place at the bargaining table when wages, hours, and working conditions were negotiated. The law was a major victory for the nation's workers. As a result, more workers joined unions.

The Clash of Unions

While the new law helped increase union membership, it also fueled a growing feud between rival labor unions. The American Federation of Labor (AFL) was a union of skilled workers that had been around since the 1880s. Its members included carpenters, electricians, meat cutters, and *teamsters* (truck drivers). AFL leaders believed that unions with only skilled workers had more bargaining power than unions with unskilled workers. But by the mid-1930s, a lot of workers wanted all workers to be in one big union. When they couldn't get the AFL to open up their membership, these workers split and formed the Congress of Industrial Organizations, or CIO.

The feud was on. Both the AFL and the CIO fought repeated battles over who should represent workers. "Goon Squads"—groups of paid thugs—were on both sides of the dispute. Baseball bats and cargo hooks were often used as weapons when the two groups confronted each other.

Lumber mills, breweries, warehouses, and shipping docks were centers of conflict. Newspapers took sides. Washington became one of the most unionized states in the nation.

In Seattle, the AFL Teamster's Union clashed with the CIO's longshoremen and warehousemen unions. *Longshoremen* load and unload ships. It was hard work and the men worked long hours. Warehousemen worked in huge warehouses where goods were stored until they could be transported to other places. The warehouses were freezing cold in winter and very hot in summer.

In spring 1939, the two unions clashed over who had the right to represent workers in the salmon-canning industry. Workers slugged it out with fists, knives, and rocks, according to newspaper reports. "Rocks were flying in all directions," reported the *Seattle Daily Times*. Four men were taken to the hospital with serious injuries, and police arrested six others. Despite the bitter rivalry, the two unions eventually merged in the 1950s.

Native Americans Get a New Deal

Indian populations reached their lowest level in the early 1900s. Poor diets and poor living conditions contributed to high death rates, especially among children. A new wave of diseases—tuberculosis, pneumonia, and influenza—ravaged the reservations. Alcoholism was also a big problem.

A Columbia University anthropologist, John Collier, was appointed to lead the Bureau of Indian Affairs. An *anthropologist* studies human societies and cultures. Collier believed the whole concept of the Dawes Act—to Americanize the Indians—had been a mistake. He thought that breaking up tribes was wrong. The tribe upheld the social, moral, and spiritual values of the group.

The Indian Reorganization Act repealed the Dawes Act and encouraged tribal governments. Tribes would again have common land and would promote Indian languages, arts, crafts, and ceremonies.

Native Americans in Washington, however, did not immediately benefit from the new law. Many Native Americans in Puget Sound had married outside of their tribes and made their living from industries like fishing and logging rather than farming on a reservation. As a result, they did not all have the tribal identities that the law attempted to preserve.

The Worst Was Over

By 1939, the worst of the Great Depression was over. Slowly, businesses opened up again. Unemployment was still high, but many people were working. They started to purchase goods. They could afford to buy more meat and other food so farmers made more money. Industry and trade in the Pacific Northwest also improved.

World War II ended what was left of the Great Depression. Similar to World War I, the fighting started in Europe. At first, the United States tried not to get involved. However, staying out of the war became increasingly difficult.

Blackfoot Indian chiefs meet with BIA director John Collier in 1934. **How is this image evidence that Collier encouraged the renewal of tribal culture?**

What Did You Learn? 2

1. How did New Deal programs like the CCC and the WPA help the unemployed and the American public?

2. What led to approval of the Columbia Basin Reclamation project?

3. How did the Indian Reorganization Act affect Native Americans in Washington?

KEY IDEAS

- When the United States entered World War II, the need for war supplies finally ended the Great Depression.

- Japanese Americans on the West Coast were forced to give up their homes and move to relocation camps during the war.

- Labor shortages in Washington led to increases in the black and Latino populations, and forever changed the role of women.

KEY TERMS

bracero
descent
detainee
ethnicity
Holocaust
radiation
reactor
relocation

An army recruit is fitted for a uniform following the Japanese attack on Pearl Harbor.

Another World War

The American economy was improving and the worst of the Great Depression was over, but there was trouble in other parts of the world. Adolf Hitler, the Nazi dictator of Germany, believed that the Germans were a superior race. Hitler set out to conquer Europe and to cleanse it of what he called inferior peoples—especially Jewish people.

Hitler sent millions of Jews to concentration camps, where more than six million were put to death in gas chambers or died from starvation. This mass murder of the Jews is called the *Holocaust*.

When Hitler's army and air force invaded Poland, England and France declared war. They were called the Allied Powers, or the Allies. Later, the Soviet Union was attacked by Germany and joined the Allies. Italy and Japan joined Germany. They were called the Axis Powers. This was the start of World War II.

Once again, Americans were determined that the United States stay out of the European war. President Roosevelt sent ships and supplies to help the Allies, and he warned Americans that someday they might have to fight Hitler.

Japanese Attack Pearl Harbor

December 7, 1941, was a beautiful day at Pearl Harbor, Hawaii. The morning sun shone over the many U.S. Navy ships anchored at the docks. Suddenly the skies darkened as wave after wave of Japanese fighter planes dropped bombs on U.S. ships.

The next day, President Roosevelt asked Congress to declare war on Japan. The United States joined the Allies and entered the war. It would be a difficult war to fight since the United States had to fight enemies in Europe and in Asia.

The Japanese attacked Pearl Harbor, sinking U.S. ships and killing many Americans. **What rescue efforts are being made here?**

Allied Powers	Axis Powers
Great Britain	Germany
France	Italy
Soviet Union	Japan
United States	

Wartime Economic Boom

While the war brought horror to millions in Europe, it brought economic prosperity to the United States. Not even the New Deal could create as many jobs as war. There seemed to be war-related jobs for everyone. Because the Northwest was located close to the Pacific war zone, the region became a shipping center for war materials and soldiers. It also became a large shipbuilding center like it had been during World War I.

Hydroelectric power from the Grand Coulee and Bonneville dams played a vital role in wartime production. The great amount of cheap power produced from the dams boosted industrial development.

Washington Industries Prosper

Aluminum

Aluminum production became the state's great new war industry. Five huge aluminum manufacturing plants were constructed. These plants were enormous consumers of electrical energy. Giant mills were built at Spokane, Longview, and Tacoma. The mills shaped aluminum into a variety of forms. Much of the metal was sent in rolled sheets to the Boeing Company in Seattle. There it was used to build airplanes.

Shipbuilding

Henry J. Kaiser, an aggressive businessman, became the world's greatest shipbuilder. Nearly 100,000 people worked in the Kaiser yards in the Portland-Vancouver region. From 1941 until the end of the war, Kaiser built 50 "baby flattop" aircraft carriers and several hundred merchant ships. Kaiser used fast, simplified methods of welding. He used steel from his own plants in California and Utah. Kaiser produced more ships than any other company in the country. Warships were built at shipyards in Seattle, Tacoma, Bremerton, and Bellingham.

Boeing workers service a new B-17F bomber, called the "Flying Fortress."

Boeing's War Planes

Just in case enemy planes flew over the area, Boeing's plant was disguised to look like a residential neighborhood. Using paint and wire, buildings were made to look like homes with trees in the yards.

At the peak of production, the Seattle plant produced 16 B-17s every day. The B-17 was the main weapon in the air war against Germany. At its Renton plant, Boeing began work on the larger B-29. The B-29 "superfortress" was the most advanced bomber of its time. It was used in the air war against Japan. Near the end of the war, six new B-29s rolled out of the plant every day.

Boeing employed 50,000 people by the end of the war. Nearly half of them were women.

By the end of the war, Boeing had built nearly 7,000 B-17s and over 1,000 B-29s. Boeing sales were 10 times the income of all other Seattle industries combined.

It seemed the state's natural resource economy based on farms, fish, and lumber had changed overnight to an economy based on aluminum, airplanes, and ships.

BUILDING THE
ATOM BOMB

Plutonium for the secret Manhattan Project was produced here at the Hanford atomic energy plant in Richland.

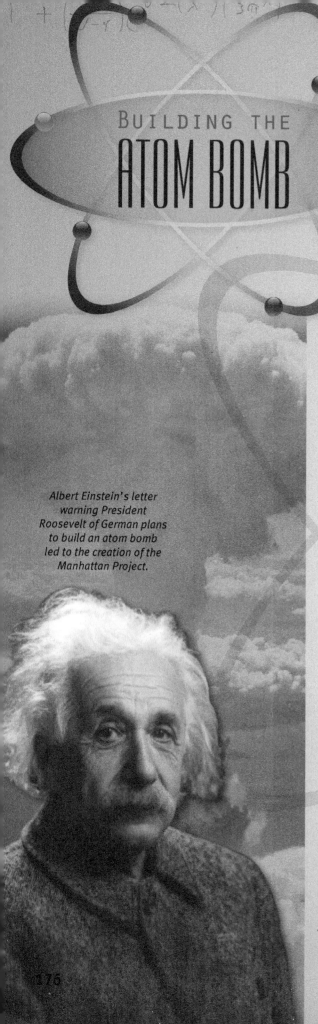

Albert Einstein's letter warning President Roosevelt of German plans to build an atom bomb led to the creation of the Manhattan Project.

In September 1939, President Roosevelt received a letter signed by the Jewish scientist Albert Einstein, warning him that Hitler's Germany might be the first country to make an atom bomb. Roosevelt started the secret Manhattan Project to develop the atom bomb for Americans.

The Perfect Location

Directed by General Leslie Groves, a former University of Washington student, the Manhattan Project built one of its research facilities at a place called Hanford. Located in a remote section of eastern Washington, the site had obvious advantages. Its location ensured both security and public safety from possible radiation. *Radiation* is energy in the form of electromagnetic waves or moving particles produced as a result of an atomic reaction. Large amounts of radiation can cause cancer.

Hanford produced plutonium, which was used for bombs. The plant's *reactors*—machines that create nuclear energy—required a huge amount of electric power and lots of fresh water for cooling. The location was perfect. Grand Coulee Dam was ready to provide the power and the Columbia River had the water.

Keeping it Secret

During the war, local newspapers agreed to keep quiet about Hanford. This meant that newspapers would withhold information from the public in order to protect the secret project at Hanford.

A "mystery city" for thousands of men and women working on the project was quietly built in Hanford. Trainloads of equipment disappeared behind the project's fences. The tiny town of Richmond was being expanded to house the administration center and a complete city for 15,000 more people. Most of the workers did not know the end product of their work.

It was not until the dropping of atomic bombs on Japan ended the war that the world discovered the secrets of Hanford.

Japanese-American children wave from a train window on their way to a relocation camp. **What do you think of their behavior in this photo? Do they seem threatening?**

Government Relocation Centers for Japanese Americans

KEY
● Relocation Camps

Pacific Ocean
CANADA
Washington
Oregon
Idaho
TULE LAKE
MINIDOKA
HEART MOUNTAIN
Wyoming
TOPAZ
California
MANZANAR
Utah
Colorado
GRANADA
Arizona
POSTON
Arkansas
GILA RIVER
ROHWER JEROME
0   500 miles

Relocation of Japanese Americans

The surprise attack on Pearl Harbor produced a hysterical fear of a Japanese invasion. Some people thought that Japanese Americans might give aid to Japan or secretly try to destroy American companies. Without any evidence to support their decision, government leaders decided to classify anyone of Japanese ancestry as a security risk.

On March 2, 1942, all persons of Japanese *descent* (ancestry) living on the West Coast were given *relocation* orders. This meant they were required to move to special camps set up by the government. Many lost their homes or were forced to sell at low prices.

They were removed from coastal areas, including Washington, and sent to 10 relocation centers. Most of the Japanese in Oregon and Washington were sent to the Minidoka Relocation Center in the Idaho desert. Minidoka was the temporary home to 10,000 people, most of whom were Japanese-American citizens of the United States. They spent the war surrounded by barbed wire and armed guards.

What Do You Think?

America was fighting Japan, Germany, and Italy during the war. Why do you think German Americans and Italian Americans were not relocated?

While in the camps, the *detainees* (people confined or imprisoned for political or military reasons) tended to small vegetable gardens or worked in the camp's cafeteria or school. Some helped produce war materials like camouflage nets. Their wages were limited to $19 a month.

The Japanese community did not resist relocation. It wasn't until later that the government admitted that the forced relocation violated the civil rights of Japanese Americans.

Japanese Americans from Bainbridge Island are assisted by soldiers in 1942, taking them to a relocation camp. **What do you think they took with them?**

Making Amends

When the war came to an end, Japanese Americans were gradually freed. The last of the camps closed in 1948—three years after the war ended. In 1988, Congress issued a formal apology and agreed to give $20,000 compensation to every surviving Japanese American who had been relocated during the war.

The Great Depression and World War II

Washington PORTRAIT

Gordon Hirabayashi
(b. 1918)

While the Japanese community as a whole did not challenge the government's relocation orders, one Seattle native did. Gordon Hirabayashi was a student at the University of Washington when he refused to comply with the relocation order.

"As an American citizen, I wanted to uphold the principles of the Constitution, and the curfew and evacuation orders which singled out a group on the basis of **ethnicity** [cultural background] violated them. It was not acceptable to be less than a full citizen in a white man's country," Hirabayashi explained.

Hirabayashi was tried and convicted for violating orders. He spent 90 days in jail. He appealed his case to the U.S. Supreme Court. The Court's nine judges ruled against him. The judges said that the evacuation orders were a "military necessity."

In the 1980s, Hirabayashi successfully challenged the Court's ruling. The Court overturned his convictions. His case made history and helped convince government leaders to issue a formal apology and provide money to surviving detainees.

A group of sailors in King Street Station excitedly read a newspaper headline announcing the end of World War II in Europe. The war raged for several more months in the Pacific.

The War Ends

In April 1945, Washington people were stunned to learn that President Roosevelt had died from a stroke. Businesses closed. Theaters emptied. Traffic slowed to a halt. For three days and nights, radio stations aired only news broadcasts and religious music.

Less than a month later, Germany surrendered, ending the war in Europe. People celebrated in the streets. Sons, brothers, and husbands were coming home. The war in the Pacific, however, was still raging. Leaders in the United States had to make a terrible decision. Should they invade Japan or should they try to quickly end the war by using their new weapon—the atomic bomb.

It was a difficult decision for the new president, Harry S. Truman. An invasion of Japan could result in the deaths of thousands of American soldiers. An invasion might also cause the war to drag on for many more months. Truman did not know very much about the bomb until he became president. He hoped it might bring a quick end to the war.

After much deliberation, Truman decided to drop the

The Washington Journey

bomb on Hiroshima, Japan. The bomb completely destroyed the city and instantly killed as many as 70,000 people. When the Japanese did not surrender, Truman gave the order to drop a second bomb a few days later. The second bomb devastated the city of Nagasaki.

It was a terrible tragedy for the Japanese people. The country's leaders knew they had to surrender. Three months after the peace treaty was signed in Europe, the war with Japan was finally over. Once again, there was celebrating all over America.

War Brings Social Change

The social impact of the war on the state of Washington was enormous. This was particularly true of the Puget Sound region. The war transformed Seattle into an industrial center and brought a large number of migrants from every part of the state.

Seattle's African-American population, for example, increased from 3,700 in 1940 to 30,000 in 1945. Many white people resented the influx of newcomers. Racial discrimination became part of daily life for black citizens. Signs that read: "We cater to white trade only" appeared throughout the city.

The demand for housing forced people to convert chicken coops, garages, and empty service stations into apartments. Some families lived in tents. Other people lived in the backseats of cars.

The *Bracero* Program

The war was a turning point for Mexican migration to Washington. After men went overseas to fight, there were not enough workers on the farms. Growers in the Yakima Valley became so desperate for help that one farm advertised for 5,000 workers.

The government's answer was the *Bracero* Program. *Braceros* were Mexican men allowed to work in the United States as temporary farm laborers. Thousands were employed in the Northwest. The program also encouraged the migration of Mexican Americans from southwestern states. Whole families made the journey from Texas and other states to work in Washington fields and orchards. The program resulted in a permanent Latino settlement in Washington. And although the extra workers were needed, Latinos faced discrimination like other ethnic groups before them.

A group of braceros harvesting strawberries. Many braceros came to work in Yakima Valley where there was a shortage of farm workers during the war.

179

The Changing Role of Women

Participation of women in both world wars forever changed their role in society. In both wars women took over at home and at work for the men who had to fight. The contributions women made during World War I helped to convince President Wilson to sign the 19th Amendment, giving women the right to vote. Women played such a vital role in the war effort that it was hard to deny them voting rights.

Women played an even greater role in World War II. They helped in all the branches of the military—the U.S. Army, Navy, Marines, Air Force, and Coast Guard. Some women even worked as spies. Alice Marble, who won 12 U.S. Open and five Wimbledon tennis titles spied on the Nazis.

While their contributions to the military were significant, women had an even greater effect on industry and the economy. Women took over for men in many industries. They became crane operators, taxi drivers, lumberjacks, auto mechanics, electricians, and firefighters, just to name a few. The number of women in the labor force grew 110 percent during the war years. In factories that made war supplies, the increase was higher. For example, before the war only 36 women worked in ship construction in the entire nation. A year later, 160,000 women worked in the shipbuilding industry. In the airplane industry, 39 percent of the workers were women.

It was expected that women would quit their jobs after the men returned home from war. After all, they did so after World War I. The Depression had forced others from their jobs in the 1930s. But World War II was different. Women had proved something to themselves, and to American society. A woman's place was no longer just in the home. They wanted more. For the next several decades, women challenged their traditional role more and more. Today, women are working as company executives, government leaders, and military officers.

This poster of "Rosie the Riveter" became the symbol of American women workers during World War II.

Women workers at Boeing rivet bolts into a B-17 bomber. At least half of Boeing's workers during World War II were women.

Working Women

- The number of women electrical workers jumped from 100,000 to 374,000 during the war.
- Women working in heavy industry went from 340,000 to over 2 million.
- The U.S. Air Force had 1,074 female pilots during the war. They flew noncombat missions, but the work was no less dangerous. Thirty-eight women lost their lives during the two years that the all-female pilot squadron existed. They actually had a survival rate better than the men flying similar noncombat missions.

What Did You Learn? ③

1. How did U.S. involvement in World War II help to end the Great Depression?
2. Why was Gordon Hirabayashi put in jail for 90 days?
3. What was the impact of the war on the state's African-American and Latino populations?

World War II Posters

World War II did not just occur on the battlefield. It was an effort that required the support of all Americans in the military and on the home front. The U.S. government launched a campaign to increase public support for the war effort. Below are two examples of posters created during World War II. Take a few moments to examine the posters and answer the questions.

Observe ---- Evaluate ---- Conclude

- What are the main topics of each poster?
- What images or symbols are used in each poster?
- Are the messages in each poster mostly visual, verbal, or both?

- Who do you think is the intended audience for these posters?
- What do the posters indicate about how women were viewed during this time period?

- What conclusions can you make about the role of women during World War II?
- Do you think these were effective posters? Why or why not?

Taking a Position

- What caused the Great Depression?
- Did the New Deal end the Great Depression?
- Was it right for the United States to drop atomic bombs on Hiroshima and Nagasaki?
- Was it right for the United States to put Japanese Americans in relocation camps during the war?

Soldiers post evacuation orders for Japanese Americans in Bainbridge Island.

These are just a few of the questions that this chapter raises. Since your textbook presents only the facts and does not offer a position on these issues, it is up to you—the reader—to take a stand.

Here are some steps to consider when preparing to write an essay or make a presentation that takes a position on a topic.

1. Pick a topic that interests you and about which you can get excited.

2. Create a question about the topic that can be answered with different but well-reasoned opinion and concrete facts.

3. In one sentence, write your answer to the question. Be sure that your answer uses words that clearly identify the position you want to take. This sentence will become your thesis statement.
   For example,

   It was wrong for the United States to imprison Japanese Americans during World War II.
   OR
   It was World War II, not the New Deal, that ended the Great Depression.

4. List three different but specific reasons that would convince a reader that your position is the most credible.

5. For each reason, identify examples and offer facts to support your position. Look for a range of evidence, such as expert opinion, primary sources, graphs, photographs, etc. You will want at least two to three supporting facts for each reason. The more you can find, the more persuasive your position will be.

6. Examine and refute the opposite position on your topic. It will help strengthen your position if you cast doubt on other views.

   You now have an outline from which to write an essay or create a presentation highlighting your position. Use the flow chart to help you organize your writing.

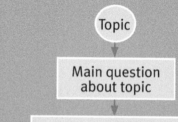

Topic

Main question about topic

Answer to question that states your position

Reason #1	Reason #2	Reason #3
Supporting examples and facts	Supporting examples and facts	Supporting examples and facts

Chapter Review Questions

1. Describe how the Great Depression was hard on Washington residents.
2. How would you describe the New Deal that President Roosevelt promised the American people?
3. What was the purpose of the Indian Reorganization Act? How did it affect Indians in Washington?
4. How did Washington's industries benefit from World War II?
5. Why was the Hanford site the perfect location for building the atomic bomb?
6. In what ways did the war change the way women viewed themselves?

Becoming a Better Reader

Compare and Contrast

Good readers often need to make comparisons to understand new information. Sometimes good readers compare and contrast ideas to see relationships between concepts. Create a Venn diagram like the one here to compare the effect of the Great Depression on workers and farmers in Washington.

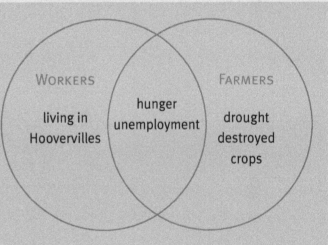

WORKERS

living in Hoovervilles

hunger
unemployment

FARMERS

drought destroyed crops

You Are the Geographer

Dams on the Columbia River

The Columbia Basin Reclamation Project forever changed the landscape of the state. Some of the changes were positive and some were not. Create a chart that compares the positive results with the negative results of building dams on the Columbia River. Do the benefits of the dams outweigh the costs? Use your chart to write a paragraph expressing your opinion.

Essential
Question?

What significant political, economic, and social challenges affected Washington State in the post–World War II era?

Washington Comes of Age

1945
- World War II ends.
- The Cold War begins.

1950–1953
Korean War

1954–1975
Vietnam War

1957
The Soviets launch *Sputnik*, the first satellite.

1940

1950

1949
- Soviets test the atomic bomb.
- Three University of Washington professors are fired during the Red Scare.

1954
The Supreme Court issues the *Brown* ruling.

1956
Interstate freeways are started across America.

Chapter 8

In the years after World War II, Washington experienced lots of change and growth. People were building new lives.

The postwar years were also challenging. The United States became involved in more wars. And there were problems at home as African Americans, Latinos, Native Americans, and women fought for equal rights.

The nation and the state began to address environmental challenges as well.

Protestors demonstrate against the Vietnam War in 1965. Some of their signs suggest issues the U.S. should be addressing. What issues are the marchers concerned about?

1961
Martin Luther King, Jr., visits Seattle.

1962
The World's Fair is held in Seattle.

1968
Martin Luther King, Jr., is assassinated.

1969
Americans land on the moon.

1986
The government releases secret reports about radioactive waste at the Hanford facility.

1960   1970   1980   1990

1963
• Washington's first sit-in is held.
• Wing Luke is the first Asian American elected to public office in Washington.
• President Kennedy is assassinated.

1972
An equal rights amendment is added to Washington's constitution.

1974
Indian fishing rights are upheld in the *Boldt* ruling.

1980
The Northwest Power Act is passed.

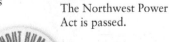

185

KEY IDEAS

- The G.I. Bill enabled WWII soldiers to go to college and buy a home.

- The Cold War between the United States and the Soviet Union was a tense time for all Americans.

- Washington's aerospace industry helped the United States lead the Cold War arms race and the space race.

KEY TERMS

arms race
cold war
Communism
crusade
dictator
propaganda
refugee
stalemate
suburb
superpower

Postwar Washington

When World War II ended, people everywhere breathed a sigh of relief. The news on the radio would no longer contain stories of evil and death. The country celebrated and then eagerly returned to normal life.

Washington residents were grateful that the war was over, but they were worried about what was to come. Factories that manufactured chemicals, aluminum, steel, tanks, airplanes, and many other products slowed down. In 1944, shipyards employed 150,000 people. Boeing Airplane Company employed nearly 50,000 people. Would thousands of workers lose their jobs now that the war was over? Would the nation again sink into a great depression?

The G.I. Bill

Most soldiers had joined the war right out of high school. When they returned from war, they needed to readjust to civilian life. They needed a home and job training. The federal government passed the G.I. Bill of Rights to assist former soldiers as they returned to the United States. Part of the bill provided money for college tuition. Many veterans took the opportunity and were the first in their family to attend college.

World War II veterans were able to afford college because of the G.I. Bill. The money they received was used for tuition and school supplies. **How do these college students compare to college students today?**

The Sawdust Empire

The G.I. Bill also helped veterans buy houses. This sparked a building boom across the nation. Families were able to get mortgage loans with no down payment. There had been little building during the war because the entire nation's resources had gone to the war effort. Once the war was over, however, the demand for housing created a rush for timber.

The timber industry in the Pacific Northwest boomed for two decades after the war ended. There continued to be thousands of jobs in logging and sawmills.

Farms changed, too. Many farm families moved to town. Other farmers bought more land, so farms got bigger in size.

The Baby Boom

An explosion of childbirths came in the years following World War II. The "baby boom" lasted from 1946 to 1964. During that time, 77 million babies were born. Today, the "baby boomers" are grown and have children and grandchildren of their own.

Families with young children wanted to have homes of their own. That meant a move to the suburbs. *Suburbs* are places where many homes are built together outside a city center. Schools, parks, and shopping centers were often built in the suburbs, too. People bought homes instead of renting an apartment in town.

Living in the suburbs meant new ways of shopping. The Northgate Shopping Center opened north of Seattle. It was the first shopping center in the world and was described as a small town because it had over 100 shops, a hospital, and a movie theater all in one place.

Within a few years, suburbs ran together and entire cities such as Redmond, Bellevue, and Lynnwood had been created. By the 1950s, two-thirds of Washington's families lived in the suburbs. The other third still lived on farms or in small rural towns.

John Graham Jr. created this architectural drawing of the Northgate shopping mall. Northgate was one of the nation's first suburban shopping centers. **Identify the main features of the mall shown in this image.**

A housing boom after World War II led to the creation of suburbs. **How is this home different from what might be found in a city?**

From Hot to Cold War

During World War II, the United States and the Soviet Union were allies. Both countries had a mutual interest in defeating the German Nazis. Their alliance was shaky, however. Deep down, the United States did not like the Soviet government because it was Communist. Once the war was over, so were any chances of a friendly relationship between the two nations. Both countries emerged from the war as superpowers. Despite the devastation of war, they both had huge military and defense systems. Their military might along with economic strength and political influence made the two nations *superpowers*. Each country feared that the other might attack at any time. The Cold War had begun.

What is a Cold War?

A *cold war* is an intense economic, political, military, and cultural competition between nations. The war is considered cold because there is no direct fighting between the nations. Instead, the nations are hostile and fight each other with propaganda. *Propaganda* is information that is designed to persuade and sometimes mislead. Each nation does all that it can to make the other country look bad. The Cold War that started after World War II between the United States and the Soviet Union lasted nearly 50 years.

Capitalism vs. Communism

Capitalism is an economic system that allows for private (individual or company) ownership of land, property, and businesses. In the United States, the government has a limited involvement with businesses. 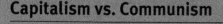 *Communism* is an economic and political system where the government owns all land, property, and businesses. A Communist government is very rigid. The leader is a *dictator*, meaning he is not elected and has complete control of the country. Citizens do not have freedom of speech or religion. Also, citizens are not free to leave the country without permission.

These U.S. Army missiles could be used to launch nuclear weapons. During the Cold War, the United States and the Soviet Union competed with each other to build the most weapons.

Protestors march outside the Washington State Armory, where the state's Committee on Un-American Activities (also called the Canwell Committee) held hearings to investigate suspected Communists. **How would you describe the protest?**

The color red was a symbol of the Communist Party, so anyone suspected of being a Communist was called a "Red." People who sympathized with Communists were called "Pinkos."

The Red Scare

Cold War fears included worrying that members of the Communist Party might take over the U.S. government. People suspected of being Communists were fired from their jobs. Labor union leaders, teachers, and government workers were often targeted. They were rarely given a chance to defend themselves. This time period was known as the Red Scare. This was actually the second Red Scare in the United States. The first came right after World War I.

Probably the most well-known anti-Communist of the time period was Wisconsin Senator Joseph McCarthy. He went on a *crusade* (a passionate campaign) against suspected Communists. He claimed that there were hundreds of Communist spies working for the U.S. government and even in the U.S. Army. Although he had no proof to back up his charges, many Americans believed him. His recklessness ruined the lives of many people.

Suspected "Reds" Fired

The University of Washington was one of the first universities in the country to fire professors who were suspected Communists. The university fired three professors during the Red Scare. The three were dismissed because they refused to answer questions asked by the state's Committee on Un-American Activities.

Professor Ralph Gundlach was one of the three teachers fired by the committee. In his remarks to the committee and to the university's president, he said, "No legislative committee has the right to ask about one's personal beliefs and associations. No one can prove I'm a Communist, and I cannot prove that I am not."

What Do You Think ?

Why do you think labor leaders, teachers, and government workers suspected of being Communists were targeted? Do you think it was right for them to lose their jobs? Why or why not?

Police remove E. L. Pettus, vice president of the Washington Pension Union, after Pettus stood up and declared that the Canwell Committee was unconstitutional. **What appears to be the mood of the audience?**

Seattle citizens receive instructions in front of the Armory during a civil defense drill. **What are they wearing on their faces? For what kind of attack were they preparing?**

Ravenna's Bomb Shelter

Fear of nuclear attack prompted many communities and families to build bomb shelters. Shelters were built underground and stocked with food and supplies. Washington built a bomb shelter underneath Interstate 5 in Seattle's Ravenna neighborhood. It was designed as a command center for the Washington State Patrol. Inside it had a squad room, a radio dispatch room, beds, toilets, and decontamination showers. The showers could be used in case of exposure to radiation. The shelter also had emergency food and water supplies.

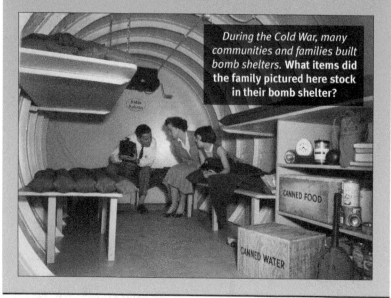

During the Cold War, many communities and families built bomb shelters. **What items did the family pictured here stock in their bomb shelter?**

New Technologies and Industries

The fear of Communist spies in the United States was boosted by several events right after World War II. Only a few years after the United States dropped two atomic bombs on Japan, the Soviets tested their first atomic bomb. The secret plans for the bomb had been leaked to the Soviets by American spies. This event sparked a race that would last for the entire Cold War. The Cold War **arms race** was a competition between the United States and the Soviet Union to have the most powerful weapons.

Fear of Nuclear Attack

The arms race further fueled fears that the Soviets might attack at any time. People in Washington State talked about being a good target because of the large Boeing plant and the Hanford nuclear site. Towns held civil defense drills and practiced how to evacuate buildings and streets in case of a bomb attack.

The entire city of Spokane practiced an evacuation drill. It was the first city in the nation to do so. Other cities had plans, too, but most people realized it would be impossible to escape if a bomb hit a city.

Students at Hazel Valley Elementary School in Burien crouch under a table during an air-raid drill in 1958. **Do you think they will be protected from a nuclear attack? Why or why not?**

The Space Race

The arms race was not the only race of the Cold War. A little over a decade after the end of World War II, Americans were shocked to learn the Soviet Union had launched the world's first satellite. Called *Sputnik*, it made Americans aware that they were not leading the way in space. By this time, the United States and the Soviet Union had become bitter rivals.

President Dwight Eisenhower reacted to the news of *Sputnik* by signing a law requiring more focus on science and math education in America's schools. American students were to be the nation's "secret weapon." Within a few years, the U.S. space program had caught up and was beating the Soviets. American satellites were used to spy on the Soviet Union. They took photos and gathered information in space. America's greatest achievement of the space race was the 1969 moon landing.

Astronaut Buzz Aldrin planted the American flag on the moon's surface in 1969.

Seattle World's Fair

The Space Needle, now an emblem for downtown Seattle, was built for the World's Fair in 1962. The Space Needle was a symbol of the nation's space program, which was pushing hard to get a man on the moon before the Soviets did.

The World's Fair was a chance to show what the future might bring in science and technology. A huge science exhibit stressed more science education for American students. The monorail was an example of future transportation. It still operates in downtown Seattle.

GM's Firebird III was an experimental car exhibited during the Seattle World's Fair. Instead of a steering wheel, it had a control stick that could steer the car.

The Lunar Roving Vehicle (LRV) was developed at Boeing's Kent facility. It traveled at 10 miles per hour and could carry four times its weight. **Does it look like any vehicles we use on Earth?**

Washington's Aerospace Industry Takes Flight

Once again, war—even a cold war where there was no actual fighting—provided jobs. Aircraft factories and shipyards continued to build planes and ships in case of a Soviet attack. Thousands of workers were able to find good jobs working at Boeing's aircraft plants.

Boeing's greatest growth was during the Cold War. The company expanded its production to include aircraft that could fire missiles. Also, the company began producing space vehicles. During the Vietnam War, Boeing was the main supplier of helicopters to the U.S. military.

Richland was the site of the Hanford Engineer Works atomic energy plant. During the Cold War, plutonium was produced there. **What geographic features shown here were important in selecting the location for the plant?**

●Richland

What Do You Think?

A popular saying at the time was "When Boeing sneezes, Seattle catches cold." What did that mean?

Led by the Boeing Company, Washington State has the largest number of workers in the aerospace industry. In 2005, the industry employed 65,400 workers. Boeing accounted for 89 percent of those workers.

Hanford Nuclear Facility

Hanford had been part of the development of the atomic bomb during World War II. During the Cold War, nuclear fuel for atomic weapons was produced at the Hanford site. In fact, Hanford was the nation's largest producer of plutonium during the Cold War. Plutonium is a key ingredient in nuclear weapons.

The town of Richland was proud to be the location for the Hanford facility. Before the plant was built, there were less than 250 residents in Richland. By 1950, there were more than 11,000. Richland called itself "The Atom-Bustin' Village of the West." It celebrated its good fortune annually at the Atomic Frontier Days celebration. The Richland High School sports teams were called the "Bombers." The town's logo and the school's symbol was a mushroom cloud.

Atomic FRONTIER Days

A NEW LIGHT ON THE OLD FRONTIER

RICHLAND WASHINGTON   SEPT. 3-4-5-6   1948

Improved Transportation

The Cold War created a lot of prosperity for Americans. Because many people had good jobs, they could afford automobiles. Families who had moved to the suburbs preferred driving their own cars to work instead of riding city buses. The roads, however, were narrow, and driving was slow. Traveling across town took a long time because drivers had to stop at every traffic light.

The U.S. government began building a national network of superhighways called freeways. They made it easier to travel across the country quickly. President Eisenhower had seen such highways in Germany during the war. He knew they would make it easier to evacuate cities if a Cold War attack ever came.

The Interstate Highway System linked Washington State to the rest of the nation. The new freeways let travelers zoom right past towns and cities without getting off the freeway.

Before he was elected president, Eisenhower was an heroic general who led U.S. troops in Europe during World War II.

Drivers can travel on Interstate 90 into Spokane. **Where else in the state can you travel on I-90?**

What Do You Think ?

What do you think was the impact of the Interstate Highway System on transcontinental railroad travel?

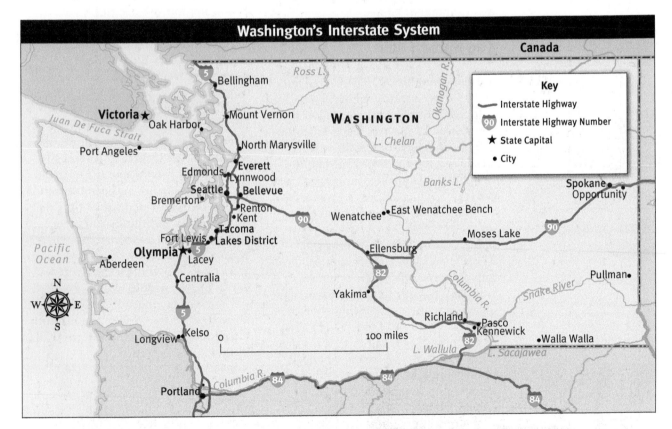

Washington's Interstate System

Washington Comes of Age

U.S. troops returning from Korea are welcomed in Seattle during a homecoming parade. **Are similar parades held today for returning troops?**

Cold War Turns Hot

Although there was no direct fighting between the United States and the Soviet Union during the Cold War, American soldiers battled Communists in other parts of the world. Two hotspots of the Cold War were Korea and Vietnam in Asia. The troops that American soldiers fought were funded and supplied by both the Soviet Union and Communist China.

The Korean War

In 1950, Communist North Korea invaded South Korea. The United States and 15 other nations sent troops to help South Korea defend itself. At first, Americans did not pay much attention to the war. Everyone felt the war would quickly end after four months of fighting. "Home by Christmas!" was the cry.

But the war dragged on for three years. Of the 33,000 American men killed, 528 were from Washington. The war ended in a stalemate. A military *stalemate* occurs when two sides stop fighting but cannot reach an agreement. As a result, the border between North and South Korea is one of the most heavily militarized (having a lot of soldiers and weapons) zones in the world. Thousands of soldiers from both countries still guard their common border.

The Vietnam War

Shortly after American troops left Korea, the United States became involved in another Asian war. This war was in Vietnam. Few Americans even knew where to find Vietnam on a map. They would soon learn, as American troops would be involved there for the next 20 years. Vietnam became America's longest war. Thousands of soldiers trained at military bases in Washington. Washington's young men were drafted and joined other Americans in Vietnam.

The Vietnam War divided Americans. Many people believed the war was wrong. They argued that the Vietnamese people were fighting a civil war that did not concern the United States. Others thought it was the duty of the United States to fight Communism everywhere in the world.

Protest marches and demonstrations against the war were held all over the United States. In Seattle, 500 people walked from the courthouse to where Westlake Plaza is now. One march in downtown Seattle filled the street with nearly 25,000 people.

The war finally ended in 1975. More than 58,000 Americans died in Vietnam. Between two and three million Vietnamese also died.

Postwar Job Losses

Several large Washington industries relied on government war contracts. Many residents depended on those manufacturing jobs to make a living. They built weapons, ships, and planes. After the war finally ended, war materials were no longer needed. Unemployment soared in the Puget Sound region.

The Cold War Ends

The Cold War lasted until 1991. At that time, the Communist governments of the Soviet Union and many other countries in Eastern Europe fell apart. The United States emerged from the Cold War as the world's main superpower.

During the time of the Cold War, the United States dealt with more than Communism. Americans struggled with racial inequality, women's rights, and growing concern for the environment.

Refugees Flee Asia

A wave of refugees fled the war zone to make their home in Washington State. A *refugee* is a person who leaves his or her country during a time of crisis and goes to another country for safety. About 55,000 refugees fled the countries of Southeast Asia because of the Vietnam War. Their lives were changed completely.

Hanh Nguyen was a child in South Vietnam. She remembers her family trying 15 times to escape by boat after the war ended. Her father was imprisoned each time. The government allowed them to leave in 1991. They had to learn a new language and new ways. "We do lose our identity—our language, our culture, ourselves—so we're trying to maintain that," she says.

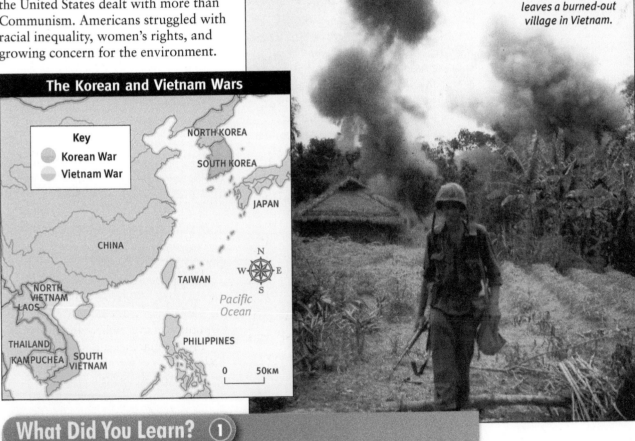

A U.S. marine leaves a burned-out village in Vietnam.

The Korean and Vietnam Wars

Key
- Korean War
- Vietnam War

NORTH KOREA
SOUTH KOREA
JAPAN
CHINA
TAIWAN
Pacific Ocean
NORTH VIETNAM
LAOS
THAILAND
KAMPUCHEA
SOUTH VIETNAM
PHILIPPINES

0   50KM

What Did You Learn? ①

1. How did the G.I. Bill help World War II veterans?
2. Give two examples of what made the Cold War such a tense time for people in Washington?
3. How did Washington's aerospace industry help the United States win the space race?

KEY IDEAS

- Activists all over the country, including Washington, helped bring an end to racial discrimination and segregation during the Civil Rights Movement.

- Latinos, Native Americans, and women also fought for more rights in the years following World War II.

- Today Washington is a multicultural state with a large and growing population of Latinos and Asians.

KEY TERMS

activist
boycott
civil disobedience
feminism
Jim Crow
minority
multicultural
oppressive
segregation

Second-Class Citizens

African Americans fought heroically in both world wars. They helped to free Europe from the control of *oppressive*, or unjustly harsh, governments and dictators. However, back in the United States, black Americans were still second-class citizens.

The U.S. Constitution guaranteed black Americans the same rights as whites, but those rights were largely ignored. In many states, blacks could not vote or run for office. They were not allowed to serve on a jury or testify in court against a white person.

In many Southern states, Jim Crow laws separated the races. *Jim Crow* was the name given to laws that made *segregation* (the separation of races) legal. Jim Crow laws applied to most public places. For example, public schools were segregated—black children could not attend the same schools as white children. Blacks were required to sit in the back of movie theaters and buses. And public parks had separate drinking fountains.

In Washington, like in most other states, blacks experienced discrimination and segregation. They were not welcome in most restaurants or hotels, and they could not use public swimming pools.

Housing Discrimination

Blacks could buy houses only in certain sections of cities, including in Seattle and Spokane. At the Bremerton Navy Base as well as the Hanford Nuclear Reservation, blacks and whites worked together but lived in separate areas.

A Spokane Valley real estate code of ethics said,

> A realtor should never introduce into a neighborhood any race . . . whose presence will [lower] property values in that neighborhood.

Guidelines for an Ephrata neighborhood said,

> No persons other than those of the Caucasian race shall ever occupy any building in this subdivision, except domestic servants . . . employed and living in the building occupied by said owner.

Challenging Inequality

By the 1950s, a movement in the black community began. Blacks began to challenge the inequality they faced. Reverend Martin Luther King, Jr., from Atlanta, Georgia, emerged as the leader of the Civil Rights Movement. He led peaceful protest marches, sit-ins, and boycotts. King and his wife, Coretta, visited Seattle to help efforts in Washington.

The first major victory of the Civil Rights Movement was the Supreme Court's decision in *Brown vs. the Board of Education*. This important ruling declared that segregation in public schools was illegal. Other victories soon followed. Reverend King and his followers challenged segregation on buses during the Montgomery Bus Boycott. A *boycott* is a form of protest where people refuse to buy or use the products or services of an organization whose practices they dislike. For more than a year, blacks refused to ride the buses in Montgomery, Alabama. Their actions resulted in another Supreme Court ruling that banned segregation on public buses.

Black and white citizens march together in a 1965 protest in Seattle. **What are they protesting?**

Civil Disobedience

Civil disobedience is a nonviolent form of protest. It involves peacefully breaking a law to make a point. Martin Luther King, Jr., believed that civil disobedience was the best way to challenge unjust laws. Sit-ins and boycotts are examples of the type of civil disobedience that King and his followers practiced.

Seattle experienced its first sit-in in July 1963 when civil rights activists occupied the mayor's office for 24 hours. The group was protesting housing discrimination. The protest was peaceful, and the protestors left the next morning.

Later that month, however, a group of protestors was arrested after occupying city council chambers for four days. After a councilman tripped and fell over one of the protesters, they were ordered to leave. When they refused, police officers took them to jail.

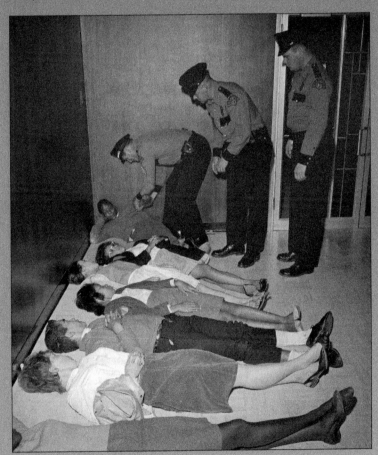

What Do You Think ?

Why do you think nonviolent protests were more effective than violent protests?

Police arrest a group of teens and young adults participating in a sit-in in Seattle's municipal building. **What makes this a nonviolent protest?**

It took a long time, but civil rights activists finally scored several major victories in the 1960s. For example, the U.S. Congress passed the following laws:

- The 1964 Civil Rights Act prohibiting any kind of discrimination in public places
- The 1965 Voting Rights Act that eliminated literacy tests for black voters
- The 1968 Fair Housing Act that prohibited discrimination in the sale or rental of property

Linking the Past to the Present

Many Americans saw the 2008 election of Barack Obama as the nation's first African American president to be the crowning achievement of the Civil Rights Movement.

The Turbulent Sixties

Unrest over civil rights and the war in Vietnam erupted in a wave violence in the 1960s. Among those assassinated were:

- President John F. Kennedy
- Malcolm X, an outspoken African-American leader who did not always agree with King's methods
- Martin Luther King, Jr.
- Senator Robert Kennedy, President Kennedy's brother who was a civil rights advocate and presidential candidate

In Washington, Edwin Pratt, the director of the Seattle Urban League (a civil rights group), was also killed.

Washington PORTRAIT

Carl Maxey
(1924–1997)

Carl Maxey was the first black attorney in Spokane. He worked hard to end discrimination and segregation in the city since he had experienced both as a young man. Before becoming a lawyer, Maxey served in the U.S. Army. He had wanted to become an army pilot, but blacks were barred from joining the air corps at the time.

When he became the city's first black lawyer, Spokane still had no black doctors, dentists, or teachers. He wanted to change that. When the Spokane School District refused to hire an extremely qualified black teacher, Maxey came to his aid. He successfully persuaded the district to change its policy. By 1969, there were 20 black teachers in the Spokane School District.

Maxey also challenged a local barbershop when it refused to serve a black student from the African country of Liberia. Maxey took up the cause after a group of black and white students picketed the barbershop. They carried signs that read: "Prejudice Prevents Progress: Help Spokane Grow." Their protest was shown on national television. The barber was ordered to change his policy as a result of Maxey's persuasive argument to the state's Board of Discrimination.

The Movement Spreads

The Civil Rights Movement was an inspiration to other minority groups in the United States. The term *minority* refers to a group that differs in race, religion, gender, or ethnic background from the dominant group. A minority group sometimes has little power or representation compared to the dominant group.

Mexican Americans and Native Americans both adopted methods similar to black activists and fought discrimination. Women, although not considered a minority in number, also joined in the fight for rights. All three groups had some notable successes.

Uniting Farm Workers

As you read in chapter 7, many Mexicans, also called Chicanos, came to the United States as part of the *Bracero* Program. They came to Washington to harvest crops. Many stayed and settled in the central part of the state. By the 1970s, migrants were coming each year to harvest crops. Many of them settled here permanently. In Othello and other farming towns, Mexican Americans soon made up more than half of the population.

Although they came to the United States to escape poverty in Mexico, the situation here was not much better. Working conditions on the farms were terrible and the pay was very low. By the late 1960s, almost 40 percent of the Mexican farm workers in Yakima County lived in poverty. Organizing a labor union was difficult as migrant farm workers moved around a lot.

Probably the most well-known Mexican-American civil rights leader was Cesar Chavez. Like Martin Luther King, Jr., Chavez believed in nonviolent protest. He founded the United Farm Workers Union and organized a nationwide boycott of California grapes. To show support for striking grape pickers, University of Washington students convinced school officials to stop selling grapes in campus cafeterias. It was the first campus in the United States to do so.

Before the 1970s, Mexican-American citizens in Washington had to prove they could read English before they were allowed to vote. A civil rights group successfully challenged the restrictions in court and won.

Hispanic activist Cesar Chavez founded the United Farm Workers Union. He brought attention to the hardships of migrant farm workers.

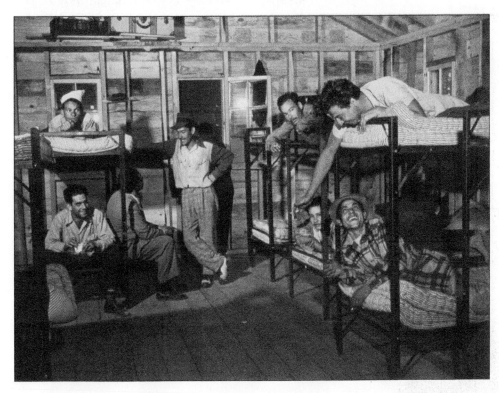

Migrant workers take a break in their barracks. **How would you describe their living conditions?**

Native American Movement

The struggle for rights in the Native American community was different from the struggle of blacks and Latinos. Native Americans were not seeking to be fully absorbed in American society. Instead, they wanted to protect the rights promised to them in treaties. Most important was the protection of tribal sovereignty and fishing rights. Additionally, Indian activists looked to improve conditions on reservations. An *activist* is a person who strongly supports a cause.

After World War II, the government's Indian policies changed again. The goal of the new policies was to move Indians off of reservations and into cities, where they might find better job opportunities. Jobs on the reservation were very limited. But Indians found that life in the city was not easy. They faced discrimination. Good jobs and decent housing were hard to find.

To raise awareness and get some help, Native Americans took over Fort Lawton in 1970. Bernie Whitebear, a member of the Colville Confederated Tribe, organized the protest. After nearly two years of negotiations, the government agreed to create the Daybreak Star Center—a Native American cultural center—on the grounds of the fort.

Fishing Rights

One of the most important court decisions in Washington's history was handed down in Tacoma by federal judge George Boldt in 1974. *U.S. vs. Washington*, or the *Boldt Decision*, has had an enormous impact on Native American rights, salmon management, and state politics. Judge Boldt ruled that fishing restrictions placed on Indians violated the treaties signed in the 1850s.

The ruling restored off-reservation fishing sites to Native Americans. It gave them the right to harvest steelhead, as well as salmon, for food. Non-Indian fishermen were outraged by the decision. Bumper stickers appeared with "CAN JUDGE BOLDT– NOT SALMON!"

One of the biggest issues facing Native Americans today is the decreasing fish population. You will read more about this in the next lesson. However, it is important to note here that nearly a third of the scientists working on salmon issues are Native Americans. Even the smallest tribes have their own scientists and lawyers, and many of them are Native Americans. It is common for half of a tribe's employees to work in natural resources.

Bernie Whitebear organized the protest at Fort Lawton in 1970. One of the signs reads: "Red Power." **What is the main message of the protest?**

The Washington Journey

Wing Luke and his mother visiting an Asian market in Seattle in 1962. Luke was the first Asian American to be elected to public office.

Women's Rights

In the 1970s, another group worked for equal rights. Although women represent about half of the U.S. population and half of Washington's population, they did not enjoy the same rights and advantages as white men.

In most jobs, women were paid less than men. There was a great separation of men's and women's jobs—men were doctors, and women were nurses. Men were business owners, and women were secretaries. School principals were nearly always men. School sports teams were open only to boys. Women had a hard time getting loans or credit cards in their own names.

The national movement for women's rights was called *feminism*, or women's liberation. The goal of the Feminist Movement was to gain equal rights, including equal opportunity.

Across the nation, people worked to add an Equal Rights Amendment (ERA) to the U.S. Constitution. It would guarantee that neither men nor women would be denied any right on the basis of gender. Although Congress passed the ERA, it failed to get approval from enough states to make it a law.

A Multicultural Washington

During the last 30 years, minority citizens and women in Washington have become more involved in government. Today, Washington is a very *multicultural* state. Washington's many ethnic groups make the state a dynamic place to live.

Asian Americans

Before World War II, many Japanese American families farmed in rural areas outside Seattle, Tacoma, and other cities. They grew fruits and vegetables and sold them to city dwellers.

After the war, the Japanese left the relocation camps and returned to their homes. Many found difficult conditions. They had been gone three years, and much had changed. Often their property had been vandalized and strangers were living in their homes.

Some Asian Americans entered politics. Wing Luke was elected to Seattle's City Council in 1963. The son of an immigrant laundryman, Luke was the first Chinese American elected to any office in the state. Luke died in a plane crash a few years later.

A DAY WITHOUT HUMAN RIGHTS IS LIKE A DAY WITHOUT SUN SHINE
THE DAWN OF AN ERA

Although the ERA was never added to the U.S. Constitution, Washington added a similar amendment to its constitution in 1973.

Gary Locke became the nation's first Asian-American governor when Washington voters elected him in 1996.

Washington's population is becoming more diverse as immigrants from Latin America and Asia continue to move here.

Who Are We Today?

There is a wide diversity of people in Washington today. Immigration, especially from Latin America and Asia, continues to grow. Latinos are the state's largest minority. Immigration of Asian and Pacific Islanders increased 60 percent since the last census. The number of Native Americans increased 20 percent.

Cultural diversity has many faces. People cannot be grouped by a census report alone. In today's world, many people have a mixed racial heritage.

"When I was younger, it was annoying when people would just assume I was Mexican," said Efrain Olivares. "I am from Venezuela. [But,] I just let it go. My wife is from Guatemala. Our neighbors are from Puerto Rico. On the census, we are all Hispanic."

"People make similar assumptions about Asians, the majority of which are Chinese," said Moon Ji. "But there are Japanese, Vietnamese, Koreans, Filipinos, Asian Indians, and others. I wish people would be more culturally sensitive. We are not all alike. We like to explain our culture to people, if they would ask."

Population Facts, 2006		
U.S. Census Data, 2006	Washington	USA
Estimated population	6,395,798	299,398,484
Women	50.1%	50.7%
White persons	84.8%	80.1%
Black persons	3.6%	12.8%
American Indian and Alaska Native	1.6%	1.0%
Asian	6.6%	4.4%
Native Hawaiian and other Pacific Islanders	0.5%	0.2%
Persons of Latino origin	9.1%	14.8%

What Did You Learn? ②

1. Give an example of how each minority group in Washington was affected by discrimination.
2. Identify the civil rights victories won by each minority group in Washington.
3. How do our state's Asian and Latino populations compare to the rest of the country?

Concern for the Environment Grows

In the 1800s, pioneers struggled across the rough terrain of the Oregon Trail. The journey was exhausting as they traveled across huge prairies, climbed snow-capped mountains, and crossed raging rivers. The travelers saw nature as something to be conquered.

One century later, people were discovering that nature was not an enemy to be defeated but a partner that was the source of all life. In the 1960s, astronauts said from outer space: "Earth looks isolated [alone] and very vulnerable [exposed]. Life is sustained only by a thin protective atmosphere."

According to writer Arthur Clarke, "Spaceship Earth" travels through the heavens with an unknown destination. One thing, however, is clear. All the supplies available for the voyage are on board. There will be no opportunity to replenish them. Starting in the 1960s and 1970s, people in Washington and elsewhere became aware of the damage that had been done to the environment.

KEY IDEAS

- The effect of human activity on the environment has been a cause of growing concern in recent decades.

- Urban sprawl, industrial pollution, and nuclear waste are key causes of environmental damage in Washington.

- Pollution, logging, and dams have all contributed to a steep drop in the state's fish population.

KEY TERMS

breach
ecology
ecosystem
leach
pollutant
radioactive

Environmental activists march against deforestation. **What familiar image is on the protestor's sign?**

The Impact of Urban Sprawl

In 1981, Seattle held a nickname contest to replace "Queen City." Promoters hoped to find a name that would lure tourists to the state's largest city. The winner was "Emerald City."

A study showed that only 7 percent of rainy Seattle was covered with plants, compared to 10 percent in Phoenix, the desert capital city of Arizona.

Rush hour traffic clogs the streets and freeways around most major cities.

It seemed perfect for a city where abundant rain helps green plants grow. The name also evoked images of *The Wizard of Oz.*

In 1999, however, satellite photos showed that Seattle's natural tree cover had declined 50 percent in 20 years. When viewed from space, Seattle looked more black than green. Asphalt and concrete had taken over. The effect of urban sprawl was obvious.

Seattle's environmental record since the 1970s is mixed. Lake Washington, which had become polluted with raw human sewage, was cleaned up. The largest problem, however, is still to be solved. Traffic congestion clogs city streets. Car exhaust pollutes the air. Building more freeways does not seem to be the answer.

Residents and tourists feel the frustration of getting from place to place on crowded freeways. Traffic woes are the main reason some people move out of town.

Spokane and Expo 74

Spokane—the smallest city to ever host a world's fair—hosted Expo 74. The fair called attention to a wide range of environmental issues.

The entire community worked together to make Expo a success. Before construction, the site of the fair was an ugly complex of warehouses and railroad tracks along the Spokane River in the heart of the city. The railroad companies were persuaded to donate most of the land. When the fair ended, the site was converted to a downtown park.

Expo's theme, "Progress without Pollution," was appropriate for Spokane. It encouraged the city to stop using the Spokane River as an open sewer, which it had been doing for years. A modern sewage-treatment plant was constructed in time for Expo.

A Spokane resident remembers the river in the 1940s and 1950s:

I lived only a half mile from the river and my friends and I played and fished along its banks. We caught large suckers from the mouths of sewer discharge pipes. Sometimes we fished an area where a large spring entered and we would catch trout, though they would stink up the kitchen if you tried to cook them.

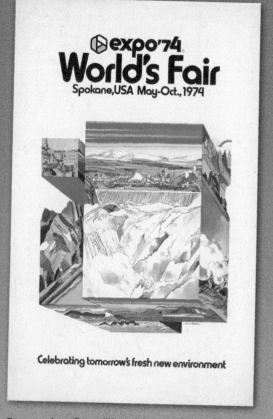

Expo 74 drew five million visitors to Spokane. The fair prompted the city to clean up the Spokane River and replace ugly warehouses with a new park.

Industrial Pollution

Over the years, many of the state's rivers have been polluted with industrial waste. The Spokane River is one example. Heavy metals from mining operations in Idaho's Coeur d'Alene region seeped into the ground and the water underneath. The dissolved metals then made their way into Idaho rivers and lakes. Eventually they flowed into the Spokane River.

The *leaching*, or filtering, of mine wastes through groundwater has increased by massive clear-cuts in the mountains. A clear-cut is a huge land area that was once a forest. The trees and other vegetation were cut down by timber and other industries. Without the trees and ground cover, there is nothing to slow water runoff down a mountain. The excess water and its pollutants get absorbed into the ground. *Pollutants* are waste material that contaminate air, soil, or water.

In the 1970s, lead poisoning from a smelter (a factory where metal is melted) in Idaho produced the highest lead levels in human blood ever recorded. Lead poisoning in children produces serious health problems, including mental retardation.

Large amounts of toxic metals leached from mining operations in Idaho during a severe winter flood in the late 1990s. The cleanup is ongoing. Every day the South Fork of the Coeur d'Alene River carries a ton of dissolved heavy metals downstream. The Coeur d'Alene Indians have sued eight mining companies, the Union Pacific Railroad, and the State of Idaho for polluting the water.

Pollution at Grand Coulee

At first, no one noticed the growing pollution in Lake Roosevelt, the reservoir behind Grand Coulee Dam. Then a U.S. Fish and Wildlife study showed that fish from the lake had high levels of metal.

The Spokane River

In 2001, the Washington Department of Health warned that the Spokane River was the most polluted river in the state. Officials reported that the river is polluted with PCBs. PCBs are cancer-causing chemicals from industrial sites. Fish from the river are a health threat to everyone who eats them, especially pregnant women.

Contaminated water from industrial sites has polluted many of the state's rivers.

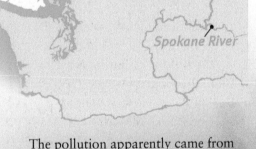

Spokane River

Industrial emissions contribute to air pollution and global warming. **Can you tell if it's a sunny day in this photo? Why not?**

The pollution apparently came from a paper mill and a smelting company in British Columbia. Both these companies dumped all their untreated waste directly into the Columbia River. Public attention prompted the companies to improve their practices.

205

Barrels of hazardous waste are buried in a landfill. **What problems may this cause years from now?**

The Hazards of Hanford

As bad as the upstream pollution is, there is nothing that compares with the problems found downstream at the Hanford nuclear facility. Decades of producing plutonium for nuclear weapons left Hanford one of the most contaminated places on Earth.

At one point there were eight nuclear reactors in operation at the Hanford facility. Water from the Columbia River was used to cool the heat from the reactors. The *radioactive* (something giving off radiation) water was then released back into the river.

Karen Dorn Steele, a reporter with the *Spokesman-Review*, began publishing articles about Hanford's radioactive releases during the Cold War. The stories showed that nuclear tests had released high levels of cancer-causing elements into the atmosphere. The government kept this secret for years.

The toxic waste poisoned animals that grazed in nearby fields as well as fish in the rivers and streams. People were poisoned when they ate the fish or drank milk from contaminated goats or cows. Some people living in the area blame Hanford for causing their cancer and other illnesses.

In 1989, state and federal agencies agreed to a plan for cleaning up stored radioactive waste. It would be the largest and most expensive public works project in American history. Clean-up work provides many jobs as the soil and radioactive waste are removed and stored safely.

Hanford Downwinders

In 1986, about 2,300 citizens who lived downwind of Hanford, called "downwinders," sued the government. They claimed that the toxic waste from Hanford caused them to have cancer and other illnesses. The first of the lawsuits was settled in 2005, when a jury awarded two of the downwinders nearly $300,000 each.

Where Did All the Fish Go?

Biologists believe the Columbia River system once supported 16 million salmon and steelhead a year. Today, fewer than one million fish return from the ocean to spawn each year. About 90 percent of the fish begin life in hatcheries.

Biologists consider hatcheries to be partly to blame for the decline of wild fish. Why? Hatchery fish cannot find their way to natural breeding grounds. Hatcheries can also introduce diseases into fish stocks. Without fish hatcheries, however, there would be a terrible shortage of fish.

Salmon vs. Electricity

Fish runs have declined dramatically because fish habitats have been severely damaged by pollution, careless logging and grazing, and dams.

Before dams were built, rivers were too shallow and fast for barge traffic. Dams, however, hold river water in long reservoirs. The amount of water leaving the dams is controlled. This puts people, instead of nature, in charge of river flow.

Dams also control water that can be used to create hydroelectricity. This provides power to homes and businesses. And dams provide water for crop irrigation in dry regions. The downside, however, is that dams disrupt the natural environment of fish. Dams slow down the natural water flow and increase the temperature of the water. Higher water temperatures can kill fish. Dam turbines (engines) used to produce electricity kill thousands of fish swimming to the ocean.

In 1980, Congress passed the Northwest Power Act. It required that:

Fish and wildlife of the Columbia River Basin . . . be treated on a par with power needs and other purposes for which the . . . dams of the region were built.

This means that there must be a balance between needs of fish and human needs for fish, water travel, and hydropower.

Possible Solutions

Fish ladders have been built on the sides of dams. They aid fish in going upstream to spawn (breed). Water is spilled over the ladders to help salmon and steelhead make their way downstream. Some people, however, want to remove the dams altogether.

Others suggest that a good compromise is breaching of the four dams on the lower Snake River. *Breaching* means that there would be a break or hole in the dams that would allow fish to swim through. This might help the fish population to increase since it would be easier for them to get to their breeding grounds.

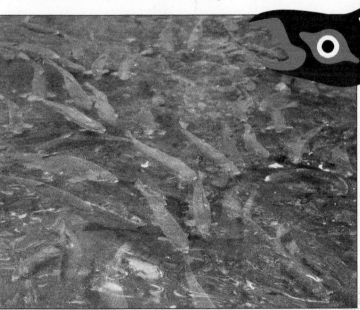

Fish ladders like this one help fish travel upstream to spawn.

Fish hatcheries help increase the fish population. But they cause problems, too. **What problems might result from this many fish in a small space?**

Timber—A Dwindling Resource

Four large Pacific Northwest companies—Weyerhauser, Potlatch, Boise Cascade, and Plum Creek Timber—have harvested trees throughout the Pacific Northwest for years. Many of the logs were sold and exported to Japan. Local lumber mills, which usually processed the logs into lumber, were forced to close as a result.

Timber companies have planted new forests for years. However, the trees will not be ready for harvest for 25 years. The shortage of trees caused timber companies to start cutting trees in national forests. Environmental groups have responded with anger.

Labeled "tree huggers," environmentalists tried to protect the forests. Some environmentalists fought by spiking trees. They hammered long metal spikes into trees so saws would be ruined when loggers tried to cut down trees. Tempers flared.

It's About More Than Trees

Environmentalists argue that the struggle over protecting forests is a lesson in ecology. *Ecology* is the study of the relationship between organisms (plants, insects, animals, humans, etc.) and their environment. Forests are more than just stands of trees. They are complex ecosystems. An *ecosystem* refers to the interaction of living things with their physical environment. Trees filter water and produce oxygen. No tree farm could match the importance to the environment of a mossy old-growth forest. When they are gone, like an extinct animal, it's forever.

Looking to the Future

It is clear that people in Washington and the rest of the world have to face the complex issue of how to both use and save natural resources. Compromise is needed so the earth's limited resources can be shared by all.

What Do You Think?

Commercial lumbering companies cut down trees in the Okanogan National Forest. How do you think this natural resource is being replenished?

Do you think environmentalists were right to spike trees to protect them? Why or why not? What else do you think they could do to protect the forests?

What Did You Learn? ③

1. Give an example of how human activity has had a negative effect on the environment in Washington.
2. How did the activities at Hanford affect people living nearby?
3. How have pollution, logging, and dams hurt the state's fish population?

Go to the Source

Report on Agricultural Workers and Migrants

This report was originally published in December 1963. The final report was submitted to the Governor's Commission on the Status of Women.

Read through the document and answer the questions.

AREA 4 – <u>Coverage of agricultural workers by state and federal labor laws</u>

Agricultural workers are exempt from most of the state and federal laws.

The Fair Labor Standards Act was amended in 1950 to make it illegal for children under 16 to be employed in agriculture while schools were in session. However, as the new amendment began to be enforced, there were many complaints that children who were not allowed to work were being refused admittance at school. School attendance officers, in general, do not make a special effort to get migrant children into schools; many communities have "crop" vacations so schools are closed for all children when the migrants arrive; and many local parents have not wanted the disadvantaged migrant children in the same classes as theirs. When the Wage and Hour and Public Contracts Divisions of the U.S. Labor Department investigated in 1959, they found 4,389 children illegally employed during school hours on 1,749 farms.

    764 or 17%, were 9 years of age or under
    2,352, or 54%, were 10-13 years of age
    1,273, or 29% were 14 or 15 years old.

Of these 4,389 children found illegally employed, 39 per cent were migrants. Agriculture is the only "big business" in the nation today that still employs large numbers of children.

Observe ———— Evaluate ———— Conclude

- List three important facts from the document.

- What evidence from the document helps you know why it was written? Quote from the document.

- Who might be interested in the information presented?

- What can you conclude about life for migrant families at the time this was written?

Comparing and Contrasting

Have you ever done comparison shopping? For example, how do you determine which ice cream to buy? Both choices are vanilla, but one is low fat and the other is sugar-free. How do you make a decision? The ability to compare and contrast information is an important skill . . . and not just in the grocery store! The process of comparing and contrasting can also help you as you read and organize information.

Creating a Chart

A good first step for comparing and contrasting two or more things is to create a chart or graphic organizer like a Venn Diagram. We'll use a chart here to compare Harry Potter books to Harry Potter movies.

Focus on one topic at a time. Fill in your chart with specific examples of similarities and differences. When you have completed the chart, review your observations. Cross out any that don't seem important. Underline the similarities and circle the differences.

Harry Potter Books	Features to Compare	Harry Potter Movies
	Main Characters	
	Plot	
	Important Events	

Organizing Your Writing

There are several ways to organize an essay comparing and contrasting two topics. Let's look at two of them.

1. Similarities-to-Differences: Here you focus on all the similarities first and then you cover the differences. So you could look at all the similarities between the books and the movies with regard to main characters, plots, and important events. Then address all the differences.

2. Point-by-Point: Here you would focus on one point of comparison at a time, such as how a Quidditch game in the Potter books is the same or different from the Quidditch games in the movies. Then move on to another point of comparison.

Transition Words

Your writing will flow better with the right transitions. Transition words help to set up a similarity or a difference. The chart to the right lists some transition words and phrases.

Comparison Words/ Transitions	Contrast Words/ Transitions
also, as, as well as, like, otherwise, in the same matter, in the same way	although, but, however, in contrast, on the other hand, instead

Your Turn

In this chapter you read about the efforts of African Americans, Native Americans, Latinos, and women to achieve equal rights. Select two groups. In what ways were the experiences, goals, and methods of each group similar? In what ways were they different? Start with a chart and then decide what strategy you will use to write about the topics.

Chapter 8 Review

Chapter Review Questions

1. What was the greatest concern of workers after the end of World War II?
2. How did the G.I. Bill help create a "sawdust empire" in Washington?
3. What was the Cold War?
4. What caused the University of Washington to fire three professors?
5. What industries were fueled by the Cold War? How?
6. Create a chart identifying the minority groups who fought for civil rights. In your chart, summarize the goals and accomplishments of each group.
7. What do you think is the biggest environmental challenge facing Washington today? How would you address the problem?

Becoming a Better Reader

Understand the Text

All writers sequence events in a story or in a nonfiction text. Sequence plays an important role in helping the reader move through the text easily. Choose four events from this chapter and write them in sequential order. Then write a paragraph telling about the events in sequential order. Use words like *first*, *next*, *then*, and *finally* to help you organize your writing.

You Are the Geographer

1. Describe how the freeway system has altered the landscape of Washington and contributed to urban sprawl.
2. In what ways have humans disturbed the habitat of fish in Washington?
3. How would you rank the efforts being made to help increase the fish population? Which is the most helpful? Which is the least helpful? Explain your reasoning.
4. What is an ecosystem? How has deforestation affected the Earth's ecosystem?

"*The happy union of these states is a wonder. Their constitution is a miracle. Their example is the hope of liberty throughout the world.*"

— James Madison, 4th president of the United States

Boeing has been one of Washington's largest employers for many years. A completed Boeing 747-400 is ready for delivery to a new customer. The 747 has six million parts. It can seat more than 500 passengers. **How many jet engines does this plane have?**

Modern Washington

How do government and civic responsibility affect the way we live?

Our Government in Action

Chapter 9

As one of the 50 states in the United States, Washington is governed by the federal government and the state government. We follow the rules established by the U.S. Constitution and the state constitution.

Additionally, we all live in cities and towns that have local governments. Each level of government works together to protect our rights and help meet our needs and wants.

As citizens, we all have certain rights and responsibilities. In exchange for protecting our rights and providing for our needs, we all must work to make our nation, our state, and our communities good places to live by being good citizens.

State officials held a competition in 1911 to select the design for the state's government center in Olympia. This architectural drawing of the capitol complex was submitted by the winners. **Why are there so many buildings?**

215

KEY IDEAS

- In the United States, political power is divided between the federal, state, and local governments.

- The principles of our government are spelled out in the U.S. Constitution.

- The separation of powers into three branches is one of the key features of our government.

KEY TERMS

amendment
bicameral
Bill of Rights
checks and balances
democracy
democratic republic
federal system
judicial review
political party
preamble
proportional
republic

Levels of Government

After the United States became a new country, Americans had a big job to do. They needed to create and organize a new government. They wanted to be able to choose their government leaders. They did not want a king or queen to lead the country. Men from each of the 13 states met to discuss what kind of government the new country should have. We often refer to these men as our nation's Founding Fathers.

Our Founding Fathers wanted a government that would be strong enough to hold the country together. They also wanted to be sure that the government did not become too powerful. A limited government could not abuse the rights of the people like England had done. To limit its power, the Founding Fathers divided the new government into three levels.

The **national government** makes decisions that affect everyone in the country. **State governments** make decisions for people in each state. **Local governments** make decisions for people in counties, towns, and cities.

*Among the many responsibilities of government is the construction and maintenance of roads like this one near Seattle. **What does the government need to do to maintain this road?***

The U.S. Constitution

The plan of government developed by our Founding Fathers is the U.S. Constitution. It was created by 55 men who met in Philadelphia, Pennsylvania, for the Constitutional Convention during the hot summer months of 1787.

The Founding Fathers wanted to uphold the ideas of the Declaration of Independence:

- People are born with basic rights.
- The power to govern comes from the people.
- Governments exist to protect the rights of people.

The Constitution says the power to rule the nation comes from the people (not from a king or queen like in England at the time). The people elect representatives to make laws for them. If voters do not like what their representatives are doing, they can elect new ones the next time they vote. In this way, the government gets its power from the people.

Our government could be described as both a *democracy* and a *republic* or even a *democratic republic* because the power to govern comes from the people through their elected representatives.

A *federal system* is a form of government where power is shared. For the United States, this means the federal government shares it power with state and local governments.

Remarkable Facts

Considering the importance of the U.S. Constitution, it is surprisingly brief. The original document is only four pages long and includes about 4,400 words. The U.S. Constitution consists of the *preamble*, or introduction, seven articles (like chapters in a book), and 27 amendments. *Amendments* are changes or revisions. The Constitution is the oldest and shortest written constitution of any major government in the world. It is a model for the constitutions of other countries. More than 100 other countries have used it to create their own constitutions!

When the Constitution was written, most American men were farmers or merchants. Most women worked at home and on family farms. Few men and women had much education. Today, most Americans live in urban areas, work at thousands of different jobs that nearly always include computers, and are educated in public and private schools. In spite of the many changes in the country, the Constitution remains a source of pride and the basis of a government for a free people.

George Washington presides over the signing of the Constitution in 1787. **Can you find Benjamin Franklin in this painting?**

Although the U.S. Constitution limited the power of government, some people were still worried that their rights would not be protected. They wanted to add a list of amendments to the Constitution to guarantee basic rights and freedoms to the American people. The first 10 amendments to the Constitution are known as the *Bill of Rights*. The Bill of Rights says our government cannot make laws that take away our rights, like freedom of speech or freedom of religion.

1st Amendment
- Freedom of speech
- Freedom of the press
- Freedom of religion
- Freedom of assembly
- Right to petition the government

2nd Amendment
- Right to bear arms: You can own guns for hunting and other legal activities.

3rd Amendment
- Protection against housing soldiers in civilian homes

4th Amendment
- Protection against unreasonable search and seizure
- Protection against the issuing of warrants without probable cause

5th Amendment
- Protection against:
  - Trial without a formal accusation
  - Being tried twice for the same crime
  - Self-incrimination
  - Property seizure

6th Amendment
- Right to a speedy trial
- Right to be informed of charges
- Right to be confronted by witnesses
- Right to call witnesses
- Right to a legal counsel

7th Amendment
- Right to trial by jury

8th Amendment
- Protection against:
  - Excessive bail
  - Excessive fines
  - Cruel and unusual punishment

9th Amendment
- Rights granted in the Constitution shall not infringe on other rights.

10th Amendment
- Powers not granted to the Federal Government in the Constitution belong to the states or the people.

Separation of Powers

One of the most important features of our government is the separation of powers. Our government separates power among three branches of government. Each branch has its own responsibilities and limits the power of the other two. This system of *checks and balances* makes sure that no single branch becomes too powerful.

The three branches of government are the executive, legislative, and judicial branches. On the national level, the three branches are often referred to as the President, Congress, and the Supreme Court.

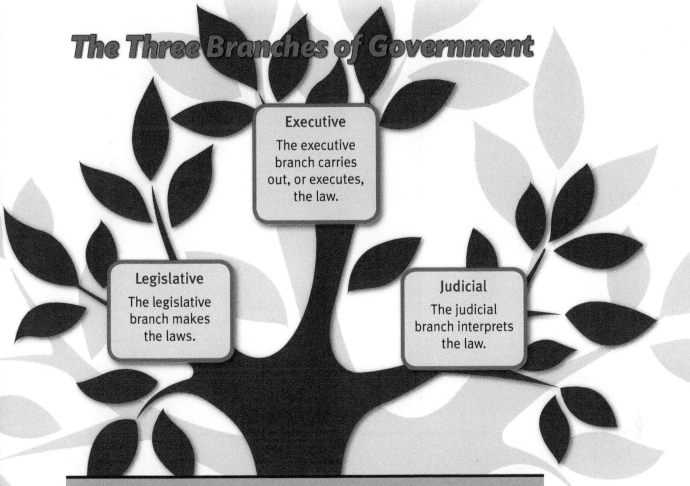

The Three Branches of Government

Executive
The executive branch carries out, or executes, the law.

Legislative
The legislative branch makes the laws.

Judicial
The judicial branch interprets the law.

Governing Principles

The U.S. Constitution is based on six governing principles:

- Popular Sovereignty: Rule by the people.
- Limited Government: The people limit the power of the government.
- Separation of Powers: The government's power is divided into three branches to limit the power of any one branch.
- Checks and Balances: Each branch of government keeps an eye on the others so that no one branch becomes too powerful.
- Judicial Review: The job of the Supreme Court is to review laws to ensure that they are not unconstitutional.
- Federalism: This is the idea of shared power between the national and state governments.

U.S. senators meet in the Senate chamber on Capitol Hill in Washington, D.C. **Why do you think the room is set up like a classroom?**

The Legislative Branch

Article 1 of the Constitution describes the legislative branch of government:

> *All legislative powers herein granted shall be vested in a Congress of the United States, which shall consist of a Senate and House of Representatives.*

Because the legislative branch has two houses, it is referred to as a *bicameral* legislature. Voters in each of the 50 states elect people to represent them in the two houses of Congress.

THE SENATE

Each state has equal representation in the Senate. This means that states with large populations have the same number of senators as states with small populations. Each state has two senators.

For example, Washington with 6.2 million people in 2006 has the same number of senators as Wyoming with 510,000 people (the state with the smallest population in 2006).

THE HOUSE OF REPRESENTATIVES

The number of people elected to the U.S. House of Representatives is *proportional*. This means that the number of representatives that each state has is based on population. States with large populations have more representatives than states with small populations. As a result, California, which has the most people, has 53 representatives in the House. On the other hand, Wyoming only has one representative. In 2006, Washington had nine representatives. If our population changes a lot, that number may change.

Even though together the Senate and the House are called Congress, representatives to the House are usually called congressmen and congresswomen. Members of the Senate are called senators.

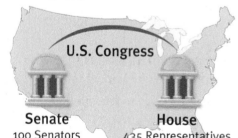

U.S. Congress

Senate
100 Senators
(Two from Washington)
Six-year term

House
435 Representatives
(Nine from Washington)
Two-year term

The Executive Branch

The president of the United States heads the executive branch. The vice president, cabinet, and hundreds of appointed offices and agencies support the president.

How is the president elected? People in all the states vote for the president. However, the president is not elected by this popular vote. Instead, the Constitution created the Electoral College to vote for the president.

Each state shall appoint . . . a number of electors, equal to the number of Senators and Representatives . . .

—U.S. Constitution, Article 2, Section 1

Therefore, Washington's 11 electoral votes all go to one candidate. This means that if 60 out of each 100 Washington citizens voted for Mrs. Blue, and 40 out of each 100 voted for Mr. Red, all of Washington's Electoral College votes would go to Mrs. Blue, and probably none would go to Mr. Red.

In fact, electors are not legally bound to vote for anyone. They can vote for whomever they want, but they nearly always cast their vote for the person who won the popular vote.

Linking the Past to the Present

There have been four times when the winner of the presidential election did not actually win the popular vote. In 1876, Democratic candidate Samuel Tilden won the popular vote by at least 250,000 votes. However, the Electoral College supported Republican Rutherford B. Hayes. Hayes became president. In 2000, Democrat Al Gore received about 500,000 more popular votes than Republican George W. Bush. But Bush edged out Gore by five electoral votes to become president.

Vice President Al Gore debates Texas Governor George W. Bush at the University of Massachusetts during the 2000 presidential election.

The U.S. Capitol in Washington, D.C., is where congressmen and senators make the nation's laws.

Washington PORTRAIT

William O. Douglas
(1898–1980)

William O. Douglas became the only justice of the U.S. Supreme Court from the Pacific Northwest. His father was a minister who brought his wife and young children to eastern Washington. His father died shortly after arriving in Washington. Young William grew up in Yakima. As a child, he suffered from polio and had trouble walking. Determined to fight his disability, he took long, slow, painful hikes.

Douglas grew up and became a high school teacher in Yakima but quit to attend law school in New York. He hitchhiked east, hopping freight trains, and arrived in New York with six cents.

After graduating from law school, Douglas held several important positions in government. He worked closely with President Franklin D. Roosevelt, who appointed Douglas to the Supreme Court. He served longer than any other justice in history.

In addition to Douglas's respect for law, he strongly supported conservation and the environment. He spent his summers in Goose Prairie, about 25 miles from Mt. Rainier National Park. The William O. Douglas Wilderness in the Cascade Mountains was named in his honor.

The Judicial Branch

The U.S. Supreme Court is the highest court in the land. Its nine judges determine if laws made by Congress are constitutional. This process of interpreting the law is called *judicial review*. For example, in the *Brown* decision that you read about in chapter 8, the Court ruled that segregation in public schools was unconstitutional. That ruling overturned state laws that required separate schools for black children and white children. The decisions of the Supreme Court can be very far reaching.

Unlike the legislative and executive branches, Supreme Court judges are not elected officials. The president appoints them. As part of the system of checks and balances, Congress must approve of judicial appointments.

What Do You Think?

Why do you think Supreme Court judges are appointed and not elected to their position?

This is the front of the U.S. Supreme Court building in Washington, D.C. **What are the main features of this building?**

The Washington Journey

Political Parties

Our Constitution does not provide for political parties, but they have become important to our government. A *political party* is a group of people with similar political ideas who organize to gain and exercise political power. Political parties work to get members of their party elected to office. Most people in Washington and the rest of the United States belong to either the Democratic Party or the Republican Party. There are also third parties, such as the Socialist Party, Libertarian Party, Green Party, and Reform Party. Some citizens run for office or vote as Independents. They do not belong to any party.

In 10 presidential elections starting with 1972, Washington voters appeared to lean toward the Democratic Party. Many Washington voters say that party membership does not influence their voting. Instead, they make voting decisions based on their views of the key issues.

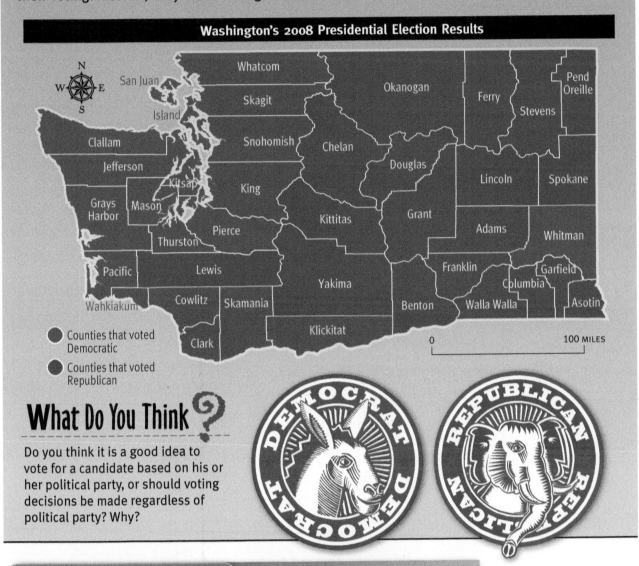

Washington's 2008 Presidential Election Results

- Counties that voted Democratic
- Counties that voted Republican

0   100 MILES

What Do You Think ?

Do you think it is a good idea to vote for a candidate based on his or her political party, or should voting decisions be made regardless of political party? Why?

What Did You Learn? ①

1. Identify the three levels of government in the United States today.
2. Describe two of the six principles on which the U.S. Constitution is based.
3. What is the main job of each branch of the national government?

KEY IDEAS

- Our state government has broad powers to make laws and institute policies for the people of Washington.

- Counties, cities, and towns have governments that oversee local issues and provide services for residents.

- Washington's Indian tribes have their own governments that can make laws separate from the state and local governments.

KEY TERMS

bill
debate
legislator
municipality
ordinance
override
resolution
veto
violate

Washington's Government

The 10th Amendment to the U.S. Constitution is very important. It states that the national government has only the specific powers given to it by the Constitution. All other powers remain with the states or the people. This gives states broad powers. As a result, all states must have their own constitution outlining the structure of the state government and its laws. Recall from chapter 4 that Washington's constitution was adopted in 1889, and it is much longer than the U.S. Constitution.

The State Legislature

Like the federal government, our state government includes three branches. However, the state legislature makes laws only for the state of Washington. The state legislature is bicameral—just like the U.S. Congress. There is a state senate and a state house of representatives. Washington is divided into 49 districts of about equal population. Each district sends one senator and two representatives to the state legislature in Olympia. The legislature meets in January each year and stays for a minimum of 60 days. Because the legislature is not in session all year, many of the members have other jobs. Sometimes the governor calls special sessions. When

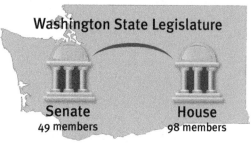

Washington State Legislature

Senate
49 members

House
98 members

this happens, *legislators* (lawmakers) must return to Olympia. Legislators are paid a salary for their work as representatives of the people.

Legislative Responsibilities

The legislature oversees:

- **Tax policies:** Legislators determine what to tax and how much the tax will be.
- **Spending:** Legislators decide what the state will spend tax money on.
- **Business and trade:** Legislators make policies that govern the conduct of business and regulate trade within the state.
- **Local governments:** Legislators oversee the activities of local governments and give authority to counties and towns.
- **State constitution:** Legislators can amend the constitution when necessary.

Committees

The work of the legislature is done in committees. Both political parties appoint members to serve on various committees. All legislators serve on more than one committee. Committees review proposed laws before they are sent to the full house of representatives or senate for a vote.

National
The United States

State
Washington

Local
Your County, City, or Town

This photo shows Washington's state capitol building in Olympia. **How is it similar to the U.S. Capitol shown on p. 221?**

How a Law Is Made

1 A *bill* is a written proposal for a law. Anyone can suggest an idea to a legislator. But only legislators can introduce a bill to the state legislature.

2 Once the bill is drafted, the legislator sponsoring it presents it to either the senate or house. The bill is given a number and read aloud. The bill then goes to a committee.

Committee Rooms

3 The committee reviews the bill. If it is approved, the bill moves on to a hearing. Any interested person can testify for or against the bill. After the hearing, amendments can also be made to the bill. The committee can let the bill "die" by not taking further action.

4 If the committee sends the bill on, it goes to the rules committee and gets on the calendar to be discussed on a certain day. Legislators *debate*, or discuss, the bill and then vote.

VOTING BOARD

House Bill 22		
Representative	YES	NO
ADAMS	●	○
ANDERSON	○	●
BOYER	○	●
COLLINS	○	●
DAVIS	●	○
EDWARDS	○	●
FARMER	●	○
FRANKLIN	●	○
GAINES	○	●
GODDARD	●	○
HANSEN	○	●
HARRIS	○	●
HUGHES		

5 If legislators pass the bill, it is reviewed once more by the rules committee. Once it leaves the rules committee, it goes for a final vote before either the house or senate.

6 When the bill is passed by one of the houses, it moves on to the other house. The bill must then go through the same process.

Governor's Office

9 The governor can also *veto*, or reject, the entire bill or parts of it. However, the legislature can *override*, or cancel, the governor's veto. To do this, a two-thirds majority of both houses is needed. This is one of the checks and balances of power—neither the legislative nor executive branch can make a law alone.

7 Once the bill is accepted by both houses, it is signed by their leaders and is sent to the governor. At this point, citizens can contact the governor to voice their opinion on the bill.

8 The governor reviews the bill. If the governor signs the bill, it becomes a law. If the governor does nothing, the bill becomes a law in five to 10 days.

Equal Rights Amendment

In 1972, Washington voters approved a state Equal Rights Amendment (ERA). Washington's 61st Amendment reads: "Equality under the law shall not be denied or abridged on account of sex." The effort to have a national ERA failed, however. Therefore, in Washington, women have more protection under state law than federal law.

Linking the Past to the Present

Washington women have come a long way since winning the vote in 1910. In 1976, Washington voters elected Dixy Lee Ray as the state's first female governor. In 2004, Chris Gregoire was elected the state's second female governor. Both of Washington's U.S. senators are women—Patty Murray and Maria Cantwell. There are more than 40 women currently serving in the state legislature.

Dixy Lee Ray, a marine biologist, was Washington's first female governor and one of the first female governors in the nation. She was elected in 1976.

The Amendment Process

At times the legislature has found it necessary to amend the state constitution. This has happened 98 times since the constitution was adopted in 1889. The most recent amendment was made in 2006. The amendment process involves a two-thirds vote by each house of the legislature, followed by a majority vote of the people in a general election.

Some amendments have had great influence on the state's history. Probably the most important of these is the 7th Amendment, adopted in 1912. This provided for the initiative and referendum, which you read about in chapter 6. These measures of "direct democracy" allow voters to approve or reject laws passed by the legislature (referendum) or pass laws themselves (initiative). After securing a required number of signatures, a measure goes on the public ballot at the next general election.

The Executive Branch

The chief executive of a state is the governor. The following are among the governor's main duties:

- Hiring a staff of hundreds of people
- Presenting the legislature with the "State of the State" (a report of how the state is doing and what the governor's plans are for the next year)
- Commanding the Washington State National Guard
- Submitting bills to the legislature
- Signing bills into law

Washington's governor has a power the president does not have. Our governor may veto an entire bill or use a "line-item veto" for single sections of a bill.

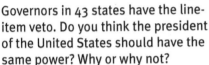

What Do You Think?

Governors in 43 states have the line-item veto. Do you think the president of the United States should have the same power? Why or why not?

After a powerful storm swept through Washington in 2007, Governor Gregoire called on the National Guard to help rescue people, deliver supplies, and control traffic. **How is the National Guard helping in this photo?**

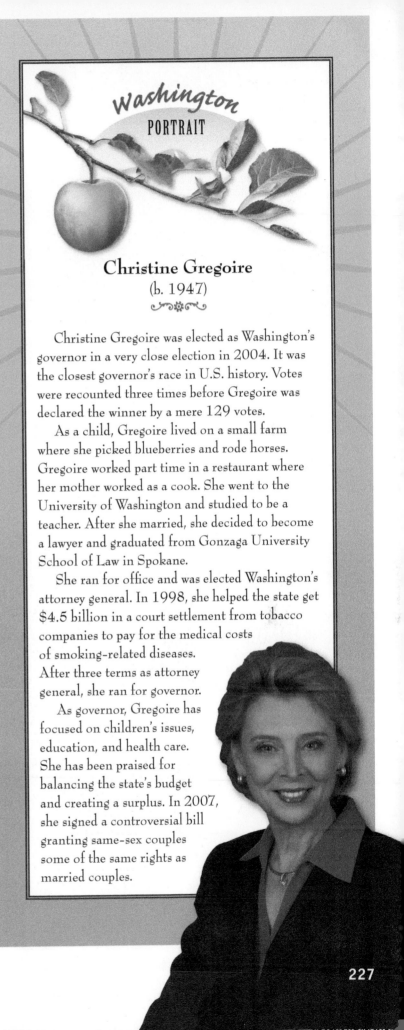

Washington PORTRAIT

Christine Gregoire
(b. 1947)

Christine Gregoire was elected as Washington's governor in a very close election in 2004. It was the closest governor's race in U.S. history. Votes were recounted three times before Gregoire was declared the winner by a mere 129 votes.

As a child, Gregoire lived on a small farm where she picked blueberries and rode horses. Gregoire worked part time in a restaurant where her mother worked as a cook. She went to the University of Washington and studied to be a teacher. After she married, she decided to become a lawyer and graduated from Gonzaga University School of Law in Spokane.

She ran for office and was elected Washington's attorney general. In 1998, she helped the state get $4.5 billion in a court settlement from tobacco companies to pay for the medical costs of smoking-related diseases. After three terms as attorney general, she ran for governor.

As governor, Gregoire has focused on children's issues, education, and health care. She has been praised for balancing the state's budget and creating a surplus. In 2007, she signed a controversial bill granting same-sex couples some of the same rights as married couples.

These are the nine justices of Washington's supreme court. Back row from left to right: James Johnson, Susan Owens, Mary Fairhurst, Debra Stephens. Front row from left to right: Richard Sanders, Charles Johnson, Chief Justice Gerry Alexander, Barbara Madsen, Tom Chambers.

Washington's Court System

THE SUPREME COURT
- Administers the state court system
- Hears appeals from the Court of Appeals

COURT OF APPEALS
- Hears appeals from lower courts except those in the jurisdiction of the Supreme Court

SUPERIOR COURT
Handles the following matters:
- Civil matters
- Domestic relations
- Felony criminal cases
- Juvenile matters
- Appeals from courts of limited jurisdiction

COURTS OF LIMITED JURISDICTION
Handle the following matters:
- Minor criminal cases
- Traffic, non-traffic, and parking violations
- Domestic violence protection orders
- Civil actions of $50,000 or less
- Small claims

Executive Officers

There are a number of people who work within the state's executive branch. They are all elected officials.

- The **Lieutenant Governor** is similar to that of the vice president. If the governor is unable to finish a term, the lieutenant governor would replace him or her. The lieutenant governor acts in the place of the governor if the governor is out of the state or temporarily unable to do the job. Also, the lieutenant governor serves as president of the state senate.
- The **Secretary of State** runs state elections, registers corporations, and maintains records.
- The **Treasurer** manages the state's finances.
- The **Auditor** prepares the state's financial records.
- The **Attorney General** acts as the state's chief lawyer. He or she gives legal advice to members of the executive branch.
- The **Superintendent of Public Instruction** oversees public schools, state education standards, and funding for education.
- The **Commissioner of Public Lands** heads the Department of Natural Resources. He or she manages state-owned lands, forests, and water.
- The **Insurance Commissioner** regulates insurance companies and serves as the state fire marshal, setting safety standards and investigating fires.

Judicial Branch

The judicial branch determines exactly what the laws mean. Judges can overturn laws that *violate* (go against) the U.S. Constitution or the state constitution.

The highest court in Washington is the state supreme court. It is made up of nine judges, each elected by state voters. Judicial candidates run for election without being sponsored by any political party. Below the state supreme court are lower courts.

Local Governments

In addition to the federal and state government, Washington citizens are governed by local governments. Local governments include counties, cities, and towns. The power of a local government is divided much like it is on the federal and state level.

County Government

Washington is divided into 39 counties. One town in each county is the county seat where the county government is located. Each county is run by three county commissioners. They are elected to four-year terms.

The job of a county commissioner includes:

- Creating and adopting the county budget
- Imposing and collecting taxes
- Making spending decisions
- Enacting ordinances
- Issuing *resolutions* (formal statements)
- Negotiating government contracts
- Adopting land-use policies and rules for development
- Making appointments to advisory committees
- Supervising county road construction and maintenance

Depending on the county, commissioners may also serve on other county boards, such as the county health board or public transportation board.

Washington's two largest counties—King and Pierce—are ruled by a county executive and a council.

What Do You Think ?

Most of Washington's counties have just a county commission that acts as both the executive and legislative branches. Why do you suppose Washington's two largest counties have a county executive and a council?

The Lincoln County Courthouse in Davenport. Counties have district courts that handle civil and criminal matters.

Municipal Government

Washington has about 270 municipal governments. A *municipality* can be a city or a town. Each is governed by one of the following:

- Mayor and city council
- City manager and city council
- Commissioners

The city council acts as a legislative branch while the mayor or city manager acts as the chief executive.

Both counties and cities make laws called *ordinances*. They also collect tax money and spend it on services for citizens.

City governments usually provide services only to people living in the city. They may provide police and fire protection, water, sewage, streets, libraries, and hospital services.

State and Local Government Organization			
	Executive	**Legislative**	**Judicial**
State	Governor	State Senate, State House of Representatives	Washington Supreme Court, Court of Appeals
County	County Executive	County Commissioners	Superior Court, Juvenile Court, District Court
City or Town	Mayor and/or City Manager	City Council	Municipal Courts
Tribal	Chairperson	Tribal Council	Tribal Courts

Indian Sovereignty

The issue of Indian sovereignty—freedom from outside control—is particularly important in Washington, where there are 30 tribes. In Oregon, by comparison, there are only nine tribes.

Congress gave additional powers to Indian tribes when it passed the Indian Self-Determination and Education Assistance Act in 1975. The new law gave Indian tribes more sovereignty. Also, the government promised to improve the quality of education on reservations.

The New Buffalo

Since Indian sovereignty means tribes on a reservation can make many of their own laws, some tribes run gambling casinos. This is against the law in other parts of the state.

The "new buffalo" is the term used for tribal gambling operations. Long ago, buffalo supplied the needs of Native Americans. Today, casinos are helping modern Native Americans by creating jobs.

Casinos, however, have triggered sharp criticism. Non-Indians point out that they do not have the same right to open casinos. Some Native Americans worry about the influence gambling will have on tribal youth.

So far, however, tribes believe the results of casinos are mostly good. The Spokane, Tulalips, and Coeur d'Alene tribes have reduced unemployment and funded social programs. The Tulalips have used casino profits to build retirement homes for their elders. The small Kalispel tribe has opened a casino just west of Spokane. The Kalispels have suffered generations of extreme poverty and unemployment. Most tribal members believe the "new buffalo" has arrived.

The Spokane, Coeur d'Alene, Tulalip, and other tribes have opened gambling casinos. Why are the casinos called the "new buffalo"?

Tribal Government

Tribal governments are separate from state and local governments. Tribal governments can make their own laws. Members of the tribe vote to elect their leaders and decide how the tribal government will be run. Then, the leaders meet in a tribal council to make laws. These laws may or may not be the same as the laws and rules of the state government.

In one example, the Spokane, Tulalip, and other tribes have opened gambling casinos. Gambling is against the law in the rest of Washington. The tribal leaders opened the casinos to make money and provide jobs for the people of the tribe.

Tribal Law

Tribal councils are also made up of representatives. They make policies and laws for the whole reservation.

The leaders of the Yakima Reservation, for example, banned drinking alcohol inside the reservation. Drinking alcohol is not against the law in other parts of Washington. However, the Yakimas said alcohol abuse was a serious problem. There were many deaths caused by drunk drivers. There were many family problems when family members drank alcohol.

What Did You Learn? ②

1. What are the similarities and differences between our state government and the federal government?
2. List five responsibilities of county and municipal governments.
3. How are tribal governments different from the state and local governments?

Government Services

National, state, and local governments do more than make laws and enforce them. They do more than tax people. Governments establish agencies that regulate many activities of the citizens and provide services.

State and local governments collect taxes to pay for public education, roads, police and fire protection, libraries, public health services, employment services, state parks, welfare support, and even sports stadiums. Washington State helps the unemployed, disadvantaged children, the elderly, disabled people, and the mentally ill get cash for food, clothing, and shelter.

Education

Public schools are a government service. Tax dollars are used to pay for school buildings, teachers' salaries, and textbooks. If you attend a private school, however, your parents pay for all or most of your education.

Since state and local tax money is used to pay for public education,

the state legislature can require school districts to do certain things. In 2000, Washington's legislature gave new guidelines that stated that students must attend 180 days of classes each school year. They must meet standards in core subjects—reading, writing, science, social studies, communication, mathematics, and health and fitness.

Washington students can study a wide variety of subjects after high school graduation. The state has five universities, one state college, and 27 two-year colleges. Other schools teach subjects such as auto mechanics, welding, carpentry, secretarial work, and other subjects designed to help people make a living. There are colleges for future dentists, doctors, and nurses.

What Do You Think

- How do government services affect you?
- How might they affect other residents of the state?
- What other services do you think the government should provide?

KEY IDEAS

- Our government not only makes laws but also provides services like public education, road construction, and help for the needy.
- Tax dollars are used to support the services the government provides.
- Taking part in our government is both a right and a responsibility.

KEY TERMS

ballot
civics
graduated
   income tax
levy
lobby
poll watcher
uniform tax

Tax dollars are used to fund the construction of new public schools like the one pictured here. **Besides educating students, how might the community benefit from the construction of a new school?**

Each year Americans must file federal income taxes using one of the forms pictured here. **Does Washington have a similar income tax form?**

Even though Washington residents don't pay a state income tax, they must still pay a federal income tax.

Seahawks Get a New Stadium

One example of how the state government and its citizens work together is the construction of Qwest Field and Events Center. The stadium was built for the Seattle Seahawks football team and Seattle Sounders soccer team. Citizens gave the green light for the project in 1997 when they approved Referendum 48. In supporting the referendum, the public agreed to provide $300 million of public money (tax dollars) to finance the new stadium.

The vote on the new stadium was close. It took a promise from Microsoft's cofounder, Paul Allen, to buy the Seahawks, keep them in Seattle, and pledge $100 million of his own money toward building the new stadium. Additionally, he donated $10 million to the state for youth and community athletic facilities.

In order to build the new stadium, the old Kingdome had to be demolished. About 97 percent of the concrete from the Kingdome was recycled and used in other construction projects, including the new stadium.

Qwest Field arena is home to the Seattle Seahawks and Seattle Sounders. **Why do you think this location next to the interstate was selected as the site for the new stadium?**

Tax Policy

The government must have revenue (money coming in) to pay for the services it provides. It gets the revenue from imposing taxes.

How does the government get the tax revenue it needs? One of the most important parts of our state constitution reads: "All taxes shall be uniform upon the same class of property. . . ."

Income Tax

During the Great Depression, the state legislature passed a law authorizing both a corporate and an individual income tax. The taxes were based on a graduating scale, which means people with lower incomes pay less tax, and people and businesses that make more income pay more taxes.

However, Washington's supreme court ruled that a **graduated income tax** is not uniform. A **uniform tax** would be a tax that is the same for everyone. Therefore, the court ruled that the income tax was unconstitutional. This means that residents in our state do not pay a state income tax.

So, how does Washington get the money it needs? In 1935, when the Depression was still a part of American life, Washington lawmakers created a tax system that is still used today. Taxes are **levied** (charged) on property (homes and land), retail sales (items bought in stores), public utilities (electricity, gas, water, and sewer), tobacco, and alcohol.

Other than the state lottery, adopted in 1983, there has been no major change in Washington's tax system since 1935.

Our Civic Duties

Civics is the branch of political science that deals with the rights and duties of citizens. Citizens have a responsibility to take part in government. Adults get to choose who will lead the country, their state, and their community. They do this by voting in elections. People who are citizens of the United States and who are at least 18 years old can vote.

Voting is a very important privilege. Voters can influence government by voting for representatives and leaders who support the issues that are important to them. If elected officials don't do the job voters elected them to do, they may be replaced in the next election.

Volunteering in Your Community

Some people help their communities by being volunteers. Volunteers help elderly people take care of their homes. Some volunteers also help people learn to read, or they may volunteer to walk or feed the animals at a local shelter. What kind of volunteer work have you done?

Rights and Responsibilities

Right	Responsibility
You can vote when you are 18 years old.	You should learn about the candidates and issues.
You get to help make the laws.	You must obey the laws.
You have the right to meet with any group you choose as long as the group doesn't hurt others.	You should respect those same rights for other people.

Citizens wait in line for an available voting booth on election day. **What measures are being taken to protect the privacy of voters?**

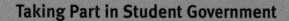

Taking Part in Student Government

My name is Elena, and I am in seventh grade. There was a problem at our school. The dirt path to our school was too narrow and close to a busy road. It was dangerous to walk to school. I thought a sidewalk would make the route to school safer.

I talked with my teacher about this problem. She said I should run for student government so that I could try to get the money for the sidewalk.

I ran for student government, and I actually won a seat! I talked with the other members of the student government about my idea for the sidewalk. The council voted to go forward with a plan to get money to build the sidewalk.

A teacher helped us fill out paperwork to get help from Washington's Department of Transportation. The state gave us the money for the sidewalk and then the county roads department did the work.

I learned that if you see a problem in your community, instead of giving up, you can sometimes get the government to help you. The government is here to serve us— the people.

Voter Registration

At least a month before a citizen can vote for the first time, he or she must register to vote. This is so people don't vote in different places or more than once in the same election. Thanks to "motor voter" laws, in many states a person can register to vote when applying for a driver's license.

Citizens are eligible to vote when they turn 18. Registered voters are then assigned a polling place, a place to vote on election day.

On election day, *poll watchers* (the people who monitor voting) have a list of registered voters. Registered voters must check in with the poll watcher. Once a voter has checked in, he is given a ballot. The *ballot* is a piece of paper, a ticket, or a card used to vote. Voting in the United States is by secret ballot, meaning your vote is private. As a result, voting is often done in booths with curtains so that no one can see how a person votes.

It is important for citizens to vote when elections are held. It is even more important that they know as much as possible about the political parties, the candidates, and any amendments or initiatives they will be voting on. There is always a lot of information in newspapers around voting time.

Democrats gather after a debate during the 2008 presidential primaries. From left to right is Barack Obama, Christopher Dodd, John Edwards, Dennis Kucinich, Joe Biden, Bill Richardson, and Hillary Clinton. **Who did Democrats choose as their candidate? Who won the general election?**

Students from a local school organized a clean-up day in their community.

Citizens can do more than elect people to office. There are many other ways for citizens to be involved in government. For example, citizens can do the following:

- Give ideas for laws to their legislators. Many ideas for bills start this way.
- Attend a public hearing on the day the bill is debated. It is a good idea to bring as many people as possible to the meeting. Legislators may ask citizens to share their experiences.
- Call or write to the governor's office to give an opinion on signing or vetoing a bill.

Although you are not yet 18, here are some things you can do to participate in and learn more about how government works:

- Ask adults in your family to vote.
- Volunteer to work on a campaign.
- Write a letter to the editor of the local paper to get attention for an important issue.
- Organize a mock presidential election in your school.
- Start a Model Congress club in your school.
- Participate in a Model United Nations.

"Never doubt that a small group of thoughtful, committed citizens can change the world; indeed, it's the only thing that ever has."

—Margaret Mead

Parents Lobby for Becca Bill

In 1993, the body of 13-year-old Rebecca Hedman was found along the bank of the Spokane River. She was a runaway who had been beaten to death by a man who picked her up on a Spokane street. Hedman had repeatedly run away from her foster parents and was addicted to drugs. At the time of her murder she had run away from a drug treatment center.

The tragic story prompted her parents and others to *lobby* (to try to influence lawmakers to take a specific action) the state legislature to change laws concerning runaways. The result was the Becca Bill. The Washington state legislature passed the law in 1995. The law's main purpose is to "protect, treat, and stabilize children while empowering parents." The law allows parents to request that a runaway be taken to a counseling center and held there. Under an old law, runaways had to agree to go to a counseling center. The Becca Bill enables parents of runaways under 18 years old to get their child into treatment without the child's consent.

How Can You Serve Your State?

You might think about applying to serve as a page in the state legislature. Pages help legislators and staff with tasks while the legislature is in session. Student pages work for one week and are paid. Pages must:

- Have a grade point average of C+ or better
- Get parent's/guardian's permission
- Get permission from school
- Be sponsored by a state senator
- Be between 14 and 17 years old

To request an application or find out more, contact the senate security office at the following address:

P.O. Box 40482
Olympia, WA 98504-0482
(360) 786-7560

A page distributes papers for lawmakers before they arrive for a legislative session.
What other tasks do you think the page helps with?

What Did You Learn? ③

1. Identify three services that our national, state, or local government provides.
2. Why do Americans pay taxes?
3. How can you participate in government even if you are not old enough to vote?

Go to the Source

A Resolution in Stevens County

One of the responsibilities of county commissioners is to pass resolutions. A resolution is an official statement of policy, opinion, or intention. Resolutions are passed by many different types of governmental bodies, such as the U.S. Congress, state legislatures, and even international organizations like the United Nations. Examine the resolution passed by the three commissioners of Stevens County.

BEFORE THE BOARD OF STEVENS COUNTY COMMISSIONERS
IN THE MATTER OF INTRODUCTION OF GRIZZLY BEARS
RESOLUTION NO. 20-2003
REQUESTING THAT BRITISH COLUMBIA THOUGHTFULLY RECONSIDER THE INTRODUCTION OF GRIZZLY BEARS

WHEREAS, it is the understanding of Stevens County that the Province of British Columbia is considering the release of grizzly bears near our common border with full knowledge that the natural range of grizzly bears will extend well into the United States. . . .

. . . NOW, THEREFORE, BE IT RESOLVED that this governmental unit of Stevens County makes the following requests to British Columbia, its neighbor to the north:

Stevens County first requests that the Province of British Columbia refrain from the release of grizzly bears in locations where the range of the released bear is likely to extend into our county.

If the Province of British Columbia determines that such release of grizzly bears is necessary, we request that British Columbia obtain, record and transmit, in a timely manner, DNA samples from each released grizzly bear to the Director of the Fish and Wildlife Department. We also request that British Columbia implant each released grizzly bear with a microchip containing, at a minimum, the date and location of original capture, the date and location of any release, and DNA tracking information specific to that individual grizzly bear. We request that DNA samples and documentation recording each of the actions described above be transmitted in a timely manner to the Director of the Washington State Fish and Wildlife Department.

However, we demand that any grizzly bear identified as Canadian in Washington State be trapped by Washington State Fish and Wildlife Department and sent back north to British Columbia to point of origin or be destroyed here by the Washington State Fish and Wildlife Department.

Passed by the Board of Stevens County Commissioners meeting in regular session at Colville, Washington, by the following vote, then signed by its membership and attested to by its Clerk in authorization of such passage the 11th day of February, 2003.

Observe

- What words or phrases make this document sound official?

Evaluate

- How does this document fit the definition of a resolution? Support your answer with quotes from the document.

Conclude

- What does this document tell you about the job of a county commissioner?
- As a citizen, would you support the resolution? Why or why not?

Preparing for a Debate

Debate is a key feature of our government. Politicians engage in debate regularly. Debate is an important part of lawmaking. When a bill is proposed, legislators debate its pros and cons.

What Is Debate?

Debate is a formal discussion or argument. But it's not the kind of argument where people yell and get angry. Debate can be very emotional and intense, but it is organized and polite.

Debate does not just occur in politics, however. Debating skills are useful in many areas. Good debating skills can help you get a job, increase your pay, purchase a car, or just change someone's mind about an issue.

Many of the issues you read about in this chapter were subject to debate at one time. For example, our Founding Fathers debated about how to organize the legislative branch and whether the president should be elected by the people or through the Electoral College. The Equal Rights Amendment was debated around the country. Although the ERA was not added to the U.S. Constitution, Washington voters were convinced and added an equal rights amendment to the state constitution.

Effective Debating

An effective debate is a lot like an effective essay. A debate has a central argument, or thesis. Facts are used to support the central argument. And there is a conclusion summing up the main points of the central argument. The difference is that an essay is written, while a debate is presented orally.

Research and confidence are keys to effective debating. Here are some additional guidelines to prepare an effective debate.

1. Pick a side to debate.

2. Gather information about the main point (central argument) you support. You will want at least three strong pieces of evidence to support your view.

3. Gather information about the opposite view or views on the topic. Your argument will be more effective if you can point out the weaknesses in the opposing viewpoint.

4. Get to know your position by practicing out loud. This will help build your confidence. An oral presentation is much more convincing if you sound sure of yourself and if you do not read from your notes.

Your Turn

Think of an issue that is of importance to your school, your community, or even the whole country. For example, maybe you want your school to remove soda machines to help students cut back on sugar. Or a major intersection in your town needs a traffic light to reduce accidents. You might even want to debate allowing the president to use the line-item veto. Organize a debate to discuss the pros and cons of your proposal.

Chapter Review Questions

1. Why did the Founding Fathers divide the government into three levels and separate the branches of government?
2. Why does the House of Representatives have more members than the Senate?
3. Give an example of how each branch of government can check the power of the other branches.
4. What are the chief responsibilities of our state legislature?
5. What options does the governor have when a bill reaches his or her desk?
6. How is the "New Buffalo" helping Washington's Indian tribes?
7. List three ways the government uses tax dollars.
8. What do you think is your most important duty as a citizen? Why?

Becoming a Better Reader

Recognize Point of View

You may have heard, "Everyone is entitled to their opinion." While this is true, it is important to base your opinions on facts. Even with the same facts, people will have different opinions. Every person has a different viewpoint on important issues. A viewpoint is the way someone thinks about something. Someone's viewpoint is affected by where they live, how they were raised, by their education, and many other factors. Good readers recognize what is fact or opinion and how opinions are formed based on a person's viewpoint. Choose an idea from this chapter that people have different opinions about. Write a couple of sentences about the idea from two different points of view.

You Are the Geographer

The Geography of Voting

The way people vote often has something to do with where they live. For example, people who live in large cities often vote differently from people who live in rural communities. Why do you think geography plays a role in voting decisions?

Take a look at the map on page 223 of how Washington counties voted in the 2008 presidential election.

1. What geographic features do counties that voted Democratic have in common with each other? What about the counties that voted Republican?
2. How did counties with large populations tend to vote? Why do you think they chose one party over the other?
3. Which county voted differently from the majority of counties in the same region? Why do you think that county voted differently from the others?

Essential
Question?

What is Washington's
role in the national and
global economy?

Our State Economy

People in Washington have always used the land to meet their needs. Even today, our geography and natural resources help us make a living. They affect the kinds of jobs we have in our great state.

People choose to live and work in Washington because it has much to offer. In turn, Washington's workers produce things they can sell all over the world.

The Skagit Valley Tulip Festival is an annual event held every April in Mt. Vernon. **What economic activities might occur during the festival?**

241

What Is Economics?

Economics involves money, business, people, and the government. It has to do with how people in a country make a living and how they interact with each other. It also has to do with how the country interacts with other countries.

Let's just look at the United States. The United States has the largest economy of any single country. That means the United States has the highest *gross domestic product* (GDP) compared to other countries. GDP measures the value of all the goods and services produced by a country in a year. In 2008, the GDP of the United States was estimated to be $14.6 trillion.

How is it possible that the United States produced $14.6 trillion worth of goods and services in one year? We'll need to take a closer look at how the economy works to answer that question. First, let's look at a formal definition of economics. *Economics* is the study of how individuals, businesses, government, and society make choices. Choices about what? The choices made involve how best to use limited resources.

Scarce Resources

The resources of the world are scarce, or limited. Economists look at four types of resources:

- **Land:** All natural resources like forests, water, minerals, and fossil fuels, etc.
- **Labor:** The work of individuals needed to produce goods and services
- **Capital:** The money, tools, machines, and other products needed to make goods and services
- **Management ability:** Comes from a skilled person who combines land, labor, and capital in a way that will make a profit

The basic question of economics is how best to use these scarce resources to meet the needs and wants of society. That's where choice comes in. Since resources are limited, people must make choices about how best to use them.

*Pikes Place Market in Seattle is full of vendors selling many different goods. **What is for sale here?***

A Balancing Act

Consider this: You have $25. You need a new notebook for social studies, a ruler for math class, and a pocket thesaurus for English class. At the same time, you want that new CD. The $25 won't cover it all. You will have to make some choices. You will have to balance your "needs" with your "wants" so that you can use your limited resource ($25) in the best way possible.

Your parents, businesses, and the government are faced with similar decisions every day. How they go about making such decisions is what economics is all about!

Economic Systems

An economic system is a way of producing and selling goods and services. Different countries use different systems, but all economic systems answer three basic questions:

1. What goods should be produced and what services should be provided?
2. How will goods be produced and services provided?
3. Who will buy the goods and services?

The Free Market System

In the United States, we have a *free market system*, also called capitalism. In this kind of system, people, not the government, own most of the companies. Company owners decide what products to produce and sell or what services to provide. They also decide where their company will be located, how much they will charge for their product or service, and who will work for them. In a free market, anyone can start a business and make or sell goods or services.

Although business owners make their own decisions, they must follow government regulations. They can choose not to follow the laws, but then there are consequences!

Consumers must always balance their wants with their needs since money is a limited resource.

Opportunity Costs

Economists use the term *opportunity costs* to describe the trade-offs a person makes when making a decision. For example, the opportunity cost of going to college is the money you would have earned if you went to work instead. Sometimes the opportunity cost is high, and sometimes it is not.

For most people, going to college is worth the opportunity cost of not going to work right out of high school. It is an easy decision to make since college graduates make about 50 percent more money during their lifetime than a person without a college education. However, this is not always the case and some people are willing to take a risk by not going to college or dropping out.

For example, Microsoft founder Bill Gates dropped out of college. For Gates, the opportunity cost for staying in college would have been huge. He had an idea for a business. Waiting until after college to pursue his idea may have cost him a lot. Microsoft may not have been the success that it is today had Gates not taken such a risk.

Businesses are started to provide consumers with goods and services. **Are these cooks providing a good or a service?**

The Business World

Why do people start businesses? People create businesses to make money. In order to make money, businesses sell either goods or services, or both.

Entrepreneurs Take Risks

People who own their own businesses are called entrepreneurs. An *entrepreneur* is a person who has a business idea as well as the capital to start the business and keep it running. Recall that *capital* is the money, tools, machines, and other products needed to make goods and services.

The entrepreneur organizes the business, hires employees, and takes the risk of entering the market. Entrepreneurs are one of the limited resources in an economy. These are the people who have the management ability to make a business succeed.

Entrepreneurs hope to make a profit from selling their goods or services. *Profit* is the money left over after a company has paid all its expenses. Business owners have many different kinds of expenses. They pay for the materials to make their products. They pay employees to make products or provide services. Many businesses spend money on advertising to get people to buy their product or service. They might also pay rent for their factory or office building.

Entrepreneurs take risks. Their business might not succeed. Many times they start their business with their own money or they take out bank loans that they have to repay. What happens if no one wants their product or service? What other risks might entrepreneurs face?

Goods and Services

Everyone needs basic things to survive—food, clothing, and shelter. Other things—such as certain brands of clothes, books, computers, sports equipment, televisions, CD players, musical instruments, and automobiles—are not necessities but are probably important to your lifestyle. Whether they are "needs" or "wants," all of these items are goods that are sold.

Many goods, such as computer software and skateboards, are manufactured. Other goods, such as apples and wheat, are grown and harvested. Trees are cut down. Fish are caught and frozen. All these things are goods.

We also need services from people who have skill and training. We need the services of nurses and doctors when we get hurt or sick. Teachers educate students, pilots fly business people on business trips, plumbers install pipes in homes, and computer programmers develop software. People pay other people for these services.

Supply and Demand

Another important part of selling goods and services is supply and demand. Business owners determine how much to produce and what price to charge based on supply and demand. Supply refers to the amount of goods and services that businesses produce. Demand has to do with the willingness and ability of people to buy the goods and services available.

While there are exceptions to every rule, it is safe to say that the higher the demand for a good or service, the higher the price. On the other hand, the lower the demand, the lower the price.

When there is a shortage of something people want, the price goes up. In the summer of 2008, for example, there was high demand for gasoline but low supply. As a result, the price of gasoline reached almost $4 a gallon. People had to make choices. Those who could afford it paid the higher gas prices and didn't change their behavior. Others limited their driving, bought smaller cars or scooters, or carpooled to save gas and money.

The Labor Market

The forces of supply and demand also apply to workers in the labor market. Employers compete with each other to find workers. If thousands of teenagers want to cut lawns during summer vacation, they will probably all earn low wages. However, if most teenagers want to work at Starbucks, the few who are willing to cut lawns could earn a lot of money.

Paying Employees

Most businesses hire employees and pay them wages or salaries. A wage is figured by the hour. A salary is a set amount. It is usually calculated as an annual amount. An annual salary is paid out by the month or by the week. Unlike wages, salaries are not paid according to how many hours a week the employee works.

What Do You Think ?

Why do you think a business might lower its prices when demand for their product is low? Why might they raise their price if demand is high?

The Minimum Wage

In Washington, the state minimum wage applies to all workers 16 years of age or older. A *minimum wage* is the lowest amount a worker can be paid per hour. Younger workers must be paid 85 percent of the minimum wage. If you must work more than 40 hours a week, the employer has to pay overtime pay. Overtime pay is one and a half times your regular wage for time you work past the 40 hours a week.

Who sets the minimum wage? The federal government sets a minimum wage, but states may set their own. Workers must be paid the federal minimum wage if the state minimum is lower. Farm workers, who usually receive low wages, must now be paid at least the minimum wage. As of January 1, 2009, the minimum wage in Washington was $8.55 per hour. That is the highest minimum wage in the country. The federal minimum wage is $7.25 per hour.

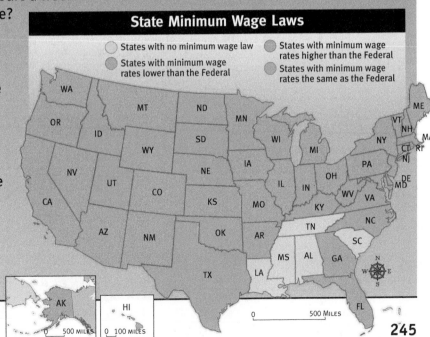

State Minimum Wage Laws

- States with no minimum wage law
- States with minimum wage rates lower than the Federal
- States with minimum wage rates higher than the Federal
- States with minimum wage rates the same as the Federal

Insuring Your Savings

Have you ever noticed when entering a bank that there is a sticker on the door or window with the letters FDIC boldly displayed? FDIC stands for Federal Deposit Insurance Corporation. It was created by President Roosevelt as part of the New Deal. During the Great Depression, many Americans were afraid to put money in the bank. When banks failed, customers lost all of their savings. The FDIC was created to insure against such losses. The FDIC insures bank accounts for up to $100,000. That means if the bank fails, the federal government will refund your money. In 2008, the government increased the coverage to $250,000. This was a temporary measure to address a banking crisis in the country.

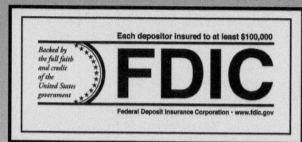

Each depositor insured to at least $100,000

Backed by the full faith and credit of the United States government

FDIC

Federal Deposit Insurance Corporation · www.fdic.gov

There are many different ways to pay for goods and services. **What form of payment do you think this woman is using?**

A Penny Saved

Saving money is as important as earning it. Most people save their money in a bank instead of putting it in a shoebox or under the mattress. A bank is a business that provides a service. They provide savings and checking accounts, and other financial services. Often, the bank will pay you interest on your savings as an incentive for you to save.

Like any business, banks want to make a profit. When you deposit money in a bank, the money doesn't just sit there waiting for you to withdraw it. The bank uses your money to make loans to other people. Those people pay interest on the money they borrow. They pay a higher rate of interest than the bank is paying you for saving your money. This is how banks make a profit and stay in business.

Spending Money

People spend money on products or services they need. They also spend on things they want. Remember, it's all about choices. Most people want to spend their money wisely. They want to get the most they can for their money. They compare prices of products from different stores. They also compare the prices of different brands.

There are many different ways to pay for goods and services. Cash, personal checks, credit, and debit cards are all ways to pay for things. When you use checks or debit cards, money is subtracted from your bank account. Credit cards, on the other hand, are a way to postpone paying for things you buy. When people buy something with a credit card, they get the item now, but they pay for it later. Credit card companies charge people interest to use the card.

Borrowers Beware

When credit card companies or banks loan money, they charge interest. Interest is good if you are a saver or an investor because you will earn money. But interest can be bad if you borrow money. With interest, it is possible to pay back more money than you originally borrowed. For example, you borrow $10,000 to buy a new car. The interest rate on the loan is 10 percent. You plan to repay the loan over a five-year period. Because of interest, your total repayment will be $16,105 at the end of five years. As a result, the $10,000 loan cost you $6,105 in interest. Does this mean you should never borrow money? What considerations should you make before getting a loan or using a credit card?

PLASTIBANK

0012 3456 7890 0000
0012

MR FIRSTNAME SURNAME

MASTER PASS

VALID FROM 05/08 EXPIRES END 05/13

Making Choices

People want to make a good income so they can meet their needs and wants. How can you make sure you will earn a good salary? The choices you make will affect how much money you will earn.

Your education will play a big part in how much money you will earn. People who do not finish high school usually make much less than people who graduate from college.

People's skills and talents can also affect how much money they make. Some people have special skills. People who are good at working with their hands might find jobs as woodworkers. Maybe you are good with computers or you can draw well. Some people turn these talents into careers.

Career choices also affect how much money people make. A doctor makes more money than a construction worker. A police officer makes more than a person who works in a fast-food chain.

In the next lesson, you will learn about the many different industries in Washington. Additionally, you will read about how the choices of some of our state's leading entrepreneurs have shaped their lives as well as the state's economy.

Linking the Past to the Present

Americans used to save money and carry little debt. But habits tend to change. Because of easy credit, many Americans have a lot of debt. The Institute for American Values reported that in 2004, the typical American family spent more than 18 percent of its income paying off debt. And at least 44 percent of college students have credit card debt of more than $2,000.

To decrease the amount of interest you pay, borrow less, get the lowest interest rate you can, and pay off the loan as fast as you can.

People's skills and interests play a role in career choices. **What skill is this person using to make a living?**

What Did You Learn? ①

1. What is meant by the term *economics*?
2. How do supply and demand affect the price of goods and services?
3. What are some of the dangers of using credit or borrowing money?

KEY IDEAS

- Washington is home to a variety of industries from high tech to agriculture.
- Renewable energy and alternative fuels are growing industries in Washington.
- Bill Gates, Eddie Bauer, and Gary Larson are just a few of the entrepreneurs who got their start in Washington.

KEY TERMS

agribusiness
aquaculture
biodiesel
competent
ethanol
philanthropist
renewable energy

Working Around the State

From north to south and east to west, in small towns and larger cities, Washingtonians are working. Teenage workers may have part-time jobs in the summer. College students juggle work for pay with the hard job of getting an education. Adults work in many kinds of jobs that require different levels of education and skill.

People work to earn money to take care of themselves and their families. They work to feel satisfied when they complete a job and do it well. They work to contribute to their community and enrich their own lives.

Washington workers are *competent*. This means they have suitable skills, knowledge, and education. They work in many different industries, including computer, aerospace, lumber, fishing, agriculture, and health care.

Food for the Nation

More than one-third of the state's land is used for agriculture. In the Puget Sound area, greenhouses and nurseries are built on tiny plots of land. The land west of the Cascade Mountains is used mostly for dairy cows and for growing fruits and vegetables. In the eastern part of the state, wheat farms are often several thousand acres in size. In the Columbia River Basin, farmers plant nut, peach, apricot, cherry, and apple orchards as well as potatoes, corn, hops, and grapes.

Cattle, pigs, poultry, and milk production are also important to our economy. Farm animals are raised in different regions, just as crops are. Dairies and poultry farms are common on the west side of the state. Sheep are raised in the southeast. Cattle ranches are most common in central and eastern regions where livestock graze in the mountains and river valleys.

Cattle graze on a farm in Colville.
What natural resources do ranchers need to raise cattle?

Agricultural Research

Chemical fertilizers were developed after World War II and resulted in larger harvests. Nitrogen fertilizer, the most common type used on wheat farms, was made by combining natural gas with air. The inexpensive fertilizer was spread by the ton on huge farms.

Agricultural research at Washington State University in Pullman resulted in plants that grew faster, repelled diseases, and matured at the same time, making harvesting by machine possible.

The Fishing Industry

Washington's coastline and many rivers make fishing a major source of income. Fishing crews work on the lower Columbia River, the waters of Puget Sound, and off the coast as far as Alaska. Salmon, albacore tuna, herring, halibut, rockfish, cod, flounder, crabs, and ocean perch are caught and sold.

Fish farming, called *aquaculture* or aquafarming, is also becoming more common. Fish farms along the coastline raise salmon, oysters, and other seafood.

The Logging Industry

Washington is second in the nation for lumber production. The forests are made up of Douglas firs, ponderosa pines, and hemlocks. Most logging operations and sawmills are located between Puget Sound and the Columbia River. Trees used to be cut just for lumber, but now they are also used to make pulp for paper and cardboard.

In the 1990s, many smaller sawmills went out of business because the supply of trees was limited. When sawmills closed, thousands of jobs disappeared. Towns in timber areas experienced great economic difficulties.

Job losses in the lumber industry are also the result of Washington's trade relations with Japan. Japan buys a lot of lumber from Washington. But rather than processing the raw lumber in Washington sawmills, it is shipped directly to Japanese sawmills. This has hurt Washington's lumber industry. There has been less demand for workers in the industry and so some people have had to find new jobs.

The Columbia Basin Project

The waters held by the Grand Coulee Dam are used to irrigate semiarid land in central and eastern Washington. This has turned a desert wasteland into a lush farming area. Sugar beets, potatoes, apples, cherries, grapes, and other crops are easily grown in the sandy soil with irrigation water. Towns like Moses Lake and Othello have grown quickly as people moved in to begin farming following completion of the dam.

The Columbia Basin Project was planned to create 20,000 new farms. When it was completed, there were only 6,000 farms. Instead of creating small farms for many farm families, the irrigation system created large profits for big corporate farms. The new approach to farming is called *agribusiness*.

The project eventually irrigated 550,000 acres of land. Alfalfa, grapes, asparagus, corn, onions, and potatoes were grown. Farm workers pick, clean, and sort crops. Then they ship them fresh (in cans or frozen) to markets. Processing plants create jobs, but many are seasonal and employ workers only during the harvest.

Moses Lake•
•Othello

Washington State leads the nation in the number of apples grown. We are second in the nation for potatoes, third for winter wheat, and fourth for barley.

Juice boxes advance on the assembly line in a factory. **What is this worker's job?**

Job Losses in the Aerospace Industry

Between 1998 and 2004, Washington lost 50,000 jobs in the aerospace industry. The Boeing Company relocated its headquarters to Chicago in 2001 and began hiring workers in foreign countries to build parts. The final assembly of planes is still done in Washington, but fewer workers are needed here now.

What Do You Think ?

Many companies, like Boeing, are hiring workers in foreign countries for jobs previously done by Americans. The companies say that foreign workers cost less than American workers. This is an economic choice that companies make. Is it better for a company to save money or to keep Americans employed? What do you think?

Manufacturing

Washington's most important manufacturing industry is aircraft, but companies also build boats, trucks, and other equipment. Aluminum plants, such as Kaiser Aluminum in Spokane, create aluminum used to make airplane parts and soft drink cans.

Many industries came to the state because of the large supply of hydroelectric power. Most industries are near Seattle and Tacoma because of close access to rail lines, seaports, and a large supply of workers.

Food-processing plants are important in Washington, too. Flour mills operate in Spokane, Seattle, Tacoma, and Vancouver. Cleaning, sorting, canning, and freezing fruits and vegetables are important jobs. Workers and machines make apples into apple juice and grapes into juice and wine. Dairy products such as milk, cheese, butter, and ice cream are made and sold, too.

That's Electric!

Washington's dam system provides hydroelectric power that is used in the state, but it is also exported. Canada and California get electrical power from Washington. The power is delivered through heavy-duty power lines that run along the West Coast. When power supplies are low in Washington, electricity can run north along the lines as well.

The dams provide most of the state's electrical power, but coal-fired electric plants produce 11 percent of the electricity. A single nuclear plant at Hanford produces 7 percent of the state's electric supply.

Other Energy Sources

About one-third of Washington homes use natural gas for heating. Washington relies on natural gas imported from Canada through underground pipelines running into the eastern and western regions of the state.

"Wind farms" provide electrical power for a growing number of Washington homes. Puget Sound Energy (PSE) built large turbines that turn wind into electrical energy at Wild Horse Wind Facility in Kittitas County and Hopkins Ridge in Columbia County. They power more than 100,000 homes. A solar-power project is underway at Wild Horse to provide future supplies of renewable energy. *Renewable energy* refers to energy that comes from unlimited natural resources like wind or solar energy and that does not contribute to pollution or global warming.

There are several biodiesel production plants in Washington that could produce up to 135 million gallons of fuel per year. There are more than 50 gas stations selling biodiesel in the state. *Biodiesel* fuel is made from vegetable oil or animal fat. In 2007, farmers grew 18,000 acres of oil seed crops to make biodiesel. More biodiesel could be produced, but when farmers get higher prices for other crops, they don't plant oil seed crops.

The state's ethanol fuel production faces the same problem. *Ethanol* is fuel made from corn. The resources for making biodiesel fuels and ethanol are limited, so farmers must choose which crops to plant in order to make the most profit.

Wind Farms in Washington provide electricity for a growing number of Washington homes. **Where have you seen wind turbines in Washington?**

Wild Horse Wind Farm

Hopkins Ridge Wind Facility

This is the main entrance to Microsoft's headquarters in Redmond. **Why do you think the headquarters site is described as a campus?**

Washington's Key Industries and Companies

Washington is home to many different industries and companies. The goods and services produced in Washington are sold throughout the state, nation, and around the world. While our state is best known for its aerospace and high-tech industries, it is also a leader in agriculture and forest products. Washington serves as the headquarters location for many of the nation's top companies.

Washington's Top Industries
Aerospace
Agriculture
Biotechnology & Pharmaceuticals
Computer Software
Electronics & Computers
Food Processing
Forest Products
Health Care
Marine Services
Telecommunications

Companies with Headquarters in Washington
Amazon.com
Boeing
Costco
Immunex/AMGEN
Microsoft
Nintendo America
Nordstrom
Starbucks
Weyerhaeuser

(Source: Washington State Department of Community, Trade & Economic Development)

The Computer Industry

The computer software industry plays a big role in Washington's economy. Most computer-related businesses are located in the Seattle area. Microsoft Corporation, in Redmond, is the world's leading software manufacturer for personal computers. In 2007, Microsoft sold about $60 billion worth of software and video games. The company has 90,000 employees in 105 countries. It also owns part of the cable news network MSNBC.

Microsoft founder Bill Gates

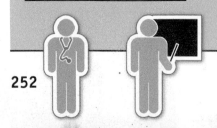

The Health Care Industry

Washington is a pioneer in health care. The first HMO (health maintenance organization) in the nation was formed at the end of World War II in Seattle. Union members and farmers joined together to hire their own doctors. Four hundred families formed Group Health Cooperative of Puget Sound, and bought a clinic and hospital. Known today as Group Health, the idea has been widely copied across the nation. Members pay a monthly fee for health services from doctors who work in a company clinic.

The state has a medical school at the University of Washington in Seattle, where physicians are trained and researchers work on new treatments. The state's school for dentists is also at the University of Washington. Washington's animals are taken care of, too—the state has a school for veterinarians at Washington State University in Pullman.

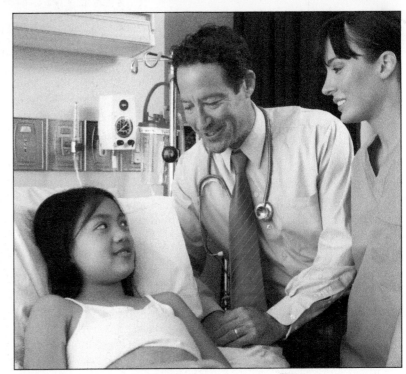

A doctor meets with a young patient. Washington is a pioneer in health care with the first HMO in the nation. **Do doctors and nurses provide a good or a service?**

Jobs for Everyone

Today's economy and job market change constantly. The occupations on the chart are expected to have the most new job openings in Washington between 2006 and 2014.

- Which occupations will need the most workers?
- Which jobs require the most education?
- Which jobs will probably pay high salaries?

Jobs in logging, mining, and fishing are not listed. Why do you think the number of jobs in those fields is not growing? Look at the list of exports on page 257 and you'll see that lumber products are major exports, but machines have replaced many jobs in those industries.

Most Job Openings

Cashiers

Salespersons

Waiters/Waitresses

Food preparation

Office clerks

Laborers

Registered nurses

Janitors

Child-care workers

Teachers (high school and college)

Bookkeeping and accounting clerks

Customer service representatives

Stock clerks and order fillers

Computer software engineers

Sales representatives

(Source: InfoUSA, 2009)

Washington's
Leading Entrepreneurs

In lesson 1, you learned that economics is about making choices about how best to use scarce resources to meet the needs and desires of society. One of the limited resources is management ability. Economists also refer to this as "entrepreneurial ability."

Some of Washington's most creative and hard-working entrepreneurs are highlighted here. Do you recognize any of them?

Armen Tertsagian and Mark Balaban

Aplets and Cotlets are candies that were created in 1918 by two young men. Armen Tertsagian and Mark Balaban had both emigrated from Armenia. They met each other in Seattle and decided to start a business. First they tried a yogurt factory, but few people had heard of yogurt then.

The men moved to Cashmere, where they bought an apple orchard. Fresh apples were not selling for good prices at the time, so they sold dried apples. Their company, called Northwest Evaporating, was a good idea because it supplied dried apples to soldiers fighting in World War I.

The men finally decided to use surplus apples to make *rahat locoum*, a popular candy they had enjoyed as children. They called the candy Aplets. Then they created Cotlets from apricots. Today, Aplets and Cotlets are sold around the world.

Debbie Mumm

Debbie Mumm is a Spokane artist who draws designs used on T-shirts, cookie jars, dishes, calendars, rubber stamps, and fabric. She started by selling books of her own quilt designs. Her company, called Mumm's the Word, employs 40 people in Spokane. Over $90 million of her products sold in 2000.

As a young girl, Debbie enjoyed art. She learned drawing, painting, cartooning, and calligraphy. After high school, she studied art at college. Debbie's advice to entrepreneurs: "Start small, find a niche [a market to sell your goods], and promote yourself."

Eddie Bauer

Eddie Bauer began selling sporting goods in Seattle in the 1920s. At first, he sold mostly tennis and golf equipment, but his business really grew when he began including fishing tackle and hunting gear. Bauer enjoyed sports and used his experience to help customers choose the best equipment.

The photograph shows Bauer outside his store in downtown Seattle. He is showing off his fishing tackle and a catch of steelhead trout. Later, he included outdoor clothing, opened other stores, and became a national success.

254

Floyd Paxton

In the early 1950s, Floyd Paxton realized there was a need for a simple way to close plastic fruit and bread bags. The fruit-growing industry in the Yakima area was growing quickly, and much of the fruit was shipped to stores in plastic bags. At the grocery store, customers picked out their own fruit and put it into plastic bags.

Floyd, who had never completed high school, whittled a sample clip out of plastic. When he showed it to the executives at Pacific Fruit Company, they ordered a million. Other orders followed, and eventually bread bags were sealed with his Kwik-Loks. Floyd became wealthy, and now bread stays fresher longer.

Harry Brown and J. C. Haley

In 1914, when World War I was beginning in Europe, two young men in Tacoma got an idea for a candy bar they named the Mount Tacoma Bar. They sold the mounds of chocolate in boxes printed with Mount Tacoma on the front. Then Seattle residents began calling the mountain Mount Rainier instead of Mount Tacoma. So in 1923, the men changed the name of their candy bar to just plain Mountain Bar. Machines can now make 592 Mountain Bars per minute, each one complete with a cherry in the middle!

Brown and Haley continued experimenting with different recipes until they came up with a log-shaped candy bar coated with chocolate and almonds. They called it Almond Roca.

Gary Larson

Gary Larson is a world-famous cartoonist. He was born in Tacoma and now lives in Seattle. His clever comics, known as "The Far Side," have been published in more than 17 languages in 2,000 newspapers worldwide. He has sold 31 million books. His animal cartoons are printed on calendars, mugs, and T-shirts. Larson is now retired, but his cartoons live on.

Where did Gary Larson get his ideas? As a child, he loved to draw but did not study art. He was a science student at Washington State University when he began publishing cartoons.

Larson's offbeat humor has made him wealthy, and it also earned him the honor of having a species of biting lice and a butterfly named after him!

Bill Gates

Bill Gates is probably Washington's most famous citizen. His father was a Seattle attorney, and his mother was a schoolteacher. He started programming computers when he was 13 years old.

In college, Bill met other young men who shared his interest in computers. They created software for home computers and started a company called Microsoft. Windows became an important part of their programs. The company has made Bill Gates the world's wealthiest man.

Bill and Melinda Gates and their children live in the Puget Sound area. The Gates are *philanthropists*—people who give money to charities. The Gates Foundation gives millions to support health and learning in poor countries. It also gives college scholarships and develops housing for homeless families.

What Did You Learn? ②

1. How has the Columbia Basin Reclamation Project changed agriculture?
2. What is a "wind farm" and how do they contribute to the state's economy?
3. Identify three products that were developed by Washington entrepreneurs.

KEY IDEAS

- Washington's location on the Pacific Rim makes it a great trading partner with the world.

- Global competition has helped and hurt the state's economy.

- International trade agreements have had mixed results in Washington.

KEY TERMS

commodity
consensus
deplete
domestic
free trade
globalization
tariff

The Global Market

International trade has always been an important feature of Washington's economy. In earlier times, furs, lumber, canned salmon, wheat, and fruit were exported to distant markets. Washington's location on the Pacific Rim has been a big advantage in overseas trade. Washington is the nation's fourth-largest exporter.

One in every four state jobs depends on international trade. By the end of the 20th century, globalization was a reality. *Globalization* refers to the spread of capitalism and free trade around the world. Computers and the Internet have linked the entire globe in a web of information, trade, and finance.

Canada is America's largest trading partner. Trade with Canada has increased over the years because of geography and trade agreements. However, trade with Asian countries, especially Taiwan, China, and Japan is growing rapidly.

Washington's biggest trading partner is China, followed by Canada. In 2008, The total value of Washington's exports was $66.9 billion. Exports to China were $9.9 billion. Exports to Canada were $9.2 billion.

Washington's Top Exports

Boeing airplanes lead Washington's exports. Computer software, electronics, medicines, aluminum, frozen french fries, and wines are also traded in addition to the traditional exports of lumber, wheat, fruit, and fish. More than half of the region's wheat crop is exported, with most going into Asian countries.

"Washington offers to our companies some of the best global trade connections and infrastructure in the world. That makes our economy stronger and more competitive."

—Governor Chris Gregoire

A container ship is docked at the Port of Seattle. **Why is it called a container ship? What country is the ship from?**

Global Competition

The global market can be brutal. Washington's Red Delicious apples once got a high price overseas. Then newer varieties such as Fuji, Braeburn, and Gala apples became more popular. These apple varieties are grown in Chile and China, where workers are paid less than in the United States. As a result, apples from these countries are sold at a lower price than apples grown in Washington.

China is now the world's leading apple producer. This competition has hurt apple growers in Chelan and Okanogan counties. Now many growers are planting sweet cherries instead of apples.

Lumber Exports Drop

Washington's lumber and wood products used to be the state's third leading export. But trading of these products has dropped since the 1990s. Reduced timber supplies and trade agreements have contributed to the decline. During the 1990s, the exports of lumber and wood products dropped by 4 percent.

What Do You Think?

How do you think employment in the state's lumber industry has been affected by the decrease in lumber exports?

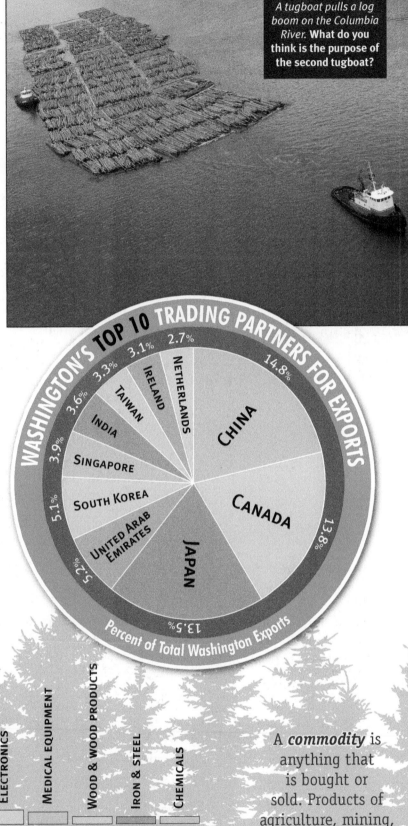

A tugboat pulls a log boom on the Columbia River. **What do you think is the purpose of the second tugboat?**

WASHINGTON'S TOP 10 TRADING PARTNERS FOR EXPORTS

Percent of Total Washington Exports

- CHINA 14.8%
- CANADA 13.8%
- JAPAN 13.5%
- UNITED ARAB EMIRATES 5.2%
- SOUTH KOREA 5.1%
- SINGAPORE 3.9%
- INDIA 3.6%
- TAIWAN 3.3%
- IRELAND 3.1%
- NETHERLANDS 2.7%

WASHINGTON'S TOP 10 EXPORTS (Percent of Total Washington Exports)

Export	Percent
Aircraft & Spacecraft, including parts	50.6%
Cereals	8.0%
Oil Seeds from Grains, Fruits, & Plants	7.3%
Computers & Industrial Machinery	4.0%
Mineral Fuel & Oil	3.9%
Electronics	2.8%
Medical Equipment	2.4%
Wood & Wood Products	1.5%
Iron & Steel	1.4%
Chemicals	1.4%

A *commodity* is anything that is bought or sold. Products of agriculture, mining, or manufacturing are commodities.

(Source for Charts: World Institute for Strategic Economic Research & U.S. Census Bureau Foreign Trade Division)

Trade Agreements

The United States has many trade agreements with other countries that affect industries and workers in Washington. Two of the most significant agreements are the North American Free Trade Agreement (NAFTA) and the Pacific Salmon Treaty.

What Is Free Trade?

NAFTA is a trade agreement between the United States, Canada, and Mexico. It took effect in 1994. It created one of the largest free trade areas in the world. *Free trade* is trade between countries that is free of tariffs and strict regulations. *Tariffs* are taxes on imported goods. Often they are called "protective" tariffs because they protect domestic industry from foreign competition. *Domestic* industries operate inside the country.

For example, to encourage Americans to buy more Washington apples, the U.S. government could charge a tariff on apples imported from Chile. The tariff would make Chilean apples more expensive than Washington apples. Since many people make purchasing decisions based on price, they might buy more Washington apples as a result of the tariff.

The Good with the Bad

NAFTA reduced many of the tariffs between the three countries. This made goods and services cheaper for everyone. The hope was that the agreement would also create jobs in all three countries. However, the results of NAFTA are mixed. It has created jobs and reduced prices on many goods and services. But it has also created problems. Critics of NAFTA point to the loss of manufacturing jobs in the United States. Some American companies relocated their factories to Mexico. They did this because it was cheaper to hire Mexican workers than to hire American workers.

Critics also argue that NAFTA hurts the environment. They say that NAFTA encourages companies to pollute. For example, laws protecting the environment in Mexico are not as strict as U.S. laws. As a result, American companies have moved their operations to Mexico so they don't have to follow strict rules.

Effect on Washington

NAFTA's effects on Washington industries are mixed, too. The apple industry did get a boost. The elimination of tariffs expanded the market for Washington's apples. Mexico has become a big importer of Washington apples. However, when it comes to asparagus, the outcome is different. Asparagus growers in Washington and California now compete with Mexican asparagus growers. The reduction of tariffs on Mexican asparagus has made it cheaper to buy than American asparagus.

The leaders of Mexico, the United States, and Canada signed NAFTA in 1992. Which U.S. president signed the agreement?

The Washington Journey

A protester stands among flaming trash bins during WTO protests in Seattle. How might images like this actually hurt the cause of environmentalists?

THE BATTLE IN SEATTLE

When the World Trade Organization (WTO) decided to meet in Seattle in 1999, city officials were pleased. The WTO is an international body that promotes free trade. This important meeting would bring business and publicity to Seattle. Seattle boasted of its export industries and its Pacific Rim connections.

But Seattle also has a history of labor problems and environmental unrest. Activists from the United States and around the world planned to bring their concerns about free trade to Seattle. Local protesters joined them. The result was a huge demonstration. The angry words and the tactics of the protesters seemed a throwback to the days of the Seattle General Strike and the Wobbly free speech fights. In some ways they were.

The protesters considered the WTO to be an organization of capitalist greed. Protesters said that WTO member nations favor profit over workers' rights and the environment. They argue that rich nations are getting wealthier at the expense of poor nations.

About 40,000 protesters marched through downtown Seattle, completely disrupting the opening session of the meeting. Seattle police, aided by the National Guard, finally cleared the area. They used armored cars, officers on horses, tear gas, pepper spray, and

What Is the WTO?

The World Trade Organization (WTO) is an international organization based in Switzerland that oversees trade between nations. Its main purpose is to promote free trade by enforcing international trade agreements like NAFTA and the Pacific Salmon Treaty. It also helps to settle trade disputes between countries like the "fish war" between the United States and Canada.

The WTO has 153 member nations that account for 97 percent of world trade. Decisions are made by consensus. *Consensus* requires all the member nations to compromise to reach an agreement.

rubber bullets. There were more than 600 arrests and several million dollars in property damage and lost business.

Seattle Mayor Paul Schell had been a civil rights and antiwar protester in the 1960s and 1970s. "I remember the sixties. I remember the protest marches," he said. "It hurts me deeply to be the mayor that called out the National Guard, but I had to protect my citizens."

The "Battle in Seattle" was front-page news around the world. For better or worse, Seattle would serve as a symbol of the promise and the peril of global trade for years to come.

The Fuss Over Fish

In the 1980s, the United States and Canada signed the Pacific Salmon Treaty. The agreement helped settle a dispute over fishing rights. At issue was the interception, or capture, of migrating salmon between Canada and the United States. American fishermen were catching Canadian salmon and Canadian fishermen were catching American salmon. For example, Coho, Chinook, and other species of salmon returning to the Columbia River were being intercepted by Canadian fishermen along the Pacific Coast. This hurt the salmon industry in Washington. For their part, the salmon were unaware that they were causing a commotion.

Without a treaty, the concern was that one country would *deplete*, or exhaust, the salmon stock of the other. The treaty allowed both countries to fish equal amounts of the other country's salmon. The agreement seemed to work until the late 1990s. At that time, Canadian fishermen accused American fishermen of violating the treaty. It seemed like another pig war was about to start, but this time over fish!

In an attempt to calm the waters, the Canadians offered to take fewer fish heading for rivers in Oregon and Washington. In return, they wanted fishermen from Alaska to reduce their take of Canadian salmon.

The two nations signed a new 10-year agreement in 2008. Among other things, the agreement should help restore Chinook salmon stocks in the Puget Sound region. Chinook salmon are an endangered species. Governor Gregoire called the agreement "historic." She said, "We now have a fighting chance to save the salmon."

Fishermen haul in a large catch of salmon in Friday Harbor, off San Juan Island. **How will they get the fish on the boat?**

What Did You Learn? ③

1. How has Washington's location contributed to international trade?
2. How has global competition affected the state's apple industry?
3. What was the goal of NAFTA?

Go to the Source

Fish Troubles

"Name one salmon you know who ever came back from a spawning run!"

Observe --- Evaluate --- Conclude

Observe	Evaluate	Conclude
• Describe the action taking place in the cartoon.	• What issue in Washington is this cartoon addressing? • Explain how the cartoon's caption fits with the image.	• How does the cartoonist use humor to make a point? • What do you think is the message of the cartoon?

Reading Graphs

Graphs and charts help us "see" information. There are many different types of graphs. This chapter includes two types of graphs—a circle graph and a bar graph on page 257. Graphs can sometimes be confusing. The following guidelines will help you be able to read graphs easily.

Guidelines for Reading Graphs

- How is the graph set up? What type of graph is it?
- What is being represented in the graph?
- What is the scale of the graph? How much of something is being shown?
- If there is a legend to the graph, what information does it provide?
- What conclusions or assumptions you can make from studying the graph?

Your Turn

Washington's exports are just one small part of the total trade between the United States and other countries. Use the guidelines from above to examine the graph. Then answer the following questions.

1. How does this graph compare to the other graphs on page 257?
2. What additional information does this graph provide?
3. Which top trading partners of the United States are also top trading partners with Washington?
4. Why do you think the lists are not the same?
5. Does the United States sell more (export) to foreign countries than it buys (imports)?
6. What conclusions can you draw about United States trade with other countries

Top 10 Trade Partners of the United States

KEY
Exports
Imports

Chapter Review Questions

1. What is an opportunity cost?
2. How do entrepreneurs take risks?
3. How does Washington's minimum wage compare to other states and the national minimum wage?
4. Why has there been job loss in the aerospace industry?
5. Who are Washington's top three trading partners?
6. What three industries export the most from Washington?
7. What is free trade?
8. What was the purpose of the Pacific Salmon Treaty?
9. Why did Seattle become a battleground during the meeting of the World Trade Organization?

Becoming a Better Reader

Draw Conclusions

You have become a better reader by learning new strategies for reading informational books. Write about the most important thing you learned about Washington. Be sure to include facts to tell about what you learned.

You Are the Geographer

Many of Washington's largest companies are in the Puget Sound region. Why do you think this is so? Use what you have learned about spatial patterns, closeness to natural resources, location on the Pacific Rim, and other geographic and cultural features to draw conclusions about why companies do business in the Puget Sound region.

Washington State Symbols:

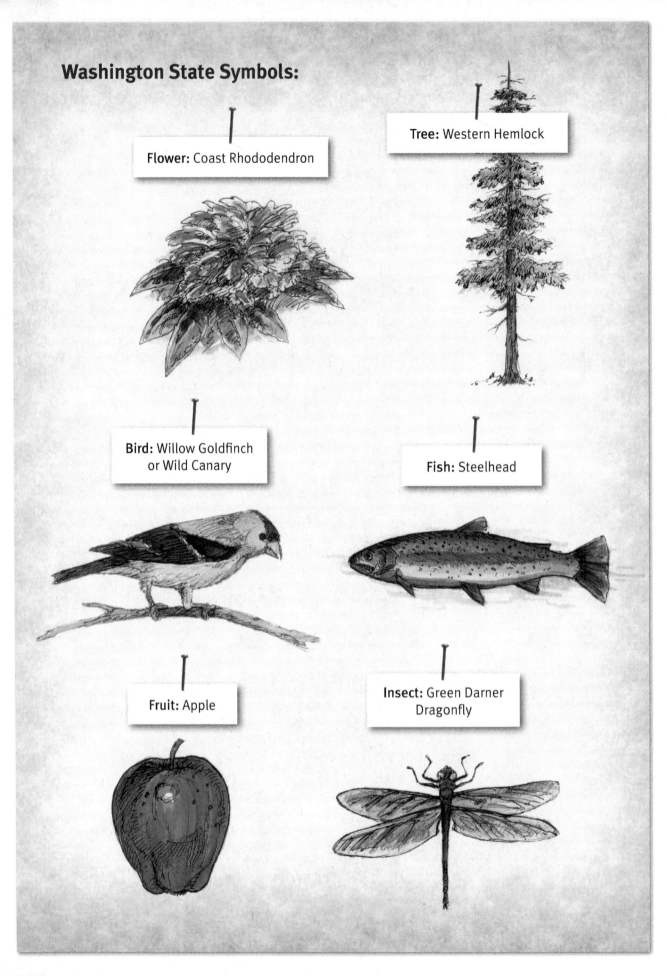

Flower: Coast Rhododendron

Tree: Western Hemlock

Bird: Willow Goldfinch or Wild Canary

Fish: Steelhead

Fruit: Apple

Insect: Green Darner Dragonfly

Washington–Counties and County Seats

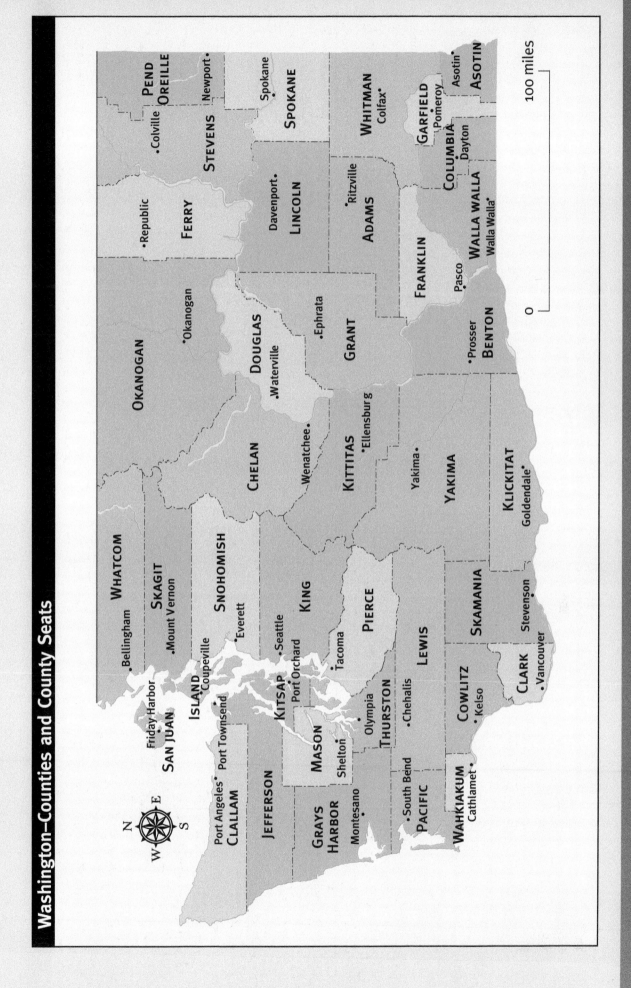

United States–Political

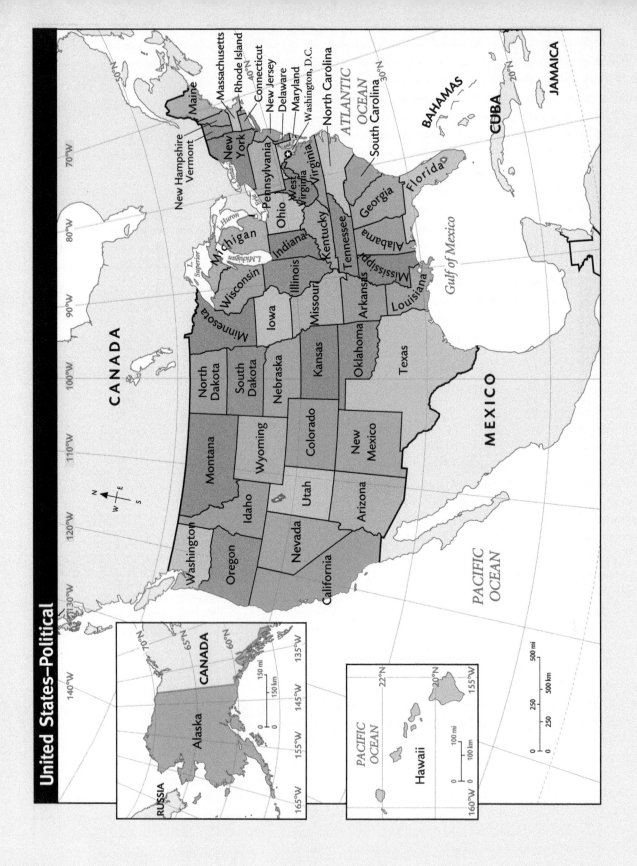

266

United States–Physical

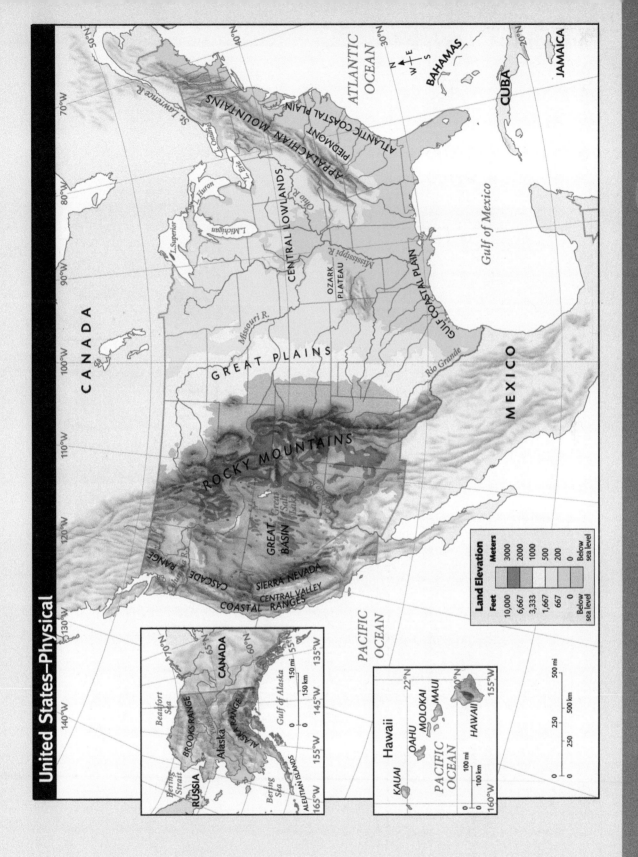

CANADA

ATLANTIC OCEAN

St. Lawrence R.

APPALACHIAN MOUNTAINS

PIEDMONT

ATLANTIC COASTAL PLAIN

BAHAMAS

N
W—E
S

CUBA

JAMAICA

L. Ontario

L. Erie

L. Huron

L. Michigan

L. Superior

Ohio R.

CENTRAL LOWLANDS

Mississippi R.

OZARK PLATEAU

GULF COASTAL PLAIN

Gulf of Mexico

Missouri R.

GREAT PLAINS

Rio Grande

MEXICO

ROCKY MOUNTAINS

Great Salt Lake

GREAT BASIN

SIERRA NEVADA

CASCADE RANGE

CENTRAL VALLEY

COASTAL RANGES

PACIFIC OCEAN

Land Elevation

Feet	Meters	
10,000	3000	
6,667	2000	
3,333	1000	
1,667	500	
667	200	
0	0	
Below sea level	Below sea level	

RUSSIA

Bering Strait

Beaufort Sea

Bering Sea

BROOKS RANGE

ALASKA RANGE

Alaska

Gulf of Alaska

CANADA

ALEUTIAN ISLANDS

150 mi
150 km

Hawaii

KAUAI

OAHU

MOLOKAI

MAUI

HAWAII

PACIFIC OCEAN

100 mi
100 km

0   250   500 mi
0   250   500 km

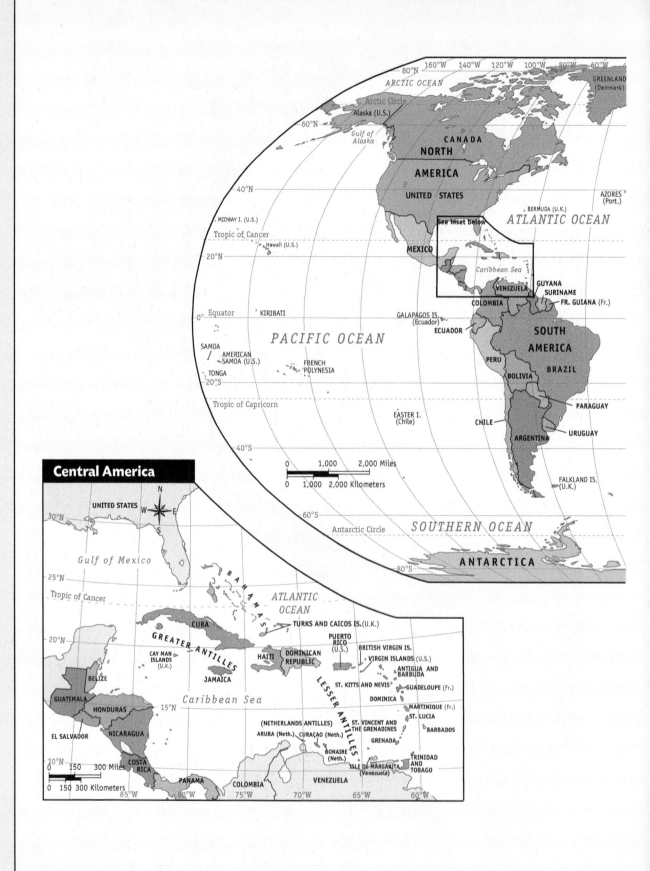

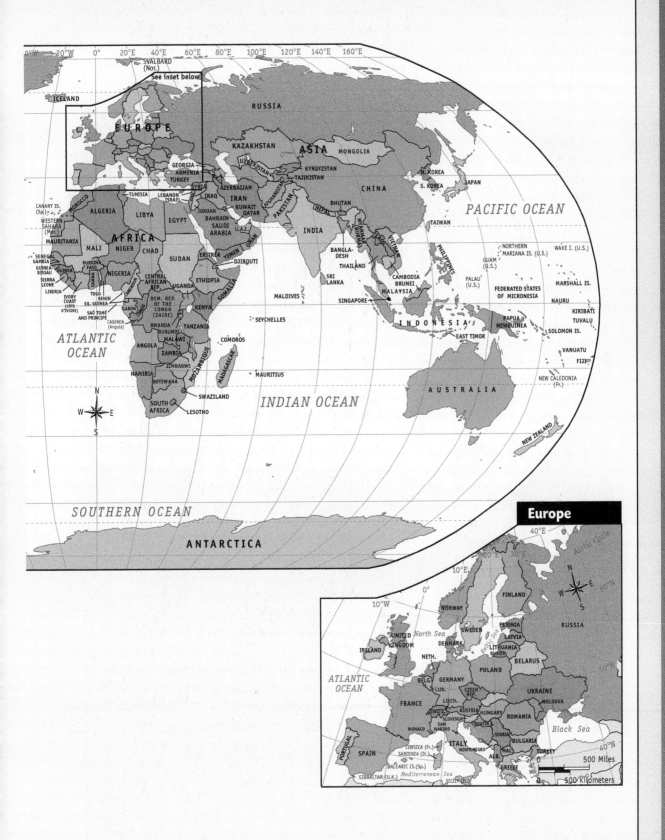

20°W   0°   20°E   40°E   60°E   80°E   100°E   120°E   140°E   160°E

SVALBARD
(Nor.)
See inset below

ICELAND

RUSSIA

EUROPE

ASIA

KAZAKHSTAN

MONGOLIA

UZBEKISTAN   KYRGYZSTAN

GEORGIA   TAJIKISTAN
ARMENIA
TURKEY   CHINA

N. KOREA

S. KOREA   JAPAN

SYRIA   AZERBAIJAN
LEBANON   IRAQ
TUNISIA   ISRAEL   IRAN   AFGHANISTAN
CANARY IS.   MOROCCO   JORDAN   KUWAIT   PAKISTAN
(Sp.)   QATAR
WESTERN   ALGERIA   LIBYA   EGYPT   BAHRAIN   U.A.E.   NEPAL   BHUTAN
SAHARA   SAUDI   TAIWAN
(Mor.)   ARABIA   MYANMAR   VIETNAM

PACIFIC OCEAN

MAURITANIA   OMAN   INDIA   (BURMA)

AFRICA   YEMEN   BANGLA-   LAOS
MALI   NIGER   CHAD   DESH   NORTHERN   WAKE I. (U.S.)
SUDAN   ERITREA   THAILAND   MARIANA IS. (U.S.)
SENEGAL   DJIBOUTI   GUAM
GAMBIA   BURKINA   SRI   PHILIPPINES   (U.S.)
GUINEA-   FASO   NIGERIA   ETHIOPIA   LANKA   CAMBODIA   FEDERATED STATES   MARSHALL IS.
BISSAU   GHANA   CENTRAL   UGANDA   MALDIVES   BRUNEI   PALAU   OF MICRONESIA
SIERRA   AFRICAN   SOMALIA   MALAYSIA   (U.S.)   NAURU
LEONE   TOGO   BENIN   REP.   SEYCHELLES   SINGAPORE   KIRIBATI
LIBERIA   EQ. GUINEA   KENYA   TUVALU
IVORY   SAÖ TOMÉ   GABON   DEM. REP.   INDONESIA   PAPUA
COAST   AND PRINCIPE   OF THE   TANZANIA   NEW GUINEA   SOLOMON IS.
(CÔTE   CONGO
D'IVOIRE)   CABINDA   (ZAIRE)   RWANDA   EAST TIMOR
(Angola)   BURUNDI   VANUATU
ATLANTIC   ANGOLA   MALAWI   COMOROS   NEW CALEDONIA   FIJI
OCEAN   ZAMBIA   (Fr.)
NAMIBIA   ZIMBABWE   MADAGASCAR   MAURITIUS
BOTSWANA   MOZAMBIQUE   INDIAN OCEAN   AUSTRALIA
N
W   E   SWAZILAND   NEW ZEALAND
SOUTH
S   AFRICA   LESOTHO

SOUTHERN OCEAN

ANTARCTICA

Europe

40°E
20°E   30°E   Arctic Circle
10°E   60°N
0°   FINLAND   RUSSIA
10°W   NORWAY
UNITED   North Sea   SWEDEN   ESTONIA
IRELAND   KINGDOM   DENMARK   Baltic Sea   LATVIA
NETH.   LITHUANIA   50°N
BELG.   GERMANY   RUSSIA   BELARUS
ATLANTIC   LUX.   POLAND
OCEAN   FRANCE   LIECH.   CZECH   UKRAINE
REP.
SWITZ.   AUSTRIA   HUNGARY   MOLDOVA
MONACO   SLOVENIA   ROMANIA
SAN   CROATIA
MARINO   SERBIA   BULGARIA   Black Sea
CORSICA (Fr.)   ITALY   MONTENEGRO   MAC.   40°N
PORTUGAL   SARDINIA (It.)   ALB.   TURKEY
SPAIN   GREECE   0   500 Miles
BALEARIC IS.(Sp.)
GIBRALTAR (U.K.)   Mediterranean Sea   SICILY (It.)   500 Kilometers

269

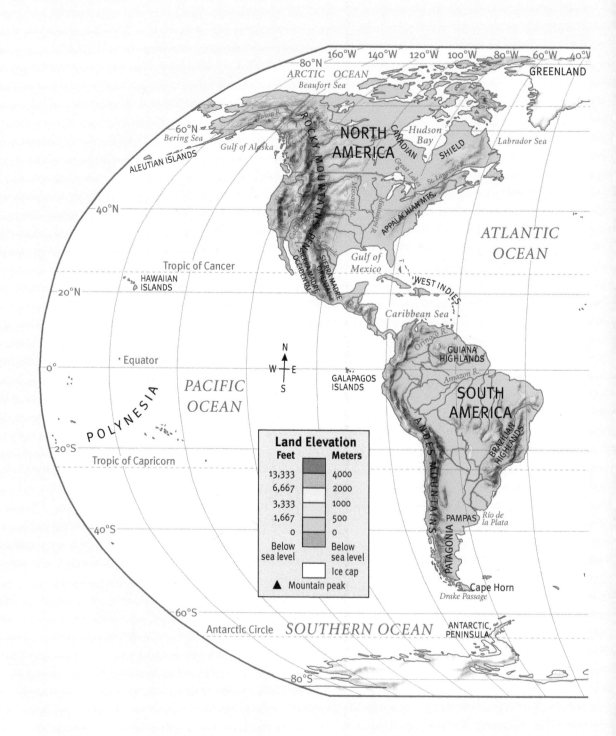

ARCTIC OCEAN
Beaufort Sea
GREENLAND
80°N
160°W 140°W 120°W 100°W 80°W 60°W 40°W
60°N
Bering Sea
Yukon R.
Gulf of Alaska
ROCKY MOUNTAINS
NORTH AMERICA
Hudson Bay
CANADIAN SHIELD
Labrador Sea
ALEUTIAN ISLANDS
40°N
Great Lakes
St. Lawrence
Missouri R.
APPALACHIAN MTS.
ATLANTIC OCEAN
Tropic of Cancer
HAWAIIAN ISLANDS
Gulf of Mexico
SIERRA NEVADA
SIERRA MADRE OCCIDENTAL
20°N
WEST INDIES
Caribbean Sea
Equator
Orinoco R.
GUIANA HIGHLANDS
PACIFIC OCEAN
GALAPAGOS ISLANDS
Amazon R.
SOUTH AMERICA
0°
POLYNESIA
N
W E
S
20°S
Tropic of Capricorn
ANDES MOUNTAINS
BRAZILIAN HIGHLANDS
PAMPAS
Rio de la Plata
40°S

Land Elevation

Feet	Meters
13,333	4000
6,667	2000
3,333	1000
1,667	500
0	0
Below sea level	Below sea level
	Ice cap
▲ Mountain peak	

PATAGONIA
Cape Horn
Drake Passage
60°S
Antarctic Circle
SOUTHERN OCEAN
ANTARCTIC PENINSULA
80°S

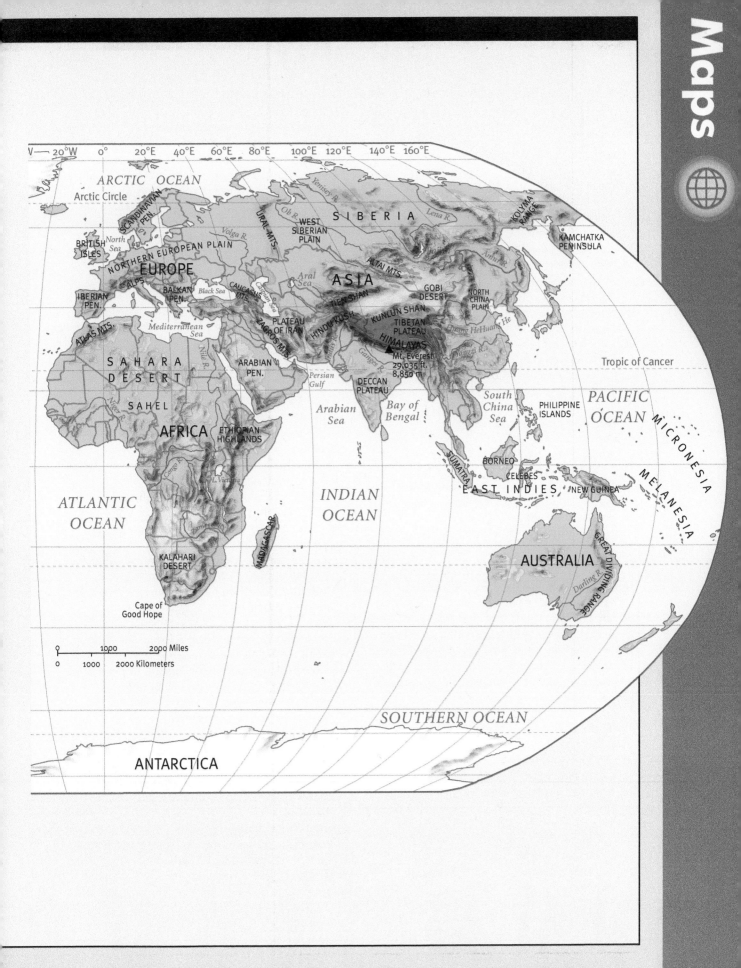

20°W   0°   20°E   40°E   60°E   80°E   100°E   120°E   140°E   160°E

ARCTIC   OCEAN
Arctic Circle

SCANDINAVIAN PEN.

BRITISH ISLES
North Sea

Yenisey R.

SIBERIA

Ob R.
Volga R.

URAL MTS.

WEST SIBERIAN PLAIN

Lena R.

KOLYMA RANGE

KAMCHATKA PENINSULA

NORTHERN EUROPEAN PLAIN

EUROPE

ALPS

BALKAN PEN.

Black Sea
Caspian Sea
CAUCASUS MTS.

Aral Sea

ASIA

ALTAI MTS.

Amur R.

IBERIAN PEN.

ZAGROS MTS.

PLATEAU OF IRAN

HINDU KUSH

TIEN SHAN

KUNLUN SHAN

GOBI DESERT

NORTH CHINA PLAIN

Indus

ATLAS MTS.

Mediterranean Sea

Nile R.

SAHARA DESERT

ARABIAN PEN.

Persian Gulf

Ganges R.

TIBETAN PLATEAU

HIMALAYAS
Mt. Everest
29,035 ft.
8,850 m

Huang He Huang He

Yangtze R.

Tropic of Cancer

SAHEL

AFRICA

ETHIOPIAN HIGHLANDS

DECCAN PLATEAU

Arabian Sea

Bay of Bengal

South China Sea

PHILIPPINE ISLANDS

PACIFIC OCEAN

MICRONESIA

Congo R.

L. Victoria

ATLANTIC OCEAN

INDIAN OCEAN

SUMATRA

BORNEO

CELEBES

EAST INDIES

NEW GUINEA

MELANESIA

MADAGASCAR

KALAHARI DESERT

AUSTRALIA

GREAT DIVIDING RANGE

Darling R.

Cape of Good Hope

0   1000   2000 Miles
0   1000   2000 Kilometers

SOUTHERN OCEAN

ANTARCTICA

271

Glossary

The definitions for words are as they are used in the chapters of this textbook.

A

activist: a person who strongly supports a cause

advocate: supporter of an issue or a cause

agribusiness: a large-scale farming operation that combines the production, processing, and distribution of agricultural products; emphasizes farming as a big business rather than as the work of small family farms

allotment: a portion of something (land, money, food, etc.) set aside for a particular purpose, person, or group

amendment: a change or revision, usually to a legal document

anthropologist: a person who studies human societies and cultures

anti-Semitic: a person who discriminates against or dislikes Jewish people

aquaculture: the business of farming or breeding fish; also called aquafarming

aquifer: a layer of rock, sand, or gravel through which water can flow; an underground pool of water

arms race: a competition between the United States and the Soviet Union to have the most powerful weapons.

assimilation: the act of accepting a new culture

B

backlash: a strong reaction, usually negative, to some political or social change

baleen: a flexible whalebone that was used at one time to make clothing and other accessories

ballot: a piece of paper, a ticket, or a card used to vote

bankrupt: unable to pay debts; without financial resources

barter: to trade one good for another

bicameral: having two legislative chambers or houses

Bill of Rights: the first 10 amendments to the Constitution that establish basic civil liberties

bill: a written proposal for a law

biodiesel: fuel that is made from vegetable oil or animal fat

Black Tuesday: the largest selling day in the history of the New York Stock Exchange marking the beginning of the Great Depression

blacklist: a list that contains the names of workers who are considered troublemakers who should not be hired; to blacklist is to put someone's name on the list

booster: energetic or enthusiastic supporter

boycott: a form of protest where people refuse to buy or use the products or services of an organization whose practices they dislike

bracero: a Mexican laborer allowed to enter the United States and work for a limited period of time, especially in agriculture during World War II

breach: to make a hole or gap in; to break through

C

camas: a flowering, edible plant that has long clusters of blue to white flowers

cannery: a factory where food, mostly fish, meat, or fruit, is canned

capital: an economic resource that includes money, tools, and equipment (machinery) to produce goods and services

capitalism: an economic system in which individuals, rather than the government, own land, property, and businesses

capitalist: a person who owns a business; someone who supports capitalism

census: an official counting of the population

checks and balances: a basic principle of constitutional governments such as in the United States where separate branches monitor the action of the other branches to ensure that no one branch has too much power

civics: the branch of political science that deals with the rights and duties of citizens

civil disobedience: a nonviolent form of protest in which citizens break a law in order to make a point and bring about a change in government policies or practices

coerce: to persuade

cold war: an intense economic, political, military, and cultural competition between nations

commerce: trade; an exchange of goods between different countries or different parts of the same country

commodity: anything that can be bought or sold

Communism: an economic and political system where the government owns all of the land, property, and businesses

competent: having suitable skills, knowledge, and education

consensus: a general agreement reached by a group

consumer: a buyer of goods and services

Continental Divide: the summit line of the Rocky Mountains where water flowing toward the Pacific Ocean separates from water flowing toward the Atlantic Ocean

corporation: a company or business that is owned by stockholders

corruption: dishonest practices in business or politics

coulee: a deep valley or canyon that was formed by running water but is now dry

council: a group of people called together for a specific purpose

credit: a purchasing plan that allows consumers to purchase goods or services now and pay for them later or a little bit at a time

crusade: a passionate campaign

cultural characteristic: the central beliefs, behaviors, and social structures of a group or organization

D

debate: to discuss or argue about something

delegate: a person designated to act for or represent another person or persons

demand: the amount of goods and services that consumers want to buy

democracy: a political system in which the people hold the power

democratic republic: a political system in which the power to govern comes from the people through their elected representatives

deplete: to exhaust

descent: ancestry

destitute: needy; lacking food, clothing, and shelter

detainee: people confined or imprisoned for political or military reasons

dictator: a ruler who has absolute, or unrestricted, control in a government

dignity: pride in oneself; self-respect

diplomacy: a discussion between nations with the goal of reaching an agreement

discrimination: unfair treatment of a person or group on the basis their race, age, or gender

distribution network: a system for the marketing, transporting, and selling of any good or service

diversity: variety

domestic: of or relating to a country's internal affairs

dormant: not active

dust bowl: the name given to the Great Plains region that suffered a terrible drought during the Great Depression

E

ecology: the study of the relationship between organisms (plants, insects, animals, humans, etc.) and their physical environment

economic depression: a period of time when the economy is suffering from mass unemployment, low business activity, and a weak stock market

economics: the study of how individuals, businesses, government, and society make choices

ecosystem: the interaction of living things with their physical environment

elusive: hard to find

emigrate: to leave one country and settle in another

encroach: to go beyond the limits of; to trespass

entrepreneur: a person who has a business idea as well as the capital to start the business and keep it running

epidemic: a rapidly spreading disease

erosion: the process by which the surface of the earth is worn away by water, glaciers, winds, waves, etc.

ethanol: a fuel made from corn

ethnicity: cultural background

expansionist: a person who supported Manifest Destiny, or the westward expansion of the United States

exploit: to take advantage of

extensive: covering a large area; lengthy

extinction: the total loss of destruction of an animal or plant

F

fault: a fracture in the earth's crust

federal system: a form of government where power is shared between a central authority and its related parts such as the sharing of power between the federal government of the United States and state governments

federal: having to do with the national government

feminism: an organized movement aimed at gaining equal rights for women

fissure: a long, narrow opening; crack

fjord: a long, narrow body of water between steep cliffs

fossil fuel: petroleum, coal, or natural gas that is used as fuel and is made from the built-up remains of ancient plants and animals

franchise: the right or privilege to vote

fraud: dishonest or unlawful behavior

free market system: an economic system where people, not the government, own most of the companies; also called capitalism

free trade: trade between countries that is free of tariffs (import taxes) and strict regulations

G

Gilded Age: a time period in history marked by the growth of business and wealth, but also business and political corruption and increasing poverty among workers

globalization: refers to the spread of capitalism and free trade around the world

graduated income tax: a tax with a rate that increases as income increases

gross domestic product (GDP): a measure of all the goods and services produced by a country in a year

H

harass: to bother or attack a person

headwaters: the source of a river

Holocaust: the mass slaughter of European Jews in Nazi concentration camps during World War II

homesteader: a settler, especially one who got land through the Homestead Act

Hooverville: the name given to shantytowns created by homeless people during the Great Depression; named after President Herbert Hoover

hostility: a feeling of anger or resentment

humane: characterized by kindness, mercy, or compassion toward fellow human beings and animals

hydroelectric: referring to electricity that is created by using the energy of water currents

hydropower: power that is generated by water

I

immunity: the ability to resist or survive a disease

incentive: motivation (a reward or even a punishment) to do something

infringe: to violate or break a rule, law, or policy

initiative: the right of citizens to propose laws themselves by gaining enough signatures on a petition

insatiable: not capable of being satisfied

interest: the fee that must be paid for borrowing money or buying on credit

intolerance: a refusal to accept differences in culture, races, or ideas

intruder: one who enters or participates without invitation; an unwelcome participant

intrusion: a disturbance or interruption

irrigation: a process for supplying water to crops by redirecting it from another location

J

Jim Crow: name given to laws that made the separation of races legal

judicial review: the main responsibility of the Supreme Court to review laws and policies to determine if they are constitutional

jurisdiction: the right, power, or authority to administer justice

L

labor union: an organization of workers whose goal is to improve working conditions

lahar: a landslide or mudflow of volcanic debris on the sides of a volcano

latitude: a measurement of distance north and south of the equator; used to describe a location on the earth

leach: to slowly remove or filter out particles with a liquid, such as water

legislator: a lawmaker

legislature: the lawmaking body of a government

levy: to impose or collect

livelihood: the means for making a living or supporting oneself

lobby: to try to influence lawmakers to take a specific action

loess: a very fine-grained mud or clay, thought to have formed as the result of grinding by glaciers and to have been deposited by the wind

longhouse: a long dwelling usually shared by an extended family, especially among Native American groups

longitude: a measurement of distance east or west of the prime meridian in Greenwich, England; used to describe a location on the Earth

longshoremen: workers who load and unload ships at trading ports

lowlands: an area of land that is low compared to surrounding land

lucrative: profitable; a business that makes money

M

Manifest Destiny: the belief held by many Americans in the 19th century that it was the divine mission of the nation to expand westward to spread American ideas and culture

mediate: to settle a dispute or disagreement

menial: of or relating to work that is considered shameful or humiliating

metropolitan: having the characteristics of a city

migration: the movement of animals or humans from one place to another

minimum wage: the lowest amount a worker can be paid per hour

minority: a group that differs in race, religion, gender, or ethnic background from the majority of the population and which has little power or representation compared to the majority of the population

molten: melted or liquefied by heat

monopoly: a company that dominates or controls an industry

multicultural: of, relating to, or including many different cultures

municipality: a city or town with its own local government

N

nativist: a person who favors protecting the interests of native-born citizens over immigrants

neutral: to not take a side or participate in a war or dispute between countries

Northwest Passage: a ship route along the Arctic coast of Canada and Alaska that connects the Atlantic and Pacific oceans

O

opportunity cost: the trade-offs a person makes when making a decision

oppressive: unjustly harsh

optimism: confidence; a positive outlook

ordinance: a law or regulation, especially one passed by a local government

override: to cancel

P

Pacific Rim: the countries and land surrounding the Pacific Ocean

paternal: fatherly; characteristic of a father

philanthropist: a person who gives money to charities

physical characteristic: natural features of the land such as climate, landforms, soils, plants, and animals

pillar: a natural structure of stone, brick, rock, or other materials

plateau: a high, wide, flat area of land

plummet: a sudden and steep drop or decrease

political machine: a handful of powerful people who control the government in a city, state, or even on a national level; the machine's purpose is to stay in power

political party: a group of people with similar political ideas who organize to gain and exercise political power

poll watcher: a person who monitors voting on election day

pollutant: waste material that contaminates air, soil, or water

potlatch: a Native American ceremony where gifts are exchanged as a show of wealth

poverty line: the level of income below which a person or family is considered poor

preamble: an introduction

predominant: main; being most common or frequent

prime meridian: the reference line that passes through Greenwich, England, from which longitude east and west is measured; the prime meridian splits the earth into the western and eastern hemispheres

profit: money left over after all expenses are paid

progressive: reformers who wanted to end corruption, address economic problems, and improve society in the early 1900s

prominent: leading, important, or well known

propaganda: information that is designed to persuade and sometimes mislead

proportional: a relationship between things based on size, quantity, number, etc.

proximity: closeness

Q

quota: a part or percentage of a whole

R

radiation: energy in the form of electromagnetic waves or moving particles produced as a result of an atomic reaction

radical: extreme ideas or actions

radioactive: something giving off radiation

ratification: to give formal approval; confirm

reactor: machines that create nuclear energy

recall: the right of citizens to elect to remove an official from political office

referendum: the right of citizens to vote on a law proposed by their state lawmakers

reformer: people who seek to address social, economic, and/or political problems by bringing about positive change

refugee: a person who leaves his or her country during a time of crisis and goes to another country for safety

region: an area that has some features in common with other areas, such as landforms or economic activity

relinquish: to give up

relocation: during World War II, this referred to forced removal of Japanese Americans from their homes in western states to special camps set up by the government

renewable energy: energy that comes from unlimited natural resources, such as the wind or sun, and that does not contribute to pollution or global warming

repeal: to cancel or overturn a law

republic: a form of government where the people rule through elected representatives

reservation: land set aside for Native Americans

Glossary

A|Z

reservoir: a natural or artificial pond or lake used for the storage and control of water

resolution: a formal statement

retaliate: to pay back in kind; respond with similar behavior or action

revenue: income

rival: a competitor or opponent

rural: having characteristics of the countryside

S

sabotage: the deliberate destruction of something

sectarian: refers to a person or group related to a particular religion or set of beliefs

segregation: the separation of races

slaughter: the brutal or violent killing of a person

solvent: having enough money to pay debts

sovereign: the status of having power or authority; self-governing or independent

sow: to plant seeds

spatial pattern: the location and arrangement of natural and human features of the land

speculate: to create a theory or conclusion based on available evidence

spoils system: the practice of giving loyal supporters a government job

spoils: goods or property taken by the winners of a war or conflict

stalemate: a situation in which no progress can be made or no further action is possible

stipulate: to require or specify as a condition of an agreement

stock: a share or part ownership in a business or corporation

strait: a narrow passage of water connecting two large bodies of water

strike: a tactic of labor unions where workers refuse to work until the company meets their demands

subsidiary: a company that is owned by a bigger company

subsidy: a grant or contribution of money; or in the case of the railroads, land from the government

subterranean: underground

suburb: places where many homes are built together outside a city center.

suffrage: the right or privilege to vote

superiority: the quality, condition, or belief of being higher or more important than another

superpower: a powerful and influential nation, especially a nuclear power

supply: the amount of goods and services that businesses produce

survey: to examine or study an area in detail

T

tariff: a tax on imported goods

teamster: a person who drives a truck for a living

tectonic: having to do with the movement of the earth's crust

temperate: with respect to weather, mild; not extremely hot or cold

terrain: an area of land; ground

transcontinental: extending across the country

transient: temporary

treaty: a formal agreement between two or more independent nations

trespass: a wrongful or unlawful entry upon the lands of another

tributary: a stream that flows to a larger stream or body of water

truce: the stopping of hostilities or warfare between two or more people, groups, or nations

tule: a grassy plant that grows in marshes or swampy areas

U

uniform tax: a tax that is the same for everyone

urban: of or relating to the city

urbanization: the transformation of small communities into cities

V

vandalize: to damage or destroy something on purpose

veto: the power of a president or governor to reject a bill proposed by a legislature by refusing to sign it into law

vigilante: people who take it upon themselves to punish criminals

violate: to go against (a law or promise, for example)

W

weir: a fence or dam used to catch fish

Index

Credits

The following abbreviations are used for sources where several images were obtained:

GR – Gary Rasmussen
Jupiter – Jupiter Images Corporation
LOC – Library of Congress Prints and Photographs Division
MOHAI – Museum of History and Industry
NWPA – North Wind Picture Archives
SS – Shutterstock.com
U of W – University of Washington Special Collections
WHS – Washington State Historical Society

Cover: Front LOC; Back (t) LOC, (under) Stephen Strathdee/SS.

Chapter 1: 4-5 Chris Mullins/SS; 8(t) Bill Perry/SS, (b) Karin Lamprecht/SS; 9 (tr) Stephen Strathdee/SS, (tl)Brown54486/Dreamstime, (b) U of W; 10 Natalia Bratslavsky/SS; 11 (t) Jupiter, (b) LEVYsheckler/WA Tourism; 12 (t) Barry Salmons/SS, (m) Tischenko Irina/SS, (b) Stephen Strathdee/SS; 13 (t)Bill Perry/SS, Steffen Foerster Photography, SS; 14 Mark Payne/SS; 15 (l) Sasha Buzko/Ss, (ml) Oksanaphotos/Dreamstime, (m) dsobo/SS, (mr) SS, (R) Sharon Engstrom; 16 (t) SS, (m) David Gaylor/SS, (ml) Noah Strycker/SS, (b) Stephen Strathdee/SS; 17 (t) Oksanaphotos/Dreamstime, (tm) A-lex/SS, (m) Al Rublinetsky/SS, (b) Carolina K. Smith, MD/SS; 18 South12th Photography, nyasha/SS; 18-19 dsobo/SS; 19 Andrew Kwong/SS; 20 (tl) Paula Cobleigh/SS, (tr) Irene Pearcey/SS, (ml) My_New_Images/SS, (b) SS; 21 Sharon Engstrom; 24 (l) Harry Hu/SS, (r) Vladmir Vitek/SS; 25 Jupiter Images; 26 (t) Karen Jacobsen, (b) Doug Wilson, 27 (t) Gary Gilardi/SS, (b) FEMA; 28 Mikenorton/Dreamstime; 29 (t) LevySheckler/WA Tourism, (b) Timberland Press, Portland; 30 U of W/Mary Levin.

Chapter 2: 34-35 Tom Till; 37 WHS; 38 (t) U of W, (b) Yasu Osawa/Makah Cultural Research Center; 39(t) LOC, (b) U of W; 40 David Powell; 41 (t) WHS, (b) Francis G. Mayer/Corbis; 42 (l) Christie's Images/Corbis, (r) Robin Phinizy/SS; 44 (t) LOC, (m) Oregon Historical Society, (b) WA Secretary of State; 45 Bettmann/Corbis; 46 WHS; 47 (t) Amon Carter Museum, Fort Worth, (b) WHS; 48 LOC; 49 U of W; 50 (t) David Wright Art, (m) GR, (b) Katherine Welles/SS; 51 Northwest Museum of Arts and Culture, Eastern Washington State Historical Society, Spokane, Washington; 52 NWPA; 53 (t) Chrislofoto/SS, (ml) LOC, (mr) LOC, (b) William Henry Jackson; 54 (l) Whitman College and North West Archives, (r) Laurie Winn Carlson; 55 HultonArchive/iStockphoto.

Chapter 3: 58-59 Glen Hopkinson; 60 GR; 61 Photograph by F. O. C. Darley, Courtesy of Special Collections, Pikes Peak Library District, 257-6345; 62 Leandro Della Piana; 63 Neal Anderson; 64 (t) LOC, (b) U of W; 65 NWPA; 66 LOC; 67 Jupiter; 68 U of W; 69 U of W; 70 MOHAI; 71 (t) MOHAI, (m) Ron Zmiri/SS, (b) LOC; 72 (tl) Margo Harrison/SS, (tr) WHS, (b) U of W; 74 Architect of the Capitol; 75 LOC; 78 LOC.

Chapter 4: 82-83 WHS; 84 MOHAI; 85 LOC; WHS; 87 U of W; 88 (t) WHS, (b) LOC; 89 MOHAI; 90 U of W; 91 LOC; 92 LOC; 93 Oregon Historical Society; 94 WHS; 95 (t) WHS, (b) NWPA; 96 GS Archives; 97 LOC; 98 NWPA; 99 WA State Archives; 100 (l) MOHAI, (r) WA State Archives; 101 WA State Archives; 102 WHS; 103 NARA.

Chapter 5: 106-107 WSH; 108 WSH; 109 (t) U of W, (b) WSH; 110 Bettmann/Corbis; 111 U of W; 112 RUI FERREIRA/SS; 113 (t) U of W, (m) WHS, (b) WHS; 114 NWPA; 115 U of W; 116 WHS; 117 (t) U of W, (m) MOHAI, (b) MOHAI; 118 (t) MOHAI, (m) U of W, (b) jfergusonphotos/Dreamstime; 119 (t) MOHAI, (b) U of W; 120 (t) MOHAI, (m) WHS; 121 LOC; 122-123 LOC; 123 WHS; 124 WSH; 125 U of W, 126 U of W, 127 Puck.

Chapter 6: 130-131 WHS; 132 WHS; 133 U of W; 134 U of W; 135 U of W; 136 (l) LOC, (r) Everette Public Library; 137 (l) U of W, (r) U of W; 138 U of W; 139 LOC; 140 NWPA; 141 (t) WHS, (b) U of W; 142 LOC; 143 U of W; 144 (l) MOHAI, (r) WHS; 145 (t) WHS, (b) LOC; 146 LOC; 147 (t) LOC, (tr) LOC, (m) MOHAI, (b) MOHAI; 148 WHS; 149 (l) LOC, (r) Boeing Images; 150 (t) U of W, (b) LOC; 151 MOHAI; 152 WHS; 153 MOHAI; 154 (t) LOC, (b) U of W; 155 U of W.

Chapter 7: 160-161 LOC; 162 LOC; 163 (t) MOHAI, (b) U of W; 164 MOHAI; 165 LOC; 166 LOC; 167 U of W; 168 U of W; 169 (t) MOHAI, (m) U of W, (b) U of W, (br) LOC; 170 LOC; 170-171 LOC; 171 Lori Howard/SS; 172 (t) U of W, (b) MOHAI; 173 LOC; 174 (l) MOHAI, (r) LOC; 175 LOC; 176 LOC; 177 LOC; 178 (r) Bettmann/Corbis, (l) MOHAI; 179 Bettmann/Corbis; 180 (r) NARA, (l) LOC; 181 LOC; 182 LOC.

Chapter 8: 184-185 MOHAI; 186 Bettmann/Corbis; 187 (t) U of W, (b) Bettmann/Corbis; 188 LOC; 189 (t) MOHAI; 190 (t) MOHAI, (l) LOC, (r) MOHAI; 191 (t) NASA, (r) MOHAI, (b) U of W; 192 (t) NASA, (m) LOC, (b) LOC; 193 Floridastock/SS; 194 MOHAI; 195 LOC; 196 MOHAI; 197 MOHAI; 198 AP Images; 199

LOC; 200 MOHAI; 201 (t) MOHAI, (r) David J. Frent/
Corbis; 202 Monkey Business Images/SS; 203 Joel W.
Rogers/Corbis; 204 (t) Natalia Bratslavsky/SS, (b) WHS;
205 (t) Romanenkova/SS, (b) valentina petrova/SS; 206
Mathew Mcvay/Corbis; 207 Zack Frank/SS; 208 Tom
Reichner/SS.

Chapter 9: 214-215 WHS; 216 Maxkateusa/SS; 217
NARA; 218 Neal Anderson; 220 US Senate; 221 (t)
Reuters/Corbis, (b) LWPhotography/SS; 222 (t) Gary
Blakely/SS, (b) LOC; 224 Zack Frank/SS; 225 Neal
Anderson; 226 (l) WHS, (r) LTC William Palmer;
1-303 CAV/WA National Guard; 227 Courtesy of the
Washington State Governors Office; 228 Carl Murray,
Seattle Photography Inc./Washington Supreme Court;
229 Courtesy Danville County Chamber of Commerce;
230 U of W; 231 Capturefoto/SS; 232 (t) Robert
Pernell/SS, (b) Natalia Bratslavsky/SS; 233 (t) Matthew
Cole/SS, (b) Algerina Perna; 234 (t) Jupiter Images, (b)
AP Images; 235 Leland BobbE/Corbis; 236 Mathew S.
Gunby; 237 CLFProductions/SS.

Chapter 10: 240-241 Carlos Arguelles/SS; 242 Mariusz
S. Jurgielewicz/SS; 243 Jupiter Images; 244 olly/SS; 246
(l) Yuri Arcurs/SS, (r) Melissa King/SS; 247 James Steidl/
SS; 248 Sharon Engstrom; 249 (t) style-photographs/
SS, (b) Erics/SS; 250 Izaokas Sapiro/SS; 251 Wiktor
Bubniak/SS; 252 Courtesy Microsoft Corporation; 253
(t) Monkey Business Images/SS, (b) Edyta Pawlowska/
SS; 254 (l) Debbie Mumm, (t) WHS, (b) WHS; 255
Courtesy Microsoft Corporation; 256 Alasdair Turner
Photography/SS; 257 Carly Rose Hennigan/SS; 258
(l) Mark Gabrenya/SS, (r) Bettmann/Corbis; 259 Peter
Dejong/AP Images; 260 Josef Scaylea/Corbis; 261
Carroll Zahn/Cartoonstock.com